Robert E. Park: Biography of a Sociologist

*Robert E. Park, Berlin, 1900, from
a drawing by Clara Cahill Park.*

Robert E. Park: Biography of a Sociologist

WINIFRED RAUSHENBUSH

With a Foreword and an Epilogue
by EVERETT C. HUGHES

Duke University Press   Durham, N.C.   1979

© 1979 Duke University Press
L.C.C. card no. 77–88063
I.S.B.N. 0–8223–0402–3
Printed in the United States of America

Contents

III. Final Experiments

Foreword: Concerning the Raushenbush Biography of Robert Park

This biography is also an account of the sociological enterprise in America. In many ways the book is a "natural history," a favorite subject of Park's who took it from his study of biological evolution. The "natural history" is the story of the surviving species, and to discover the surviving species one must study social change, paying special attention to social movements. As in other social movements there were in the origins of sociology in America a number of John the Baptists who preceded the establishment of a lasting set of sociological enterprises. When Park came to the University of Chicago, its Department of Sociology was already a going concern; he had a major part in making it grow into something of national and international repute and performance. Raushenbush tells what he did and with whom he worked as he moved from one problem to another, changing his methods and his points of interest. This is what makes the biography a natural history.

The Department of Sociology at Chicago, started in 1892, was really the first big and lasting one in the country; thus, also the world. In Europe various philosophically minded persons had written books about something they called "sociology." Harvard had had a Cabot and others studying social ethics in an enlightened way. The University of Wisconsin got Edward Alsworth Ross, who stayed there (he had been somewhat peripatetic) and was part of the welfare economics group, but he built nothing like the Chicago sociological enterprise. Cooley, University of Michigan, a scholarly and thoughtful man, wrote things of lasting importance, but he also built no vigorous group enterprise to compare with Chicago. The Michigan department did not, in his lifetime, flourish. Giddings, at Columbia, had something of an enterprise from the early times of American sociology, but it faded. The present Columbia sociology is a product of a later impulse. Lester F. Ward was a competing, shining light at Brown University. Eventually a new department grew where he had been. Sumner at Yale upset the Yale curriculum and wrote a book that lasted, but a department did not develop, or at least did not come to much until his immediate successors had moved on and a new group came in. The University of Minnesota grew at a moderate rate into something of importance about the same time as the Chicago enterprise, taking its color from Stuart Chapin. This is not a complete list of the early sociological efforts.

The prime mover at Chicago was Albion W. Small, a social gospel man who had eventually got a Ph.D. in welfare economics at the Johns Hopkins University. A whole generation of American social scientists took that degree. Some of them became self-declared sociologists and affiliated themselves with the sociological movement and were eventually presidents of the American Sociological Society which was, in effect, organized and promoted by Small of the University of Chicago. As it is told in a chapter of this biography, Small had gathered an outstanding group of young men around him in the '90s, had organized the American Sociological Society with free rent on the University of Chicago campus, and had started publishing the *American Journal of Sociology* which was for forty years the official journal of the sociological society and was one of the many learned journals undertaken at that university. It was to this university that the wide-ranging, adventurous, restless Robert E. Park came in 1914. He was 50 years old and had been a newspaper man, a student of philosophy, a magazine writer, and a cotraveler and writer for Booker T. Washington. The Chicago department already had William I. Thomas whose great work was the study of *The Polish Peasant in Europe and America*. Park never assumed any official position except the surely academic one, but, in fact, he became a leading spirit in the Journal, in the graduate school, and in the research program of the department and the university, and he was within an amazingly short time after arriving in Chicago, president of the American Sociological Society. This book is the story of Park's enterprises, that is to say, his research projects. This book makes no claims for Park's theories. It tells 'how he did it.' Let someone, anyone, or many people, write their criticisms of him and his work. That is not the aim of this book. It tells the story and I am sure there will be plenty of criticism. It is not a critique in the strict sense. That is, it is not a systematic statement of Park's theories and an attempt to place them, one and all, into a stream of sociological theories. A critique, however good and broadly read it might be, could not catch the spirit of all this and certainly would never have the knowledge and sense of Park's life and documents that Raushenbush has. It is a service to American sociology and American history to have the story of this man's efforts told in this way.

EVERETT C. HUGHES
Boston College

Preface

As a sociologist, Park believed in life histories. He felt that his own life history might be worth telling. Without having taken more than one course in sociology in his life, he has been recognized as one of the most original sociologists the United States has produced. He was, in the words of John Higham of the Institute for Advanced Studies, "the first outstanding modern student of race relations." From 1914 to 1932 he was a major figure in the famous "Chicago school of sociology."

A newspaperman for eleven years, he then studied philosophy in five universities. He knew John Dewey, William James, George Santayana, Josiah Royce, Wilhelm Windelband, Wilhelm Friederich Knapp, Georg Simmel, and William I. Thomas—men who influenced his thinking and his work.

He immersed himself in diverse cultures. He knew more regions of the United States intimately than any sociologist of his generation: the Midwest, where he was born, studied and taught; Massachusetts where for years he made his home; the South where he spent seven years in intensive study of black-white relations; and the Pacific Coast with its concentrated Oriental population. He studied race relations in South Africa, Brazil, and Asia. He once said of himself: "I expect I have covered more ground tramping around in different cities of the world than any other living man." An enthusiastic researcher, he was a natural synthesizer of the phenomena he discovered. Sociologist Herbert Blumer says, "I have always felt that his mind was very like that of Darwin."

He studied many matters—revolution, anarchism, crowds, collective behavior, the newspaper, geography, peasants, cities, race relations, and human ecology. He believed the value of studying the present was to forecast the future more accurately.

Park said he wanted to write "the natural history of my mind." This book aims to be such a history. It is hoped that it will be useful to future writers on Park and to students who are attracted to the social sciences.

Acknowledgments

This biography of Robert E. Park would not have come into existence without the joint interest of Morris Janowitz of the University of Chicago, Everett Cherrington Hughes, formerly of the University of Chicago, now of Boston College, and Edgar T. Thompson of Duke University.

The papers relating to Park's working life were for the most part poorly preserved. Everett Hughes found boxes of them in the hall outside Park's office and rescued what he found. They have been supplemented by an examination of the Library of Congress's Washington-Park papers, the Americanization Studies file of the Carnegie Corporation, the Park papers at Fisk University, and other sources. In my early search for Park papers, Mr. J. Richard Philips was helpful regarding the Department of Special Collections of the University of Chicago Library.

For data on Park's early life I am indebted to his children: to the late Edward Park for an interview, to Theodosia Park Breed for writings, to Robert Hiram Park for "Memoir of My Father," and to Margaret Park Redfield, anthropologist, for describing Park's family relationships, for making family-owned documents available, and for writing chapter 14. Theodore K. Noss shared with me some of the Red Wing interviews he made while writing a "Field Study of Robert Park's Boyhood and Early Manhood."

This book could not have been written without the generous help of many of Park's students: Bingham Dai, William O. Brown, Horace C. Cayton, Robert E. L. Faris. Bernard L. Hormann, Helen MacGill Hughes, Andrew Lind, Donald Pierson, Pauline Fisk Young, Everett V. Stonequist, Edgar T. Thompson, Villa-Rojas, and two students' wives: Mrs. Donald Pierson and Mrs. Louis Wirth. Nels Anderson sent me an early version of his autobiography, later published in Holland. The considered contributions of Samuel P. Adams and Herbert Blumer were especially useful. Everett C. Hughes who has served throughout as my guide and mentor wrote the Epilogue, "Park and the Chicago Department of Sociology." The services of his secretary, Birdie Shelkan, were very welcome. I am indebted to a variety of people including Andrew Lind, Harold L. Gosnell, Louis R. Harlan, James D. Nobel, Amos T. Hawley, W. Lloyd Warner, and Emory S. Bogardus.

Reynolds Smith was a perceptive editor.

I have received valuable literary criticism from my husband, James Rorty, and—more recently—from my brother, Carl Raushenbush.

WINIFRED RAUSHENBUSH

I. In Pursuit of the Unknown End

Chapter I. Mississippi River Boy

Robert Ezra Park was born February 14, 1864, on the farm of his maternal grandfather, Dr. Simon Warner, six miles from the little town of Shickshinny in Luzerne County, Pennsylvania. His mother was a 23-year-old school teacher, Theodosia Warner; his 26-year-old father, Hiram Asa Park, was a soldier in the Union Army.

Theodosia and Hiram had a war-time romance. When the Civil War broke out, Hiram enlisted for three years as a volunteer in the 1st Regiment Iowa Cavalry. In 1863, as a first lieutenant, he was in charge of taking chained southern prisoners of war by boat to a northern prison. When a dangerous storm struck the ship, Hiram ordered the chains removed. Since only the captain could give such orders, he was court-martialed. Asked what he thought of his undisciplined action, he replied, "I would do it again, Sir." Allowed to resign on April 1, 1863, he hurried to his former home in Montrose, Pennsylvania, looked up his first cousin, Theodosia Warner—whom he had never seen—married her on June 1, 1863, and joined the 205th Pennsylvania Cavalry. After the war, he moved his young family to Red Wing, Minnesota, the town to which his father, Dr. Ezra E. Park, had moved from Pennsylvania before the war.

Robert Park was to spend the first eighteen years of his life in Red Wing—"a real rough river town"—on the west bank of the Mississippi River forty miles south of Minneapolis. For a boy with Robert's curiosity, this was an exciting place to grow up: boats came down from Minneapolis or left for New Orleans; freight cars brought in winter wheat from the adjoining prairie states; Norwegian and Swedish immigrants arrived in such numbers that Red Wing became a predominantly Scandinavian community; Indians paddled over from islands in the river to beg in the town streets. All his life, Park cherished the idea that he, like Mark Twain, was a "Mississippi river boy"; when grown, he remembered with longing "the dear old prairies and the air that smelled so good."[1]

1. Except where indicated, all of the quotations in this book are taken from sources credited in the Acknowledgments: personal letters and family documents belonging to Park's wife and children, letters and papers of former students and friends, and special collections of his papers at the University of Chicago, Fisk University, and in the Booker T. Washington Collection in the Library of Congress. Over the years in which the material for

In Red Wing, Hiram Park promptly opened a grocery store with borrowed money. He was successful and was soon involved in dealing foodstuffs like wholesale sugar and wheat. Red Wing traders bought, stored, and shipped the hard winter wheat from the adjoining prairie states, and for a time the community became an important grain market. Hiram settled his family in the less built up section of Red Wing and the household soon acquired a Norwegian "helper," Litza, who became Robert's great friend. Other Norwegian immigrants settled near the Park family and Robert grew up with Norwegian playmates.

Robert was a self-confident, genial child who made friends easily. Describing his boyhood, he said:

> I grew up with Swedes and Norwegians and among the first of my childhood heroes was "Black Pete," the son of a Norwegian blacksmith. Black Pete was two or three years older than I, and stood out ... by the fact that he had an imagination. He devised ... interesting games ... most of which had some practical purpose. Gathering slab wood from the river in summer and bringing it in on sleds in the winter was one of the . . . occupations. Black Pete had an old flat-bottomed boat that he and his father had constructed, which he used to transport his countrymen across the river, and not merely across the river, but by a winding channel through the island, across the lake in the middle of the island and then across a second channel to the Wisconsin mainland. This system of transportation was probably illegal. . . . When I was permitted to make these trips I usually pulled an oar. I learned a great deal from Black Pete. But he was merely one of a number of others, all older than myself, who assisted me in making of my early life a happy, romantic and vagabond existence.

Of the family's Norwegian servant, Litza, he said:

> Litza was, after my mother, my first and most intimate friend and remained so until she died, when I was in college. . . .
>
> I learned some things about life during this period for which I am very grateful. . . . I gained an intimate acquaintance with Norwegian peasants, so intimate that when I went to Norway . . . I felt as though I were revisiting a country with which I had long been familiar. I saw there the places and people which my Norwegian nurse had made

---

this biography was being assembled, some of the papers have changed hands, making it difficult in many cases to specify exactly the location of a particular document. Although I have been concerned to identify the source of a particular quotation—notebook, letter, etc.—it has not always been possible for me to state its present whereabouts.

me familiar with, for every night during my childhood I listened to two Norse stories before she carried me upstairs on her back to bed. I am ashamed to say that she did that until I was quite a big boy.

Years later in Japan, Park remembered Black Pete and Litza with affection:

Black Pete.—His wonderful stories—inventions—made a fairy land out of an old vacant lot. No prejudices against this family because they were always dirty. Black Pete's father—improvident—village blacksmith—big, silent, always engrossed with the problem of making a living.

Litza and the odours of the ship. How I came to like that odour. . . . Spoke to my mother about it. . . . She explained it was from the ship. Poor Litza had romantic interest for me. Grew to like it . . . because I loved Litza . . . she had a red flat pug nose. I would not have liked that in anyone else.

When he was five, Robert and his mother went to visit his Pennsylvania grandfather, Dr. Simon Warner. (Park said: "Both of my grandfathers were physicians; they grew up together in Montrose, Pa., and studied medicine with my great-grandfather Park.") When grown, Park used to tell his children about this trip and finally he wrote it down for them. The story concerned the adventures of a boy named "Bobs," who, on this trip to Pennsylvania saw mountains and "Christmas trees" for the first time. Bobs' grandfather was "tall and straight and had a long white beard . . . and very black shining eyes that seemed to look right through you and made you afraid until you got used to them and learned that it was mostly fun that made them glitter so, a quiet sort of fun that a little boy at first could not understand."

Bobs assured his grandfather one day that he could easily shell a lot of corn for him, but then he quit shelling after one hour because it was "too hard." His grandfather quoted Scripture to him: "He who putteth his hand to the plow and turneth back, the last state of that man is worse than the first." Bobs also learned something from his grandfather's sheep:

Bobs saw sheep in a field grazing. His heart leaped with joy. He even felt that they would recognize him as an unknown friend. The sheep . . . merely looked at him in a bored way. Evidently they did not recognize him. Bobs pleaded with them. . . . Suddenly one of the sheep turned on him. . . . The sheep was going to butt him. Bobs scrambled to the fence but the sheep was too quick for him. He was toppled over, rolled in the dirt, trodden on and nearly frightened to death, but he managed to get over the fence.

It was (with) a feeling rather of sorrow than of anger that Bobs trudged back home. His first ideal had been shattered. He had lost confidence in first impulses.

Although his mother would give birth to four more sons, Robert was, for the first five years of his life, an only child. This was one of his happiest periods because he had his mother's companionship.

The little boy's father . . . was in business downtown and so Bobs was left at home with his mother and he used to spend most of his time watching her work in the kitchen. He used to sit by the table in his high chair when she washed the dishes and she told him stories and scolded or sang to him all day long and they had a very good time together, only that his mother was always a little sad and lonesome and sometimes when she looked with that lonely and wistful look he learned to know so well, out of the window or when at evening she would take him in her arms and closing her dear tired eyes let her head drop back on her chair while she rocked and sang to him—at such time, I say, a curious lonesome feeling would come to him, too, and he would lie quite still and listen.

Robert was very aware of Theodosia's moods. Shortly before the trip to his grandparents' home in Pennsylvania, Theodosia's second son had died in infancy; this visit with her parents was probably designed to restore her.

A great reader, she kept a diary that is filled with honest, vivid writing and bursts of poetry. She was also musical and taught Robert songs like "Lord Lovell," "Randy, My Son," "All Alone and All Aloney," and the old hymn "Flee Like a Bird to Yon Mountains."

As a public school pupil and "Mississippi River boy," Robert cherished a love of adventure. He had distinguished himself by having the best collection of dime novels in town, and when a teacher urged him to give up this nefarious habit and read good literature, Robert's response was to hide the books. After school he loved to climb Barnes Bluff, a 300 foot cliff overlooking the Mississippi River, and throw stones at passing freight cars. In the bluff there were two caves, the Unrope Cave and the Rope Cave, into which you lowered yourself by a rope. The Rope Cave was Robert's favorite place. The most noteworthy event of these years was his encounter with Jesse James who asked Robert where he could find a blacksmith shop. The incident probably happened in 1876, when Robert was twelve. (One of James's biographers, Carl W. Breihan, notes that there was a famous bank robbery in Northfield, Minnesota, that year, and that Jesse was in the habit of asking boys, rather than adults, for directions.)

When grown, Robert Park used to say to people he knew very well: "When I was still in public school, I wanted to run away from home. I didn't then, but later I did." Although he and his father were both strong willed and independent, they were very different. Hiram was a natural athlete who loved horses, hunting and fishing; he was Red Wing's best billiard player. He was also something of a prankster. Merle Potter in *100 Best Stories of Minnesota* says that Red Wing won a boat race from Stillwater on which there was heavy betting because Hiram smuggled a ringer from a crack eastern university team on to the Red Wing crew, while concealing his identity. Robert however, though he boxed and loved to row, did not share most of his father's tastes.

Of Hiram Park's five sons, one died an infant, two as adolescents. Only two reached maturity: Robert, born in 1864, and Herbert—the second youngest—born in 1874. Hiram Park was not a cruel man, but he believed in bringing up his sons in the way that he wanted them to go; this involved whippings. Herbert decided early that the simplest way to deal with his father's whippings was to accept them and forget about them as quickly as possible. Robert, however, was angry and rebellious. He stayed away from home as much as possible; the family often did not know where he was. His father, on one particularly cold night, locked the windows as well as the doors. However, Litza saw Robert running in circles around the yard and let him in without waking the household. Robert felt that his father had been cruel. The result of such clashes of wills was that father and son were engaged in a continuing feud.

Years later, commenting on the inherent difficulties in any father-son relationship, Robert noted that his own father had not understood children very well; he thought he understood them somewhat better. When confronted with the problem of getting on with his own first-born son, known as Dink, he said: "I used to think about Dink, that the time would come when we would so quarrel that we would quit, shake each other off. Because as long as he remained with me, I would insist on having my way. But I know now that I would do just what my father did with me when it came to the point of breaking. If the boy was headstrong, I would give in and let him walk all over me. But it would never come to that. I never intended that it should. Besides I do not think he will ever be as hard a problem for his father as I was for mine, and I am sure that I understand children better than my father did."

Although Red Wing had been founded by New Englanders in 1850, it was not until 1874 that the first high school class graduated. Robert was a member of this class. Later, he said: "I never had any comprehension of how little one could learn in school until years afterward, when I discovered how much more my children knew of literature at the ages of ten and twelve then I knew when I was eighteen. The result was that I did not really begin my education until I entered college. Life was like that, in the prairie towns when I was a boy."

In high school Robert found he was interested in writing. With his friend Axel Sjoblom, a minister's son, he briefly put out a paper, *The Rambler*. He had what one of his daughters calls "a beautiful baritone voice" and sang in the choir of Christ Church, which his parents attended. He described himself as having been "an awkward, sentimental and romantic youth." He was tall, sturdy, and handsome, and his brother Herbert tells us that many pretty Red Wing girls insisted on giving him their pictures.

He was also something of a radical as he recalled: "It was true that I had read much, but not by any means the best. . . . Probably the most stimulating stuff I had encountered up to this time was Bob Ingersoll's lectures *The Ten Mistakes of Moses* and a protracted series of rather ribald debates on the subject of evolution carried on by a society of young radicals in our town. That debating society seems to have played about the same role in my intellectual life that the debates of the Hell Fire Club did in that of Benjamin Franklin. . . . However, I did discover geometry . . . and found it exciting. I made a sort of game of it, trying to work out problems, as far as possible, without referring to the text. Otherwise I was not interested in school."

But he did consider his future. Who was he and where did he belong in the scheme of things? He did not want to be a merchant like his father, or a doctor like his grandfathers, or a small town official like his ancestor Robert Parke of Wethersfield, England. In 1630, this Robert Parke had sent his eldest son to New England. In 1639 he himself migrated to Boston, became a freeman of the colony in 1640, a representative in 1642, a selectman in New London in 1649, and a representative again in 1652.[2]

As part of his search, Robert studied the careers of Red Wing's important citizens. His investigations were unusually thorough. He had already studied the Norwegian peasants of Red Wing; now he studied its middle-class Americans. These included his relatives from New England, the Foots, who lived in the older, more settled, more prosperous section of the town.

> I was supposed to belong to this group, and used to be occasionally invited to parties. I met the younger generation, too, in the school, but life at the other end of town was always on a higher plane. Now

2. James Savage, *A Genealogical Dictionary of the First Settlers of New England, Showing Three Generations of Those Who Came Before May 1762 on the Basis of the Farmer's Register*, vol. 3 (Baltimore: Genealogical Publishing Co., 1965), p. 347.

in a town of that size, everyone knows all about the few conspicious people. . . . Gradually I built up in imagination . . . the personal histories of most of the prominent people in town.

These people present themselves to me as full length portraits. I have seen them grow up, succeed and fail and . . . meet the fortunes for which they were fated. Since it is characteristic of human beings that they have not only character and personality, but that they also have careers, this knowledge has been useful to me. I mention these things because, while books have taught me to think, most that I have learned of the aspects of life in which my interests lie has come out of my personal experience.

None of the careers of Red Wing's successful citizens appealed to him. As a small boy, he had told his father that he expected to fly some time. His father ridiculed the idea as "impossible." Robert was later indignant about this, saying that if he had been encouraged at this point he might have become a scientist. His search for a future career ended with a book he read in Red Wing's Seaside Library: "The hero of it was a mining engineer . . . a strong vigorous personality who achieved success in the face of great obstacles. I determined to be an engineer, any kind of an engineer."

At high school graduation in 1882, Robert ranked tenth in a class of thirteen. His father decided that, since he was "not the studious type," there was no point in sending him to college. Robert then *did* run away from home; he joined a railroad gang, earned $50 during the summer, and enrolled at the University of Minnesota as a freshman.

It was not an easy year. Of course, tuition was free, and he rented a cheap attic room where he could cook, but he earned only $1 a week taking care of the university president's horse. At times he went hungry. His mother sent him a good Thanksgiving dinner, took him clothes and blankets, and got him to come home for Christmas. His father, too, was prepared to help. After her first visit to Minneapolis, Theodosia wrote to her son: "Your father asked me what you were doing up there. I told him. He said: 'You write . . . and tell him to tell Prof. Folwell to take care of his own horse and to send the bills to me.'" However, Robert was not prepared to accept help from his father.

Never having learned to study, he found difficulties. Because he wanted to be an engineer, he took the science course, and he did absorb some botany, chemistry, and physics. Military science was a required subject. He was sustained during this period by his warm and understanding relationship with his mother.

Theodosia and her son were two of a kind. She had graduated from a normal school at the age of nineteen and had begun teaching in a country elementary school. Her diary that year (1860) tells us about her:

> May 23. The future—the future. . . . My heart thrills with a strange new feeling. I am so young and full of life.
>
> Oct. 18. New York, one o'clock—just returned from Niblo's where I saw Edwin Forrest . . . playing King Lear.
>
> Nov. 7. Lincoln is elected.
>
> Nov. 22. Mr. Richard took me to Mrs. R. and we went to hear Henry Ward Beecher at Concert Hall. The subject was "America and the Secession." Oh what a splendid mind he has. I was perfectly delighted. Let people say what they will about mixing politics with religion, I cannot but feel that he is right.
>
> Dec. 17. While in school time passes, I know not how. But when night comes . . . then that wild unrest seizes me, what a longing for friends far away, for sweet hopes given up, for a different social life, wilder, richer, freer.
>
> Dec. 18. We may cause flowers to spring by the side of the dreariest life, it is said. Sometimes I feel like murmuring that nature formed me with tastes and desires above my station in a little country school.

Marooned in a frontier town not long after her marriage, Theodosia complained of the poor local newspapers: "When I was young we always had a good weekly, the N.Y. Tribune. Those were the days of the immortal Horace. All the best writing on Politics, Science, Literature. . . ."

Clearly what education Robert had during his first eighteen years came mostly from his mother. Understanding the difficulties he was having at the University of Minnesota, she wrote, in January 1883: "I suppose there are people who have never felt 'a sickening sense of inferiority,' but they were people who never had an aspiration above satisfying their animal wants. If we never see and feel our defects we shall never get above them."

Robert echoed his mother's letter forty-two years later in *The City*: "Most of us have known at some time in our lives 'that sickening sense of inferiority' that comes over one when, in competition with his fellows, he realizes, for the first time perhaps, the inadequacies of his personal resources—physical, mental and moral—to achieve his personal ambition."

With hard work, Robert passed all his first-year courses at the University of Minnesota. Hiram then offered to finance his further studies and suggested that he go to the University of Michigan, known as "the best university west of the Alleghanies." Robert was willing; the long feud between father and son ended.

Less than three months after Robert entered the University of Michigan his mother died—on December 2, 1883, at the age of forty-three. She had had for two years an abdominal pain whose cause was not properly diagnosed by the local doctor. Hamlin Garland, in *A Son of the Middle Border*, tells how hard frontier life was on women—a man often used up three women in the course of living there. In the spirit of one of Garland's heroines, Theodosia, who was neither a neurotic nor a complainer, wrote at thirty-seven:

> O woman of sad remembrance full
> That stir up false feelings and narrow the soul
> Rise above thinking of sorrow to come
> And try to make cheerful your husband and home.
>
> O woman you are not half as bad as you think
> It's Man that stands between you and the shimmering brink
> And man has with life's realities to deal
> And trouble unbounded that you never feel.

Red Wing remembered Theodosia as a beautiful woman, active in Sunday School affairs and temperance campaigns, and helpful to sick neighbors and the local Indians. Her obituary notice called her "one of the noblest, truest women in our city." Robert got home just in time to say goodbye. Trying to reconcile himself to her death, he read aloud Whitman's lines to death, the dark mother:

> Dark mother, gliding near on soft feet
> Have none chanted for thee a chant of fullest welcome?
> Then I chant it for thee, I glorify thee above all.

On entering the University of Michigan, where he was to spend four years, Park abandoned the study of science. He chose to major in philology, and acquired eighty-nine credits in Greek, Latin, French, German, and English studies. During his sophomore year he took his first German course—Goethe's *Egmont* and *Herman und Dorothea*—with Calvin Thomas, of whom he said:

> The teacher who "pulled the kivers off and woke me up" . . . was Calvin Thomas who was just then making his reputation as a German scholar and teacher. He was the first real scholar . . . that I had ever met. The others were just teachers. German was his subject but I learned more than German from him. After the first ten days in

freshman German we had a written quiz. On that quiz he gave me a score of ten on a scale of 100. Incidentally, he informed me on a note at the bottom of my paper, that if I was six times as good a student at the end of the semester . . . he could not possibly pass me. That note changed my career. I had been a football player, an outdoors boy. I became a consistent burner of the midnight oil.

In his senior year Park took two courses with Thomas on Goethe's *Faust*. It affected him profoundly, since he found in Faust a fictional hero even closer to his dreams about himself and his future than the heroes of his favorite dime novels or the Seaside Library engineer.

The other teacher who impressed Park was John Dewey. After a course on logic with Dewey during that sophomore year, he made a third radical shift in his interests. He decided to major in philosophy. "My interests in going to college," he said later, "had not been originally intellectual but practical. I intended to become an engineer. I became a student of philosophy and was presently possessed with a devouring curiosity to know more about the world and all that men had thought and done."

His philosophy courses at Michigan intrigued him. Three of them were historical: "History of Philosophy," "History of Philosophy in Great Britain," and "History of Leading Epochs of European Philosophy." He was in a seminar on Hegel, one on Plato's *Republic*, one on "Real Logic or Principles of Philosophy" and one on Kant's *Critique of Pure Reason*. It was during his senior year that Dewey wrote four articles about psychology and published a book, *Psychology*.

Park went to Harvard eleven years later with the avowed purpose of learning more about "social psychology".

What attracted Robert Park to philosophy? The subject itself—"all that man has thought and done"—but also the personality and mind of John Dewey, of whom he said, "My first interest in philosophy I owe above all to John Dewey. . . . With him learning was always, it seemed, an adventure that was taking us beyond the limits of safe and certified knowledge into the realm of the problematical and unknown.

In 1887—the year Park graduated from Michigan—Dewey was still under thirty and still an idealist.[3] He had not yet developed his variety of pragmatism; he was trying to combine British empirical psychology with the doctrines common to Hegel and T. H. Green. Dewey was in this period still a religious believer and was attempting to bring science and religion into harmony under the aegis of idealism. Like other idealist writers, he attempted to develop an organicist social philosophy; when

---

3. See George Dykhuizen, *The Life and Mind of John Dewey* (Carbondale: Southern Illinois University Press, 1973), chaps. 1–4.

Park was his student, he was writing an essay on "The Ethics of Democracy," in which he argued that democracy would remain an ideal unless it is "a democracy of wealth" and "that democracy is not in reality what it is in name until it is industrial as well as civic and political."[4]

Park recognized that Dewey had a mind in motion, forever adding to the sum total of its knowledge, forever exchanging old solutions for new ones. Park was also adventurous by nature. As a child he had great curiosity but had found education dull. In Dewey he found a man as interested as he in exploring the world. He saw philosophy as large enough and rich enough in content to command his attention. Having a good mind himself, he was able to appreciate Dewey's mind. Max Eastman, who taught logic at Columbia under Dewey, said of Dewey: "You felt his moral force. You felt the rigorous self-discipline behind his sagging manner. You felt also . . . that with all his taste for heresies, John Dewey knew his trade. He was an expert philosopher. . . . He wrote a great many things that drove his colleagues . . . wild, but he never wrote anything amateurish."[5]

In addition to pursuing his studies at Michigan, Park was active on the university student paper, *The Argonaut*. He was associate editor his junior year and managing editor his senior year. His satire "A Misapprehension, A Realistic Tale à la Henry James" appeared in its pages, as did an editorial on the merits of his university in which he pointed out that "Michigan University was the first to introduce coeducation, the first to introduce the seminary [seminar] method, the first to introduce freedom of studies, the first college or university to treat its students as honorable men and women."

After Theodosia's death in 1883, things did not go well for a time with the family in Red Wing. In 1885 Robert's favorite brother, Asa Eugene, died at fifteen. In the late summer of 1886, Hiram Park had a debt of $30,000 which he could not immediately pay off. Nevertheless, he married twenty-six-year-old Anna Olson, moved to Watertown, South Dakota, where, as an able and respected businessman, he set up another wholesale food business, became prosperous again, and at his death in 1911, was able to leave an inheritance large enough to be useful to his two surviving sons.

Robert Park graduated from the University of Michigan Phi Beta Kappa in 1887 with a Ph.B. degree. He hoped to get a job as soon as he

4. From "The Ethics of Democracy," an essay later delivered as a lecture at the University of Michigan and printed in the University of Michigan Philosophical Papers, Second ser., no. 1. Ann Arbor: Andrews & Company, 1888.

5. Max Eastman, *Great Companions* (New York: Farrar Straus & Cudahey, 1959), pp. 283–84.

finished his studies. He also had to pay back most of the $600 his father had borrowed to see him through his senior year. On leaving the university, he went to Red Wing and stayed with his relatives, the Foots. He was offered a job teaching in the Red Wing High School, turned it down, and persuaded his friend, Bill Brownlee, a former editor of *The Argonaut* and now editor of a Minneapolis newspaper to hire him as a reporter.

While Park's autobiographical notes about his childhood are illuminating, they are slight about his adolescence. We know, however, that he left the University of Michigan with three characteristics that were to serve him well in his subsequent career: he had a capacious memory, he had much skill as a writer, and he had learned to work very hard. He was to work hard the rest of his life. An impulsive and adventuresome young man he was, from childhood on, primarily interested in understanding people, an interest he was to pursue further as a reporter. Other members of the 1860s generation who were beginning their careers at about the same time as Park were Wilbur Wright, Henry Ford, William R. Hearst, Lincoln Steffens, Jane Adams, and the philosophers George Santayana and Josiah Royce.

Chapter 2. John Dewey, Franklin Ford, and the Newspaper

After graduating from the University of Michigan in 1887, Park spent eleven years as a newspaperman. In 1929 he described the mood in which he approached this career:

> It was there [at the University of Michigan] that I met John Dewey. He was an instructor in philosophy there, an inspiring teacher, and his influence, while not perhaps designed or intended to do so, inspired in me and encouraged an intellectual curiosity in regard to the world for which there was no justification or explanation in the tradition in which I had been reared. I conceived a scheme of life that should be devoted to merely seeing and knowing the world without any practical aims whatever. A course I had with Calvin Thomas in which he read and expounded Goethe's Faust reenforced this resolution. I made up my mind to go in for experience for its own sake, to gather into my soul as Faust somewhere says "all the joys and sorrows of the world."
>
> The result was that I went into the newspaper business. My program was to see and know what we call "Life." I worked as a newspaper man for three years on the Minneapolis *Journal*. I was a Court reporter at first, then, occasionally, a police reporter, but mainly I was devoting myself to exploring and writing about the life of the city. That was the period when, under the influence of the New York *World* and the yellow journalism which Pulitzer introduced, newspapers all over the world, and particularly the afternoon papers, which were addressed at that time mainly to the low brows and common folk, were increasing circulation so rapidly that the newspaper public multiplied more rapidly than the urban population. The Yellow Journals went in for reform, and I became a reformer. The word "muckraking" with which Roosevelt later characterized this sort of enterprise, had not been invented. The City Editor of the Minneapolis *Journal*, Billy Brownlee, who had preceded me at Ann Arbor as editor of the college paper, discovered that I would stay on a story longer than any one else, so he set me to work hunting down gambling houses and opium dens. This was the

beginning of my interest in sociology, although at that time I did not know the word. I did a lot of research, of a sort, both in Minneapolis and later in Detroit. Some of it was something more than mere muckraking.

In Detroit, for example, I looked up, and printed the record of a quaint little old woman who was an habitual drunkard. I found that she had spent some thirty years of her life serving short terms in the workhouse. The purpose of this was to raise the question whether habitual drunkenness should not properly be treated more as a disease than a crime. We had a diphtheria epidemic. I plotted the cases on a map of the city and in this way called attention to what seemed the source of the infection, an open sewer.[1]

In the 1880s newspaper salaries were low and reporters were rarely given a by-line. Park supplemented his pay by getting publicity for a circus. A granddaughter, Lisa Peattie, says:

Grandpa said that when he was young, he worked . . . as a publicity man for a small circus, living and traveling in the railroad car reserved for the performers in the side show. These people, "freaks" to the outside world, were all varied and interesting human beings to him. Some were rather pitiful, like the "Pinheaded Boy" whose tiny head held only a meager brain. However the "Dog Faced Man," whose face was all covered with hair, was quite intellectual. As they traveled, Grandpa and this man carried on long discussions on the political and social issues of the day. Then there was the "Ossified Man," a man slowly and sadly dying of some disease in which his bones became increasingly calcified and rigid. As publicity for the side show Grandpa wrote a poem about the Ossified Man, something to the effect that when he dies he will become his own tombstone. This last anecdote always gave me a thrill of delicious horror.

From Minneapolis Park moved to Detroit and Denver. Some time around 1891 he was persuaded by his long-time friend, newspaperman Hartley Davis, to go to New York City. The two arranged to live together. Davis was having some success selling articles to *Munsey's Magazine*. Park got a job on the New York *Morning Journal* as a police court reporter and also contributed stories to the New York *World*. Years later, in a speech about Walt Whitman, Park described how New York thrilled him:

1. "The Life Histories of W. I. Thomas and Robert E. Park," with an introduction by Paul J. Baker, *American Journal of Sociology* 79 (September 1973), 253–54.

When I first encountered Whitman I was . . . disturbed and unsettled, but I had my moments of ecstasy also. I was a newspaperman, then, as Whitman had been. A newspaperman, more than most people, I suspect, knows, and feels, and is thrilled by the vast, anonymous and impersonal life of the city. Walking on upper Broadway or down to the Battery on a bright afternoon, or watching the oncoming and outgoing human tide as it poured morning and evening over Brooklyn Bridge, was always for me an enthralling spectacle. . . . Crossing Brooklyn Ferry, you remember, inspired Whitman to reflections upon life and death and I felt, as he did, that there was something inspiring, majestic in the spectacle of the manifold and multitudinous life of the city. Whitman was the first one, so far as I know, to see and feel in the collective life of the city something at once moving and mystical.[2]

Lincoln Steffens notes in his autobiography that "the life of a newspaperman at that time seemed to be about eight years; after that, if he remained in the profession, his value steadily declined." Park and Davis were aware of this. They wanted to make a breakthrough into some other form of writing. They thought of condensing and selling novels. Then a publisher agreed to finance a book which they would write jointly, but Park decided it would not sell well enough to be worth the trouble. Instead, he wrote a novel, *The Isle of Enchantment* (a fragment of which still exists). It dealt with Manhattan, its social classes and their interrelationships. The themes include "the tortures of jealousy" and "possession." Among the characters are "a Labor Man," two friends, Caleb and Simon—Simon is a newspaper reporter—and Prudence, who sometimes comes to breakfast. The following is typical of the book's style:

"Good morning, fair sirs," sounded a clear, musical voice beyond the portieres. "May I come in?"
"It's the lady," muttered Caleb.
"Ah, ha, the enchantress," shouted Simon, rising in joyous anticipation.
Prudence, reeling with careless grace, trilling some careless birdlike trills, came toward them.

The Park-Davis correspondence also mentions several plays. One—by Park—was *The Right to Lie*.
In 1892, when Park was twenty-eight, he decided to quit the newspa-

2. Quoted in Florence B. Freedman, "A Sociologist Views a Poet: Robert Ezra Park on Walt Whitman," *Walt Whitman Review* 10 (December 1970), 102.

per business and work as a partner in his father's wholesale grocery business in Watertown. It had recovered from the reverses caused by the drought of 1886 and Hiram was prosperous again. On the way to South Dakota, Park made a stopover in Detroit. There he learned that his former teacher, John Dewey, was interested in starting a new kind of newspaper. He hurried to Ann Arbor to see Dewey, who introduced him to Franklin Ford. This stop-over changed the course of Park's life. He said:

> After leaving college, I gave up a position as a teacher in a High School in Red Wing, Minnesota and went to Minneapolis on the chance of getting a job as a reporter. I got the job and saw a lot of the world—the kind of a world a reporter does see. . . .
>
> Meanwhile I had gained an insight into the functioning of the newspaper. The newspaper and news became my problem. About that time I was introduced by John Dewey, who was then at Ann Arbor, Michigan, to a very interesting man named Franklin Ford. Ford had been a newspaper reporter. He had reported Wall Street and had gained a conception of the function of the press by observing the way in which the market responded to news. The market price was, from his point of view, a kind of public opinion and, being a man of philosophic temperament he drew from this analogy far-reaching inferences. I cannot go into that. Suffice it to say he came to believe, and I did too, that with more accurate and adequate reporting of current events the historical process would be appreciably stepped up, and progress would go forward steadily, without the interruption and disorder of depression or violence, and at a rapid pace.

Park's "very interesting" Franklin Ford was a visionary. A graceful writer and a widely read man, in 1880 he became editor of Dun and Bradstreet's *Journal of Trade, Finance and Economy.* The *Journal* had been founded in 1837 to enable Eastern businessmen to obtain reliable information about the credit rating of distant rural customers. In 1883 a *Journal* reader wishing to build a Western railroad applied to Ford for business information which Dun and Bradstreet did not have, offering him important money for it. Other businessmen approached Ford with similar requests, whereupon he had a "moment of clear seeing." He thought how business information and every other kind of information could be organized. Four years later Ford traveled "as far as the Rocky Mountains" trying to persuade newspaper managers to cooperate in collecting business information. They were not interested. In 1888 Ford tried to explain the importance of his ideas to professors in seven major universities. The only one who listened was John Dewey, then twenty-nine, teaching at the University of Michigan. Dewey wrote William James on June 3, 1891, recommending Ford to his attention:

Dear James,

I should say that if there is something back (and something ahead) of whatever freedom of sight and treatment there is in my ethics, I got it from Franklin Ford to whom I refer in the Preface. . . .

By some sort of instinct and by the impossibility of my doing anything in particular, I was led into philosophy and into "idealism"—i.e. the conception of some organism comprehending both man's thought and the external world. Ford, who was a newspaperman (formerly Editor of Bradstreet's in New York) with no previous philosophical training, had been led by his newspaper experience to study as a practical question the social bearings of intelligence and its distribution. . . .

He identified the question of inquiry with, in philosophical terms, the question of the relation of intelligence to the objective world—is the former free to move in relation to the latter or not? So he studied out the following questions: (1) The conditions and effects of the distribution of intelligence especially with reference to inquiry or the selling of truth as a business; (2) the present (or past) hindrances to its free play, in the way of class interests; or (3) the present conditions, in the railway, telegraphy, etc., for effectively securing the freedom of intelligence, that is, its movement in the world of social fact; and (4) the resulting social organization. This is, with inquiry as a business, the selling of truth for money, the whole would have a representative as well as the various classes,—a representative whose belly interest, moreover, is identical with its truth interest. Now I am simply reducing what was a wonderful personal experience to a crude bit of cataloging, but I hope it may arouse your interest in the man and his work.[3]

By 1892 Ford had persuaded Dewey to help him publish a paper, *Thought News*. Believing that Park would be useful in the enterprise, Dewey introduced him to Ford. A circular announcing the forthcoming publication of the *Thought News* appeared in the *Michigan Daily* and was mentioned in *The University Record*. Park reports:

3. Dewey to James, in *Philosophy and Psychology*, vol. 2 of Ralph Barton Perry's *The Thought and Character of William James: As Revealed in Unpublished Correspondence and Notes, Together with His Published Writings* (Boston: Little Brown & Co., 1935), p. 518.

On the way west I stopped in Detroit and heard of the project which Ford and John Dewey had for bringing about a revolution through a new kind of news. I stayed there and waited for it. We got out the copy for the first issue of the "Thought News," but it was never published. It was set up and then pied. My share in paying for it was about $15.

And Dewey:

It was an overenthusiastic project, which we had not the means nor the time . . . and doubtless not the ability to carry through.

Park had by this time decided not to go home and enter his father's business. He got a newspaper job in Detroit and traveled to Ann Arbor as frequently as possible to see Ford. On 1 July 1892 Ford had a manuscript called *A Draft for Action* printed privately. Park read it, for the most part enthusiastically, eventually with some disappointment. On 28 December 1892 he wrote to a young artist, Clara Cahill, about Ford's book:

Dear Miss Cahill:

I sent Ford's book to your father the other day, with two copies of the Railway Gazette containing short articles by Ford. If your father is at all interested in the book I should like to talk to him about it. I hope your interest in Mr. Ford and his idea is not momentary and that I may be able very soon to tell you more about this that Mr. Ford calls "the third fact of the century." I should consider that the "cause" had gained a great deal if it won your interest and enthusiasm. This is a "cause" you know. It is a revolution.

A Draft for Action—Ford looked on it as his magnum opus—envisioned a union between the newspaper and the increasing knowledge of the university scholar. The central pool of intelligence thus created would sell information to a variety of newspapers directed at publics with different interests and different intelligence levels. Because this pool would be informed by what university scholars know, the ordinary citizen would not have what Ford called "pre-locomotive concepts" palmed off on him. In his vision of how the newspaper business could be reorganized, Ford was a twentieth-century rather than a nineteenth-century man. He correctly foresaw the trend toward an ever greater concentration of publishing and of the gathering of all kinds of information. He quoted Greeley's prediction that "the time is coming when all newspaper matter will be handled from a single source" and Lamartine's edict that "the ultimate book will be the morning newspaper." Park was interested in Ford's perception that the reporter needed an awareness of long-term trends: "According to my earliest conception of a sociologist," Park said, "he was to be a kind of super-reporter, like the men who write for *Fortune*. He was to report a little more detached than the average, what my friend Ford called the 'Big News.' The 'Big News' was the long-time trends which recorded what is actually going on rather than what, on the surface of things, merely seems to be going on."

Ford's vision of making the world work better through better communication had a name: he called it "the revolution absolute." Park and Dewey were intrigued not only by Ford's revolution but also by his charm. When Ford gave Park the assignment of covering "the relation of art to life," Park was happy to accept.

Park was soon aware, however, of Ford's impracticality and was, very early, critical of his writing and ideas to which he later referred in some classroom notes as "the purest intellectualism." But he never denied the influence Ford had on his life and mentioned him in almost every major autobiographical note. Ford pointed Park in the direction of writing about the newspaper and public opinion. During his newspaper career, Park had conceived of himself as a writer who has not yet found his proper field. Should he write novels or plays? His contact with Ford and Dewey during the *Thought News* period focused his attention on public opinion, about which he was seven years later to write a doctoral thesis. Although he owed this interest partly to Ford, he gave Dewey the credit; in 1941, he said, "It was from Dewey that I got, to use a newspaper phrase, my first great 'assignment,' the assignment to investigate the nature and social function of the newspaper."

Chapter 3. Courtship and Marriage

After the spring of 1893 Park no longer refers to Ford in his letters to Clara Cahill. His relation with the young artist takes center stage in his life. Since Clara lived in Lansing, Michigan, while Park worked in Detroit, their friendship was initially carried on largely by correspondence.

Making a trip to Toronto to interview a famous scientist, he wrote to Clara: "You know I feel very proud when I find that I can understand and interest big original men—and measure them. There is only one thing I can do you know—[it] is to understand." He attended an execution. He persuaded a minister and a rabbi to visit the Detroit police court and write about it for his paper. As editor, he supplied a frontpage introductory article. Since *Thought News* had failed to materialize, he wanted to form a university club which would "bring people who are outside the University in closer touch with it and through them bring the University in closer touch with life. . . . The solution of all the problems of our social life is the extension of the nervous system of the social body. It is this terrible chasm between knowledge and action—between the University and life—that is the cause of all the present trouble."

He kept up his Ann Arbor associations. He wrote to Clara about meeting George and Helen Mead:

Have I told you about Mr. and Mrs. Mead? Mr. Mead is the assistant in psychology at Ann Arbor and he has a witty and delightful wife. Her name before her marriage was Castle and she has lived all her life in Honolulu. Her brother is one of the commissioners who came over from Honolulu to ask the American government to annex Hawaii. Her father is the most important person in the Islands I guess and annexation has been his dream. She is now writing an article for the papers on the situation there and I am going up tomorrow to help her.

By the time he met Clara, Park had no illusions about the social reform movements of the 1890s which were carried on for the most part by good but naïve people who often succeeded in making a situation worse instead of better. He wrote:

I will send you an article about the Women's Independent Voters' Association. I did not dare to tell all that I mean about them. I fear you would not like it because it is a trifle Mephistophelian and I cannot teach you to see the subtle delights of making people who are sincere but misguided appear ridiculous. It may help if you know that these women, consciously or unconsciously, have been malicious in their slanders and that the city democracy into whose hands they have been playing is composed of thugs, convicted thieves and gamblers. Not all of it. But the substrata. These men control the votes of the ignorant class while the silk stocking democracy of the city despises the lower class of the city democracy. Still it uses them and puts them into office.

Because of his experiences with social reformers, Park let it be known subsequently that he himself was not interested in being "a do-gooder." His function as a reporter was to give his readers enough information and background about a situation to enable them not to act stupidly about it. This desire to make intelligence about human nature and society generally available had animated Ford, Dewey, and Park to try to establish the *Thought News*.

When Clara lent him a book on Russian nihilism, it made a profound impression:

> That is a great book you sent me, little friend. . . . I am going to study the whole history of the Russian people now, you have interested me in it. . . . Nihilism is not a mere momentary explosion. It is an idea that has been slowly ripening through centuries. It has been watered with the sweat and the blood of millions of patient people. It is the red fruit of a system and a social curse that has been upon Europe for 300 years. Black and pestilent as anarchy may seem, it contains within it the germ of an idea that is the salvation of the world—I am certain of it—people die for that idea. Until a man is prepared to die for what he believes, he does not believe.

As a newspaperman, Park was aware of the spirit of revolt that animated the midwestern farmers who organized the Populist movement, which in 1892 won 8.5 percent of the popular vote. He decided to study revolution as a phenomenon. With a newspaperman friend, a Mr. Bingham, he organized a reading club to study the French Revolution and urged Clara Cahill to join. He told her not to read Carlyle until she had "mastered the history," recommended certain novels which were "historically correct," and suggested that she cover "the whole period of the German renaissance beginning with Herder and Lessing." Having set up this elaborate program, he noted that it would help himself, Clara, and Bingham to understand what was currently going on in the world. "Does it seem like a Herculean task?" he wrote to her. "It isn't I assure you. It's simply a question of directing your reading in some channel that will have a bearing on modern life."

As their friendship grew, Robert wrote Clara less about his work and more about himself and the future he hoped they would share. He was determined that Clara should not enter marriage without full knowledge about him. A man of great reserve who all his life valued privacy, he was completely candid with Clara. He did not hesitate to say: "I have been a rash youth, you know; nobody ever knew what I was going to do next."

When he first met her, he was twenty-eight and a newspaper reporter. He knew he was a hard worker, that he had the reputation of staying with a story longer than other men, and that he wrote well. However, he did not want to remain a reporter, and he did not know what his alternatives were. He wrote to Clara: "When I fall to worrying about the future—when I fear I am destined always to be a reporter at $25 a week—when I have moments of real dizziness and distrust everything as I have to-day—one look at that picture, one thought of you has made them vanish." He presently became a city editor, and his financial position was somewhat improved. He wrote to her: "I think maybe I should go into the think business like Carlyle and Emerson." This was sound: the think business was in fact to be his future career, first as a philosopher and then as a sociologist.

He told Clara rather fully about his unhappiness as a child, his uncertainties as a young man. "I have not had a home for years and I was never happy when I did." "You cannot understand what torment it is to live in hell—neither can you understand the delights thereof. But I lived it for many years, all the time I was in college and afterwards."

If Park had been merely a somewhat tormented young man uncertain about his future, Clara Cahill would hardly have been attracted to him. However, he had other qualities. He was strikingly handsome; he was genial and witty; he had gusto. He told Clara: "I love this crazy mixed-up world; if I didn't love it, I couldn't write about it."

This love relationship with the world comes out strongly in many of his letters:

> I am now convinced that the intoxicating pleasure of sharing consciously in the movement of the whole world, of making the whole world me, of feeling in my bosom all the joys and sorrows of it is the greatest pleasure, the supreme happiness of life. . . . I believe that a man's success in life is dependent on the extent to which he shares in the life of the race. . . .

Dark thoughts will come, dear. Do you think I, too, never have moments when it seems as though I doubted everything. . . . I, too, am impulsive, I, too, am tossed by waves of feeling this way and that, but it seems to me there are depths which are never disturbed. It is so with me in everything. That is perhaps the reason many people do not understand me.

Let us always be assured that these [little things] are but the waves upon the surface of our lives, the surf along the shore and that back of all is the unbounded ocean. For my part it seems to me I live two lives—one the little life of everyday activity . . . of hopes and disappointments—and one of deep unvarying currents, a life that grows broader and deeper every day and one that is able to swallow up and forget the superficial life I am leading.

Did I not say to you when I first came to know you that there are some things I believed in with all my heart, some things that I wanted to do in the world no matter in how small a way—things that I would like to die in battle for . . . that I wanted to live gayly, light-heartedly. But at the same time feeling that everything I did was a matter of life and death—with all the devotion of a saint, with the bravery of a soldier, live, live, live.

He spoke of his love of life and also of an inner serenity he claimed he had: "I live two lives, one of deep unvarying currents, a life that grows broader and deeper every day." How did he achieve that serenity? He did not have it as a New York City reporter, when he envied Whitman for *his* serenity. Looking back on his youth at a later date, he says: "When I was young . . . though I was rebellious, I was what the Quakers call a seeker, I had not found my vocation. I was unsettled, unmarried and without a program."

Park's inner serenity seems to have come from the more or less simultaneous effect three persons had on him: Dewey, Ford, and Clara Cahill. The unplanned stopover in Michigan changed him. Coming into Dewey's orbit again, he was reminded of the large world of thought in which Dewey was at home. The relation between Dewey, Ford, and himself, centering on the idea of communication, had been electric. Clara Cahill stimulated his emotions and also his mind. Because of a book she recommended, he explored nihilism and revolution. His contact with these three people gave him a renewed sense of direction. During his schoolboy years in Red Wing, he had been convinced that some day he would run away, thus escaping from much unhappiness. Now his new sense of direction came from the conviction that he was growing as a thinker, and that this was what he wished to do.

Of the three, Dewey, Ford, and Clara Cahill, it was probably Clara who more than anyone brought him serenity. To one of his children, grown at the time, he once said, "The best thing I ever did was to marry your mother." He had met Clara Cahill in the winter of 1892 and in June of 1894 he married her. The following account of their married life has been written by their daughter, Margaret.

Although there was not quite five years difference in age between Robert and Clara, there was a decided difference in experience and temperament. Robert as a newspaperman had led a strenuous, disillusioning, and often lonely life dealing with many of the unsavory aspects of the city. Though he had not lost his drive and interest in new experience, he did have periods of dark depression. Clara was the daughter of a judge in the Supreme Court of Michigan at Lansing. She had had a happy childhood in a sympathetic and lively family. She had been abroad and had studied for three years at art school—two in Cincinnati and one in New York at the Art Students' League. She had also been ill—one illness kept her in bed for a year. The man she had planned to marry had died. Small, quick-moving, and impulsive, she was basically optimistic and gay. Her new suitor was passionate, quick-tempered, and amusing, but sometimes moody or lost in thought. Clara had had many beaux, but none like Park; she was attracted both to his person and to his ideas. He in his turn was both astonished and delighted to meet a charming young woman who could listen and respond so sympathetically to his interests.

He was impressed by her talents; she had ability not only as an artist but also as a writer. When Clara showed him a story she had written, he praised it highly, criticized it a little, and said, "The net resultant impression is that you can *write* and might better be writing stories than I."

There was a philosophy of life to share, the strenuous philosophy of heroic self-sacrifice in Carlyle's writings—*Sartor Resartus* in particular, Robert's favorite from college days. If Clara had realized how seriously her Robert took this ideal, she might have given a little more thought to her parents' objections that, although interesting, Robert Park might not make a good family man. With Clara's delicate health—one doctor had asserted it was too risky for her even to think of having children—this was important. In addition, Robert at this time was supporting himself on a rather meager salary. But the couple saw no real obstacles, and they were married in June 1894. Robert entered upon years of pleasant relationship with his in-laws. They ceased to fear the dangers childbearing might have for

Clara when she bore four vigorous babies between 1895 and 1902. Robert gloried in his family, but in the pattern of the times did not take on any domestic duties—he confessed he had never changed a diaper.

It was at this time that the Robert Parks began their connection—which lasted all their lives—with the summer colony at Roaring Brook on Little Traverse Bay in northern Michigan. Judge Cahill had some years earlier visited this untouched area and bought a large tract of land. One summer Robert and Clara helped to run the newly built Roaring Brook Inn. They also managed to have a cottage of their own constructed on land given them by the Cahills. (Robert always claimed that they paid for the cottage by his giving up smoking cigars.) In the less prosperous years, they rented out the cottage "in season"; later, enlarged and improved, it was used a great deal by Robert and Clara and their guests. With other family houses, it was a site for family reunions. (The house is still in the family.)

During the first four years of the marriage, Park worked as a newspaperman in Detroit and then in Chicago. Some idea of what he was writing then can be obtained from a scrapbook made by his wife. For example, in an article about an insane asylum, he first covered the history of the region and of the institution. He described the rural surroundings of the asylum and noted that inmates tended to drift in with the first chill of autumn and to leave in the spring. He wrote an exhaustive account of the finances of the asylum and ended the article by considering the mind of the insane.

During this period Park amused himself by getting acquainted with some of Detroit's anarchist intellectuals. One made disagreeable remarks to anyone who would listen. Another talked of burning a building but never quite got around to it. A third helped Park with his German translations. Returning years later to Detroit, Park found most of them well off and no longer much interested in revolution.

Summing up his newspaper career in 1927 for the *National Cyclopedia of Biography*, Park said:

> I began my active career as a reporter with the Minneapolis *Journal*, and during the next three years developed an interest in sociological subjects, based on observations of urban life. This order of special articles I contributed to the Detroit *Times* in 1891; to the Denver *Times* in 1891–92, and to the New York *Morning Journal* in 1892–93. In New York City, I worked as a reporter at the Essex Market Court on the East Side of New York and had my first intensive experience as a police reporter. I was reporter and then city editor of

the Detroit *Tribune*, later, also, of the Detroit *News* in 1894–96. My last regular newspaper connection was in the capacity of reporter and dramatic critic for the Chicago *Journal* in 1897–98.

By 1898 Park had been a newspaperman for eleven years. He had begun to wonder whether he should not do something else; the question was what? Hiram Park was by this time very proud of his handsome son and aware of his son's problem. Hiram, a vigorous, adventuresome man, interested in sports, a good church member, had admired and married a woman who "always had her nose in a book." His son Robert had the same bent. Although Robert could at any time have become a partner in his father's now profitable business, Hiram knew that Robert had never really *wanted* to do this. Robert said: "When it came to the matter of going into business, my father said he didn't want me to do it, but that I could do anything I liked. So I went back to the University and spent altogether seven years at it—at Ann Arbor, Harvard and in Germany. I did this because I was interested in communication and collective behavior and wanted to know what the universities had to say about it."

Chapter 4. Crowd and Public

In the fall of 1898, at the age of 34, Park went to Harvard for the academic year, obtaining an M.A. in philosophy. "Until 1898, when I went to Harvard to resume my studies," he said, "I lived the life of an intellectual vagabond."

Park arrived at Harvard during the "Golden Yard" period when William James, Josiah Royce, and George Santayana formed a brilliant constellation in the philosophic firmament. He took courses with all three and also worked with Muensterberg in the psychological laboratory. This course was listed as "Experimental Investigations by Advanced Students." Of his teachers, Park said:

> Harvard was at that time a great place for a student of philosophy to be. James offered a seminar on abnormal psychology the first year I was there.... The universe was not for him a closed system and every individual man, having his own peculiar experience, had some insight into the world that no other mind could have. The real world was the experience of actual men and women and not abbreviated and shorthand descriptions of it that we call knowledge....
>
> Santayana had not at that time developed his own philosophy, as he has since done, but his lectures on the philosophy of art were immensely interesting and suggestive, and his conception of the relation of art and religion, in fact all that he has from time to time written about religion, seems to me to throw more light upon the subject and indicate a more satisfactory point of view for systematic study than anything I have read.

A breakthrough occurred for Park when James's class on metaphysics was discussing Royce's proofs for the existence of God:

> The proofs for the existence of God was a live topic in the department of philosophy at Harvard at that time. So it was that we found ourselves one day discussing the attributes of God ... Someone suggested that one of God's attributes was infinity. Infinite in what? Infinite in space? Infinite in time? "Infinitely old" said James, and that remark banished once and for all, as far as I was concerned, any further interest in the attributes of God.

It did more than that. It banished scholasticism. From that time on, logic, and formal knowledge of every sort, ceased to have for me the interest or authority they once had. Ideas were no longer anywhere or in any sense a substitute for reality and the world of things. Thenceforth my interest was in science rather than in philosophy.

Although Park valued his contact with these great men, Harvard did not give him what he was looking for. He wanted to understand communication and collective behavior and had imagined that social psychology as taught at Harvard would give him the answers. It did not. As he said later: "There was at that time no such thing as social psychology at Harvard, but a society for the study of social psychological problems was formed at this time of which I was a member and my interest in this field has been constant ever since."

In fall 1899 Park moved himself, his wife, and his three children to Berlin and registered as a student at the Friederich-Wilhelm University. Among his courses were "European Art in the Nineteenth Century" and "History of Law" with Professor Paulsen. In spring 1900 he took three courses with Georg Simmel who was then forty-one and a docent in the university. The courses were in "Ethics," "History of Philosophy in the Nineteenth Century," and "Sociology." This was the only course on sociology Park took in his entire life. Years later Park was to say that Simmel was "the greatest of all sociologists."

Although he had registered for further courses at the university, Park decided not to attend, but did not notify the university. Apparently he spent part of his time in Berlin researching and writing an article for *Munsey's Magazine* on the German army.

Park's plans changed because he discovered a man and a book that offered some kind of an answer to the questions which had sent him back to the academic world in the first place. He wrote: "In Berlin I attended Paulsen's lectures in philosophy, but it was from Simmel that I finally gained a fundamental point of view for the study of the newspaper and society. It happened that at this time I ran across a methodological treatise by Kistiakowski: *Gesellschaft und das Einzelwesen* [*Society and the Individual Person*]. Kistiakowski had been a student of Windelband and as I discovered in this book an attack upon the methodological problem that I had come to regard as fundamental, I decided to go to Strassburg and write my doctor's thesis with Windelband."

In Strasbourg (then Strassburg), Park spent the next two years at the university taking courses in philosophy and the social sciences and working on his thesis under Windelband. He also studied geography with Georg Gerland and political economy with Georg Friederich Knapp. Park admired Knapp: "I think the very best teacher . . . I ever studied under was Georg Friederich Knapp. . . . He was . . . at once a statistician and a historian, and his most popular course was a history of European, and particularly German agriculture. Among other things I got to know and to understand from him was the German peasant."

Other courses in the social sciences that Park may have taken there cannot be determined because of the absence of records. Although the university was completely reorganized as a German institution in 1841, it was made a French university again in 1918 and whatever records may have existed have since disappeared.

In 1902 Windelband was asked to teach at the University of Heidelberg and accepted. Park decided to follow him. Since Park did not expect to be in Heidelberg long, his family returned to the United States. While in Heidelberg Park studied political economy with Rathgen and took three courses with Hettner: "An Understanding of the German Language and Culture," "Geographical Exercises," and "Non-European Land Masses." Park said: "Geography, as Hettner conceived it, was a revelation to me, and it has led me to the conclusion that every student of sociology should have to know geography, human geography particularly, for after all, culture is finally a geographical phenomenon."

Between 1900 and 1903, during his Strasbourg and Heidelberg years, Park's principal occupation was writing a doctoral dissertation that he called "Masse und Publikum: eine methodologische and sociologische Untersuchung" ["Crowd and Public: A Methodological and Sociological Inquiry"].

The title shows that Park knew he was writing a sociological thesis although he was studying in a department of philosophy. In his introductory remarks about crowd psychology, he also emphasized the sociological nature of his dissertation:

This writer believes that every significant advance in sociology must, in the last analysis, proceed with research like that begun in the field of crowd psychology, that is, the description and explanation of the activities of human groups. Both an examination of material already available and a more exact definition of the relevant concepts appears not only highly desirable but essential. The following study proposes to do this in the case of two basic forms of social units: the crowd and the public.

John Dewey had told Park to study the newspaper. He was prepared to do this; after arriving in Germany he decided to study the crowd also. Studying the newspaper meant studying the role of public opinion in human affairs. As a reporter and editor Park was aware of the powerful influence which public opinion can have and also of its limitations. In his thesis he wrote: "The public is not a law giving group. The opinion through which the public controls its individual members is a purely psychological product without any normative validity. . . . Public opinion presents only a part of the changing psychological conditions of the group."

Park's interest in the crowd went back to the thorough study of the French Revolution he had made with a newspaper friend in 1893. In his dissertation he drew heavily on the writing about crowds by various European scholars, including Scipio Sighele, Gustave Le Bon, and Pasquale Rossi. Park's major conclusion was that, although the crowd and the public are distinct phenomena, they serve the same function, that of making it easier for societies to change when the necessity for some kind of change is clear. About the crowd, he wrote:

> It must be concluded that the suggestive influence exerted by people on each other constitutes the deciding characteristic of the crowd; and the social epidemic becomes the typical social phenomenon for collective psychology. . . . The great classic examples of crowds are that last vast migration of peoples, the Crusades, and the French Revolution. They serve as illustrations of the spatial and temporal effects of the social epidemic. Here the crowd appears as a great revolutionary force which shakes and overturns a whole civilization. Common experience demonstrates that people under the influence of a collective stimulus often carry out actions which as individuals they neither could nor would do. . . . It is indeed the popular riot's tendency to irrational rage and its blind destructive spirit . . . that first captured the attention of collective psychology. The equally characteristic ability of the crowd to accomplish heroic acts that none of the members would have the courage to attempt alone was first stressed by Le Bon.

Park quoted Le Bon: "Only collectivities are capable of great unselfishness and devotion." He also noted that crowds appear at times when the ties that have hitherto bound a society together are weakened:

> Precisely because the crowd proves to be a social power whose effect is always more or less disruptive and revolutionary, it seldom arises where there is social stability and where customs have deep roots. . . . It is seen that the great crowd movements of the Middle Ages, the Crusades and the smaller movements which preceded and accompanied the Reformation arose at a time when social ties were weakened. . . . But it was through these very crowd movements that a new collective spirit developed. The Renaissance followed the Crusades and out of the ruins of the Church new sects arose. Crowd

movements played a double role here—they were the forces which dealt the final blow to old existing institutions and they introduced the spirit of the new ones.

Whenever a new interest asserts itself among those already existing, a crowd or a public simultaneously develops. . . . In Europe a public reaching beyond the boundaries of states and nationalities, a tradition containing the kernel of a norm and of legislation which is international.

Park differentiated between two kinds of social groups: those which are organized to serve some special purpose, like political parties; and those which are transient and individualistic. The crowd and the public belong to the second category:

Crowd and public are different from all these. . . . They serve to bring individuals out of old ties and into new ones. . . . The historical element which plays such an important role for these other groups is partially or completely absent for the crowd as well as the public. Instead the crowd and the public reveal the processes through which new groups are formed. . . . If an attempt is made to define crowd and public according to the form in which control is exercised, it is clear that they are . . . the only forms of society which can be called individualistic. Again, a difference between crowd and public must be noted. Only in the crowd does anarchy in its purest forms exist. As members of a public, people are at least controlled by the norms of logic. The ultimate tyranny, as Max Stirner has already noted, is that of the concept.

Park's *Masse und Publikum* was submitted to the philosophical faculty of Heidelberg in 1903 and published by Lack and Grunau in Bern, Switzerland, in 1904. In 1972 it was translated into English by Charlotte Elsner and published by the University of Chicago Press. The translation, in *Robert E. Park: The Crowd and the Public and Other Essays*, has an introduction by Henry Elsner, Jr., and a further introduction by Donald N. Levine, who has also written about Park's teacher, Georg Simmel. Levine calls the thesis "a gem of sustained thought and reflection" and says it involves "a synthesis of three traditions of social thought: group psychology, individual psychology, and political philosophy." Levine also points to the detachment of mind with which Park approached the matter of the social changes continually going on in the world, and says: "Park's dissertation is notable in several respects. It is probably the first attempt to formulate a functional interpretation of crowd behavior. Previously such phenomena had been viewed merely as threats to civil order and high culture or, at best, as involving deteriorated states of human functioning. *Masse und Publikum* shows the necessity for society to have such fluid, primitive forms to enable it to make institutional change."

Although from the time when he left for Harvard in 1898 Park was heading in the direction of social psychology and the social sciences, he never regretted his study of philosophy. He said: "With the exception of Simmel's lectures I never had any systematic instruction in sociology. . . . I got most of my knowledge about society and human nature from my own observations. I am sure, however, that my observation would have been of very little use to me if I had not had a thorough training, first at the University of Michigan, later at Harvard and Berlin and finally under Windelband at Strassburg and Heidelberg in philosophy. Windelband's philosophy was mainly its history, and his history of philosophy was a history of thought. He described philosophy as a 'science of sciences,' fundamentally a science of method based on a history of systematic thought. There is, in my opinion, no other way of getting a conception of scientific method."

The years in Germany, especially in Strasbourg, were memorable for Park and for his family. His wife studied painting and his two oldest children, Edward and Theodosia, attended schools in Berlin and Strasbourg. Theodosia remembers this period of her life vividly:

> My father's years in Germany must have been some of the happiest of his life. He had with him a pretty gay young wife and three very young children. My mother had a capable woman doing the housework so she was free to study painting. My impression is that neither of my parents thought of us children as a great responsibility, rather as fun to be with. Life was very gay in Strassburg at the turn of the century. We lived in a little French villa with an enormous garden. The once formal garden complete with orange trees (an Orangerie it was called) was filled with overgrown perennials, a meadow full of wildflowers and old stumps which we children converted into houses for fairies. The house was not big, but there was a ballroom with a beautifully polished floor. When my father was not at school, he used it for a study with his desk guarded by a large black spider—his friend. It certainly kept us from messing around in his papers. He also used the ballroom to exchange boxing lessons for dueling lessons with his friends. Those were the days of duels on small pretexts. My father was always a great boxer, he even bought boxing gloves for us later. I remember my father as a great big man who laughed very loudly and seemed almost too healthy and full of vim and vigor. He was always singing and that was probably the

thing I loved best about him. He had a beautiful baritone voice and would sometimes sing me to sleep (on request).

Park's younger daughter, Margaret, says:

Robert and Clara entered into the life of the university community and made some lasting friendships. Participating in the traditional carnival was something to remember ... a whole community masked and in costume, music, dancing in the streets, and the crowds of dashing students with their duelling scars.

When Clara's parents arrived and found their daughter expecting a fourth child, they took the two oldest children back to the United States. Robert and Clara with their youngest daughter visited the Black Forest. Park had studied the German peasant at the university. Of this trip he said: "I became intimately acquainted with the Black Forest. I tramped all over it, lived in little country inns and came in this way to know German peasant life at first hand."

Chapter 5. Secretary of the Congo Reform Association

Returning from Germany in summer 1903, Robert Park secured a position as assistant in the Department of Philosophy at Harvard for 1903 and 1904, and during this time he finished writing his thesis. From 1904 on, he was editorial secretary for the Congo Reform Association, whose president was the distinguished psychologist G. Stanley Hall and whose vice presidents included Lyman Abbott, editor of *Outlook* magazine, Henry Van Dyke, Booker T. Washington, and Samuel Clemens. Regarding the beginning of this affiliation, Park says: "While I was acting as instructor at Harvard I lived in Wollaston, which was a part of Quincy, just outside of Boston. It happened that the movement directed against misrule in the Congo had its origin, as far as America is concerned, in Quincy. Any ambition that I had ever had to be a reformer had quite vanished by that time. But I had nothing to do. I was quite discouraged about the prospects in America of Collective Psychology as I had conceived it. I was ready to take up newspaper or literary work again. The Congo Reform Association offered an opportunity. I went to work as a publicity agent, and became the first Secretary of that association. Dr. Thomas Barbour, Secretary of the American Baptist Missionary Society and I formed the Association."

Sponsored by the Massachusetts Commission for International Justice, E. R. Morel, the young man who almost single-handedly had built up support for a Congo Reform Association in England, came to the United States in fall 1904 and delivered a report on the maladministration of justice by King Leopold of Belgium in the so-called Free State of the Congo. Morel had sent his friend Dr. Barbour a thousand copies of his pamphlet, *The Congo Free State: A Protest against the New African Slavery and an Appeal to the United States and to the Continent of Europe*, printed in Liverpool in 1903. Park met Morel during his visit to Quincy and was favorably impressed by his grasp of the situation. On 15 January 1905 he wrote Morel:

> I agree perfectly with what you say that this is not a fight against the Congo State alone, it is against slave labor in tropical Africa. It is simply the race issue in its most concrete forms, that is, in the cases

where you have not merely the race but its appropriate environment, the soil on which it lives as an element in the problem.

There is nothing in the world that a man of your temperament or of my temperament would rather do in this world than fight just such iniquity as this in the Congo State. It is a great privilege to be allowed to do so. It is a luxury that few men can afford themselves.

To my way of thinking, politics, I mean politics of just the sort you and I are engaged in, is the real business of human life.

Characteristically, Park proceeded to read extensively not only about the Congo but also about all Africa:

In the next year or so I picked up a good deal of knowledge about Africa. I saw . . . that King Leopold's position was wholly untenable. He claimed to be an absolute monarch in the Congo; not responsible to Belgium, for whom it was assumed that he was holding the colonies and not responsible to the international concern in whose name his government was established. Furthermore, I suspected . . . that most of the evils that had arisen under his rule were more or less endemic and incurable, the inevitable consequence of the invasion of European civilization in Africa. The whole thing presented itself as a very real, very fundamental and only incidentally as an administrative problem.

In 1884, at a Berlin conference of the great powers, the Congo basin had been declared neutral territory and Leopold of Belgium named its international guardian. Fifteen nations, including Great Britain and the United States had agreed to this guardianship.

In 1904 a group of missionaries addressed a memorial to King Leopold for reforms in his administration of the Congo Free State. In response, Leopold promised reforms but did nothing. The missionaries presented a second memorial in January 1906. By this time, international public opinion had been thoroughly aroused. Park had his friend John Daniels appointed as corresponding secretary of the Boston association. Together the two saw to it that meetings were held, speeches made, and articles written. Three articles by Park appeared in *Everybody's Magazine* on 1 November and 1 December 1906, and 1 January 1907: "A King in Business: Leopold II of Belgium, Autocrat of the Congo," "International Broker: The Terrible Story of the Congo," and "Blood Money of the Congo."

Six weeks after Park's final story appeared, the United States Senate unanimously passed a resolution condemning Leopold. A week later, Sir Edward Grey declared that the Congo Free State as a legal entity had "morally forfeited every right to international recognition." On 14

November 1908 the Congo Free State, as a legal entity, ceased to exist.

In the highly organized, international campaign to take Leopold's power from him, what excited the public were the brutalities—the natives of the Congo were whipped, their hands were cut off, they were murdered. Park did not want to rely on the horrors too much, since it was not, at a distance, easy to verify their precise number and extent. His experience with one man left Park with mixed feelings. In a private note, he said: "I did not take much stock in their atrocity stories. . . . This man got in returned missionaries and dragged stuff out of them. He made them sweat under his questions and would finally sweat stuff out of them. . . . Although he never said so, I am sure that what made him angry was that the administration of the Congo Free State favored the Belgian Catholic missions over the Protestant missions. I certainly got the low down on missionaries from this experience."

What Park thought and felt about the Congo appears in the conclusion of an article in *Everybody's Magazine*:

> To sum up: There is no trade in the Congo. There is instead forced production, extortion and an organized system of plunder. There has never been freedom. . . . The supply of ivory is exhausted. . . . The land is being depopulated at the rate of 15,000,000 in 20 years. . . . A whole fertile land, violated and despoiled, crushed under conquest, overhung by the black cloud of despotic oppression, of misery un- paralleled in the world's history today, a land from which blood and gold has been drained without mercy, a land of dying peoples. . . . Ask any missionary who has been to Africa, any traveller what they have found in the Congo Free State and they will look at one another and at you and give you one word, gravely, in answer: Hell.

Park apparently took the job of secretary of the Congo Reform Associa- tion without much enthusiasm: "I was at that time very little of a mis- sionary and my experience as a newspaperman had convinced me that reform was not enough. But the Congo looked to me like a 'good story.'"

The Congo became much more, however, than a good story for Park. Viewing the Congo, not as a reporter but as a sociologist, Park became profoundly interested in what was going on not only in the Congo but also elsewhere. He wrote: "I had become convinced that conditions in the Congo were not the result of mere administrative abuses. Rather they were the conditions one was likely to meet wherever an European people invaded the territory of a more primitive folk in order to uplift, civilize and incidentally exploit them."

The process was, as Park recognized, a painful one. But could it be made less painful? He had no confidence in reforms. What was the answer? Because he was a tireless investigator and an omnivorous reader, Park stumbled on what looked to him like an answer and told Booker T. Washington about it: "I told Washington that I was thinking of going to Africa; that there was there, I had heard, at Lovedale, South Africa, an industrial school for natives, and that if there was any solution for the Congo problem, it would probably be some form of education." Washington was a vice president of the Congo Reform Association and principal of the famous Tuskegee Normal and Industrial Institute. The upshot of their conversation about the Lovedale School was that Washington invited Park to come to Tuskegee and see *his* industrial school before going to Africa. Park accepted.

Both Park and Washington have described their first meeting, Park in various autobiographical notes, Washington in the preface to a book that the two wrote, *The Man Farthest Down*. Park approached Washington first. "Among others," Park stated later, "I went after an article by Booker T. Washington. He said he would do it if I got the facts together. I wrote up something, and then he said for me to go ahead and write it up for publication and he would sign it. He wasn't really interested in the Congo natives, or in anything else for that matter, except the American Negro and his school in Tuskegee."

Historians agree that Washington cared little about the problems of Africans. Comparing the three great black leaders of the late nineteenth and early twentieth centuries, Douglass, Washington, and Du Bois, August Meier notes that "the interest of Douglass and Washington in Africa was largely perfunctory."

Washington was interested in Park because of the effectiveness and style of the American Congo Reform Association campaign for which Park was responsible. When he met Park, Washington needed someone to handle the publicity for his institute in place of Max B. Thrasher. (Thrasher died in 1903.) In 1902 the position had been offered to Du Bois, who had been teaching sociology at Atlanta since 1896 and who was assured that he would not be allowed "to sink to the level of a ghost writer." Du Bois was to publish *The Souls of Black Folk* in 1903, and because of this and probably other reasons, he declined. A letter Park wrote to Washington's secretary, Emmett Scott, on 19 April 1904 shows that Park already had been approached about handling the Tuskegee publicity:

My dear Mr. Scott:

Your letter arrived yesterday and I note what you say about the material waiting for the right man to work it up. I hope that I am, as you suggest, the man to do it.

I distrust my ability to perform any great original task in the world, but I believe that I can do good work as a lieutenant and have no other ambition except that of doing the best that lies in me under the direction of a first class man.

At Washington's invitation, Park made his first trip to Tuskegee on 18 February 1905. On arriving in that "remote little southern town," he saw Washington's famous Normal and Industrial Institute, which (as Washington told the National Liberal Club in London in 1910) covered 3,000 acres, had 96 buildings, 170 "instructors and helpers," and 1,600 students. As late as 1933, Alabama still did not support a high school for blacks. From 1881 on, Tuskegee Institute had served and had, Washington said, sent out 6,000 graduates who "without difficulty" found employment as teachers, farmers, mechanics, housekeepers, and business and professional men.

Here was an American school which resembled in its essence South Africa's Lovedale School. Park became deeply interested in the pedagogical principles being used at the institute. However, the operations of even the most remarkable school would hardly have held Park in Tuskegee for seven years. What did keep him there was the relation of this school to the entire black community of the southern states. Of Tuskegee and its Institute he said: "I was, it seemed, at the very center of the Negro world. The real problem of the school . . . was not so much to educate a few hundred or a few thousand boys and girls as to change conditions among the masses of the Negro people. This school is simply one point in a large circle of Negro life, with which it connects through its Negro Conference, the National Negro Businessmen's League and all its other agencies for teaching and inspiring the masses of the people."

Park was still engaged with other matters, like the Congo Reform Association. He planned to begin his work as publicist for the Tuskegee Normal and Industrial Institute in fall 1905. Prior to this time, in the one and a half years between his return from Germany and his departure for Tuskegee, he had felt perplexity and a temporary loss of confidence in his destiny. "After my return to the United States in 1903," he said, "I was for two years an Assistant at Harvard. I spent most of the time putting my thesis in shape, it was a thin little book and not very easy to read. I had expected to produce something shining and was terribly disappointed and discouraged." When he received the offer to go to Tuskegee, he was holding three jobs: assistant at Harvard, secretary of the Congo Reform Association, and editor of the Sunday edition of a Boston newspaper. They provided a fairly decent living for his family, but the work gave him no satisfaction. Although he had received an offer to try teaching sociology at the University of Chicago, he had declined. He described this refusal simply: "One summer . . . I met Albion Small at Roaring Brook. I told him something about my interests and my study in Germany. He gave me some of his stuff to read but I couldn't make anything out of it. He asked me whether I would like to go to Chicago to teach some summer to try myself out, but I didn't go."

In trying, later, to describe his mood at this time, he says he was "disgusted with what I had done at the university" and was "sick and tired of the academic world." What he craved by way of relief was action: "I wanted to get back into the world of men. I had never given up the ambition I gained from reading Faust—the ambition to know human nature, know it widely and intimately."

His description of his temperament is accurate. His impulses toward thought and action were equally powerful and his whole life was a rhythm of moving back and forth from one to the other. Having spent four years in universities, he was eager for action, but not action merely. He yearned to do something worthwhile. Apparently he conveyed this desire eloquently in writing to his wife, for soon after his arrival in Tuskegee she wrote him on 25 February 1905:

> Dearest: I can hardly tell you how moved I was by your letter. . . . It certainly is a great thing when a man finds the particular spot in the universe where he feels he can count for the most, where he knows he can "positively appear." I wanted to say, "I would rather be the wife of you, and you away, than any other man's wife and have him here" and that, after all my lonesome times without you, is as strong as I could put it. . . . I wish I could be there and help too. Nothing less will ever satisfy me. If I could teach drawing. . . .

Her support was invaluable to him; he could hardly have carried on at Tuskegee without it. In 1905 the four Park children ranged in age from three to eleven. Robert and Clara's initial idea was that the entire family could live in Tuskegee winters and move to Roaring Brook, Michigan, in the summers. This did not work out. It was too upsetting to the children's schooling and too expensive and difficult. The compromise was that Robert would work winters in Tuskegee when necessary, spend summers with his family, and get home on trips as frequently as possible.

On 29 June 1905 Park wrote to Washington that he planned to visit a number of southern states before coming to Tuskegee. In an address made in 1942, he described what happened on this trip:

> Until I met Booker Washington, except for what I had learned from books, I knew nothing either about Negroes or about the South. But

what one can learn about Negroes and the South from books, as I was soon to discover, is not enough. Under these circumstances my journey to Tuskegee assumed—particularly as I travel very leisurely, reading all the local newspapers and talking with everyone I meet—something of the character of a voyage of exploration and discovery. I had at that time no notion of the extent to which the lives of colored folk and white had been articulated if not integrated into a common pattern of life. Neither knew to what extent colored and white folk lived in different worlds: worlds that touched but never really interpenetrated. "One as the hand," as Mr. Washington once said, "but separate as the fingers." Later on I discovered that if one knew his way about and had the proper passports, he could travel all through the South seeing white folk but never really meeting them. At any rate I saw and heard on this first trip South—which took me as far, finally as New Orleans—a great deal that interested and excited me. The thing that impressed me most, however, was the tragic insecurity—as it seemed to me then—under which colored people lived. . . .

All this and much more that I saw before I reached New Orleans was new and strange, not to say shocking. When I finally met Mr. Washington in Tuskegee I was eager to tell him some of the things I had seen and heard. He listened patiently for quite some time and then said: "Well, that makes it all the more interesting, doesn't it?" That was his only comment. I never told Booker Washington any heart-breaking stories after that. I found that he was not interested.

Chapter 6. The Black and the South

In going to Tuskegee, Alabama, in 1905, Park planned to play two roles. He would be a publicist, helping to keep the Tuskegee Normal and Industrial Institute in funds by writing about what Washington was doing and what the Institute was accomplishing; and he would be a student. Washington understood this from the beginning, and it was Washington who suggested to Park that the proper focus of his studies should be "the Negro and the South."

During his seven years at Tuskegee, Park met and talked with many hundreds of blacks. When possible, he wrote their life histories in the reporter's notebook he always carried. He also traveled through at least seven southern states, sometimes on his own.

The southern territory Park came to know best was Macon County, Alabama, the location of Tuskegee Institute. Part of Macon County lies in the Black Belt, whose rich black soil runs through several states, but in the part farmed mainly by black people the soil was sandy and poor. Having studied peasants at the University of Strasbourg and having known German peasants in the Black Forest, Park was now bent on getting acquainted with the black peasants of Macon County. He wrote:

> The Black Belt . . . is a strange country with a strange people. We hear the name in the paper, but there are very few of us, even those of us who know it best, who have much real knowledge either about the Black Belt, or the people who inhabit it. To begin with, it is a big region, several times as big as England . . . and it contains more inhabitants than Canada. Each section, too, has its own peculiar customs and traditions and to a certain extent each section lives its life in isolation from the rest, knowing little and perhaps caring little about the rest. . . .
>
> Tuskegee is the center of a farming district, where the blacks outnumber the whites five to one. The land is frequently poor and for that reason easy to buy. . . . Looking out from the sandy ridge on which the village stands, you seem to see on every hand a vast unbroken forest. . . . Distributed about at irregular intervals in this seemingly endless waving ocean of green are the farms and farmers of Macon County, 20,000 people in an area of 650 square miles. . . .

As the town recedes the look of things changes. The well kept barns and fences and the well ordered fields give place by imperceptible gradations of difference to buildings that lop and seem to support themselves with difficulty against the more or less confused background of the fields. The fences begin to stagger, the lines in the fields wander. Energy, system, order are in retreat.

In a handwritten manuscript called "Land of Darkness," Park described one of his first explorations of Macon County. On the first page: "There are places untouched by the influence of Tuskegee. This is the story of a visit to one of them." After an all-day buggy drive, Park and his companion arrived at the home of a respected black farmer:

At dusk we halted and took supper in the cabin of one of the important men of the town. This man, who lived in the midst of a wide tract of land that he and his sons cultivated, was living, as others in that community, within a few miles of where they had been born as slaves. Measured by the standards of the community he was well-to-do. He kept a garden, pigs and chickens and "managed"; directed all the work and business for his children, many of whom were grown up and had families. He was a man of considerable force of character and spoke with shrewdness and knowledge of farming conditions in his neighborhood. But he did not own the land upon which he lived and had never seriously conceived of himself as owning anything.

After we had washed our faces and hands in a tin basin that stood outside the house, we sat in the open corridor that connected the wings of the cabin and talked over conditions. There was a dignity and reserve about this man that it was not easy to penetrate, and though he uttered no complaint, his reflections as he sat there seemed touched with a certain bitterness. He had reached the age when he had begun to feel the weakness of old age creeping up on him. The responsibilities of his patriarchal family had given him a wider view of things about him than the others, and, no doubt, the sense of their helplessness. The condition in which they were living, of those dependent upon him, had apparently impressed itself on him. It was something in his tone and manner rather than anything he said which suggested all this to me.

"Fo the fust time in my life," he said once looking out meditatively across the furrowed fields beautiful in the moonlight, "fo the fust time in my life it seem t'me this year as if I'd like to own my home."

Considering the years of patient labor he had put in upon the land on which he lived, this remark struck me as singularly pathetic.

While we were sitting there, tardy laborers from the more distant fields came silently straggling in through the golden moonlight. I noticed that one of the mules bore a young woman, barefooted and in a sunbonnet. A young man walked by her side and led the mule. When the mule reached the house he lifted her carefully down. Some one else took the mule and they wandered away arm in arm down the path that led to the little garden. I didn't see them again until a shrill voice called out in a few minutes: "Heah, you lovers, come in to supper." We had supper in the little kitchen built apart from the house. A gigantic black woman, slim as an athlete and straight as an arrow, her black head cropped in a white turban did the cooking. A couple of young girls served the table. I have rarely seen anything human that impressed me more with a sense of power than this big, primitive, black woman.

This farmer had been born a slave. Although he and his wife were outstandingly competent farmers, they had little to show for a lifetime of hard work. Farmers of precisely this kind were the ones that Booker Washington, through his institute, was trying to reach. His first advice to them was always: buy land, if only one acre at a time.

To reach the black farmers of Macon County and adjoining counties, Washington had done many things. In 1892 he started a Negro Conference which was to have "no set speeches." In 1897 he followed this with a Negro Farmers' Conference to which he invited seventy-five farmers; four hundred came. In 1904 the institute began giving a short course for farmers, between Christmas and Valentine's Day. In 1906 farmers all over the county, both black and white, were reached by the Jessup Agricultural Wagon, which acquainted them with modern farm machinery. In 1907 the institute established demonstration farms.

Washington was extremely successful with farmers and the fact that he was fond of farming helps to explain this. "The pig is my favorite animal," he wrote in his book *My Larger Education*; "I like to touch things and handle them. I like to watch plants grow and observe the behavior of animals. I like to deal with things at first hand, the way a carpenter deals with wood." He combined directness with an ironic sense of humor. In one of his notebooks, Park recorded a fragment of a speech Washington made to some black farmers, who usually could not afford to buy the good lime-rich land of the Black Belt and had to settle for the poor sandy land. "You people down here got the pore lan'," Washington said, "but you got the haid to wuk it. We got the rich lan' but we aint got the haid. Consequence is we spend all our money fast as we get it. Some of our women spen' enough money for a bonnet to buy an acre of lan'. I make it my judgment that the worst thing we ignorant men can have is money: that's the reason we needs the schools up our way same as you have em down here."

In 1907 Park considered the situation in the Black Belt: "On the whole conditions are probably better in Macon than they are in other Black Belt counties of Alabama. This is due in part to the fact that the northern part of the county has the sandy soil upon which some of the more progressive farmers have been able to get a foothold and become independent owners. But in large part it is due to the direct influence of Tuskegee Institute. Of the 3,834 farms in Macon County in 1900 some 3,075 were run by colored farmers. But of that number only 211 were owned in whole or in part by Negroes. . . . I am acquainted with one farmer in the lower part of the county who can neither read nor write, but who conducts a plantation of 1,100 acres; he has a system of cryptic scratches on the wall of his house."

The church was, of course, the basic institution of the rural black, and Park wrote some warm and moving accounts of his visits to the black churches of Macon County. In creating or helping to create such essentially economic institutions as the Negro Farmers' Conference and the Negro Business Mens' League, Washington was interested in moving the blacks to a position where they could more readily compete with white Americans. Park noted the Conference particularly:

> Most original of these educational devices, it seems to me, was the Negro Farmers' Conference. This conference which brought together annually the Negro farmers in Macon and the neighboring counties to discuss local affairs, gained in a short time such a reputation that it brought people together from all over the South. Instead of attempting to instruct this gathering or exhort it, Washington's method was to get from its members some sort of a report, based on their own observation and experiences of the actual conditions of rural life, as they knew them in their communities. . . . The information which this procedure brought forth, couched in the quaint, homely but eloquent language of the people themselves—enlivened by anecdotes and illuminated by quaint humor and touches of pathos—was the most moving and informing, not to say inspiring report on the state of the country and the human aspects of Negro life in the rural South that one could well imagine. . . . As a method of instruction, the procedure of this conference, which lasted all day and was opened with prayer and was enlivened with the singing of hymns—hymns the people themselves had created—has not, so far as my experience goes, been anywhere equalled by any more formal type of institution.

Park's first assignment at Tuskegee was to assist Washington in writing *The Story of the Negro*, published in 1909 in two volumes. A good many people were involved with this book, including Monroe Work, who in 1908 had received an M.A. from the University of Chicago. It was not easy to collect materials on black history at this time. Park spent much time in New York and Cambridge libraries. Many items had to be purchased. One of the legacies Park left behind him in Tuskegee was this collection of materials. In a letter of 11 March 1909, he said: "Mr. Wood and I have recently doubled the number of books on the Negro in the Library. . . . In addition we have increased the resources of the Library by making a catalogue of all the references to the Negro that I have been able to find in the books and magazines in the Library. We already have a catalogue of something like three hundred fifty topics, all of which are now available for use."

Park's thinking about the situation of Southern blacks was influenced greatly by the riot in Atlanta, Georgia, 1906. In a letter to Washington, he said: "I have for a long time thought that it would be possible to get the national government to make a special study, through its department of statistics, of mob violence. One of the unfortunate things about this recent outburst is that the real facts are not known."

The United States government did not get around to making a study until sixty-two years later—the Kerner report of 1968. Park stated in one of his diaries that Du Bois, then a professor of sociology at Atlanta, hid in a country farmhouse during the riot, whereas Washington went to the scene immediately to see what he could do to calm things down. Park commented: "Washington was a man of courage; he was no white man's nigger."

It is true that Washington showed extraordinary courage in going to Atlanta during the riot. However, what Park says about Du Bois is not wholly accurate. In his third and final autobiography, written after he was ninety, Du Bois stated that he was not in Atlanta when the riot broke out but that, hearing of it, he had hurried back to Atlanta to make sure that his wife and small son were safe. On the way he wrote a poem "Litany of Atlanta." It appears that the two men acted in accordance with their temperaments and special gifts: Du Bois functioned as a poet, Washington as a man of affairs.

One part of Park's major activities was to accompany Washington on his many railway tours. Between 1906 and 1912 these tours included parts of Arkansas, Oklahoma, North Carolina, South Carolina, Delaware, Tennessee, and Mississippi. Washington traveled in a private car and was always accompanied by some of the more important blacks of the state being visited. These tours gave Park a magnificent chance to interview

Washington's guests and to visit different sections of the South free. The
tours had been suggested to Washington by the National Negro Business
Men's League, which sponsored and financed them.

In October 1907, Washington and his party were touring Mississippi.
His guests included eight black bankers. James K. Vardaman, at one time
a governor of the state and in 1907 an editor of *The Issue of Jackson*,
described in the paper of 17 October what was happening at Lula:

> The first bitter fruits of Booker Washington's visit to the state were
> plucked at Lula, Mississippi, at six o'clock last Saturday evening. A
> great crowd of Negroes had gone to Helena, Arkansas, to hear this
> apostle of social and political equality, and being stuffed full of his
> dangerous doctrine together with a goodly supply of red liquor and
> other drugs, on their return home, they became offensive in their
> manner and insulting in language, whereupon the conductor re-
> monstrated. The remonstrance was answered with more insulting
> language which in turn brought from the conductor a slap on the
> Negro's face. As the train reached Lula, the brother of the murderer
> was there to give courage and countenance to the assassination. A
> pistol was placed against the conductor's side and fired. The proba-
> bilities are that the conductor will die. The Negroes were arrested,
> put in the calaboose and a mob soon gathered, took them out and
> visited condign punishment upon them by swinging them to a limb.
>
> It is stated in the public press that the bodies were permitted to
> hang until Booker Washington passed the town in his private car the
> next morning.

Vardaman said, further:

> It is reported that this saddle colored accident of an evening's in-
> temperance is travelling through the south in a private car with a
> couple of white men, who are represented as "magazine writers
> from Boston." I presume the pale faced scribblers are travelling
> through the South for the purpose of making an impartial study of the
> race question. The reading public may expect something unique
> and interesting from their observations and coon-flavored lucubra-
> tions. . . . But it matters not what these social perverts and reportorial
> liars may say, the people of the south are going to handle these
> problems in their own peculiar way.

One of the "scribblers" was Park.

On the Tennessee tour of 1908, Washington spoke to whistle-stop
audiences and also to audiences of thousands of people in major cities.
Park wrote seven signed articles about this tour for the New York *Eve-*

ning Post, one article for the Springfield *Republican*, and another for the Boston *Transcript*. The *Post* and the *Transcript* also printed editorials. The *Post* said:

> The remarkable success of Booker T. Washington's latest speaking tour of the South emphasizes again his great usefulness to the whole country. In this role as an interpreter of one race to another, pleading for harmony, mutual respect and justice, he is performing a patriotic service that it would be hard to overestimate. One of the foremost white educators now at work in the South exclaimed on hearing the details of Mr. Washington's recent trip through the South: "Now I believe there is going to be a revolution in the South in favor of the Negro." The greatest service Washington can render to-day is plainly not at Tuskegee, and not at the White House conferring on appointments, but on the stump in the South.

The *Post* editorial noted that Washington was introduced by one Tennessee judge as "a fine type of Southern gentleman," and that another judge classed him with "the first president, Thomas Jefferson, Madison, Monroe, Lee and other Virginia worthies." The *Post* also noted the following:

> "Yo cayn't tell me," drawled one tall and stately man who might well have borne the title "colonel," if he didn't actually,—"yo cayn't tell me that man ain't inspired. Why he's inspired just as surely as Moses was, sir; yes, sir, Moses."
> "Yo are right, sir," returned his companion. "God did cert'nly raise him up to lead his people out of darkness."

Washington's purpose in making these tours was intensely practical. He wanted white Southerners to begin to feel responsible for Southern blacks and, as a first step, to see that blacks were educated. Northern white money and Southern black money had long been financing most Southern black schools. Washington now asked that—at the very least— there be more white southern trustees for southern black schools.

On what he learned during his seven years studying the black and the South, Park commented:

> Booker Washington gave me an opportunity such as no one else ever had, I am sure, to get acquainted with the actual and intimate life of the Negro in the South. . . . I became, for all intents and purposes, a Negro myself. . . . Returning from Europe, I was no longer a newspaperman, but a student. It was as a student, participating in a great enterprise but sufficiently detached to see it in more general social

and sociological significance, that I looked at the Negro and the South. . . .

I believe in first-hand knowledge not as a substitute but as a basis for more formal and systematic investigation. . . . I was not . . . interested in the Negro problem as that problem is ordinarily conceived. I was interested in the Negro in the South and that curious and intricate system which had grown up to define his relations with white folk. . . .

The study of the Negro in America, representing, as he does, every type of man from the primitive barbarian to the latest and most finished product of civilization, offers an opportunity to study . . . the historic social process by which modern society has developed. The Negro in his American environment is a social laboratory.

Chapter 7. Washington and Park Tour Europe

In 1910 Washington and Park toured Europe. Their purpose was to compare the conditions of the black tenant farmers of Alabama with those of the poorest classes in Europe. Park estimated that the trip would cost $1,850. He went to Europe before Washington, taking a slow steamer to Norway to save money; Park got Washington a first-class round trip passage. By December of 1910 Park had the first six chapters of what would eventually be published as *The Man Farthest Down* ready for publication by *Outlook* magazine.

The Man Farthest Down was reviewed on the front page of the *New York Times* literary section. It is generally considered—after *Up From Slavery*—Washington's best book. Washington and Park appear as joint authors. Washington described in his preface how they worked together:

> Dr. Park was not only my companion on all my trip to Europe, but he also went to Europe some months in advance of me and thus had an opportunity to study the situation and make it possible for me to see more in a short space of time than I would otherwise have been able to do. . . . Two people travelling together can, under any circumstances, see and learn a great deal more than one. When it comes to travelling in new and unfamiliar country this is emphatically true. For this reason a large part of what I saw and learned about Europe is due directly to the assistance of Dr. Park. Our method of procedure was as follows: When we reached a city or other part of the country which we wished to study, we would usually start out together. I had a notebook in which I jotted down on the spot what I saw that interested me, and Dr. Park, who had had experience as a newspaper reporter, used his eyes and ears. Then in the course of our long stretches of railroad travel we compared notes and comments and sifted, as thoroughly as we were able, the facts and observations we had been able to gather. Then as soon as we reached a large city I got hold of a stenographer and dictated as fully as I was able the story of what we had seen and learned. In doing this, I used Dr. Park's observations, I suppose, quite as much as my own. In fact, I do not believe I am able to say how much of what I have written is based on my own personal observations and what is based on those of Dr.

Park. . . . In another direction Dr. Park has contributed to making this book what it is. While I was dictating my own account of our adventures he would usually spend time hunting through the book stores and libraries for any books or information which would throw light on any matter in which we were interested. The result was that we returned with nearly a trunkful of books, papers and letters which we had obtained in different places and from different people we met. With these documents Dr. Park then set to work to straighten out and complete the matter I had dictated, filling in and adding to what I had written.

Of this European tour, Park said:

One of the most interesting things I did during my connection with Tuskegee was to take a trip across Europe with Booker Washington. He had a plan to take a look at the laborers in Europe. He had an impression that, in spite of all the disadvantages that the Negro laborer lived under in America, his condition was not so much worse than that of the laborer in Europe. In one way he was right about that; in another he was wrong. In Europe the status of any class is pretty well defined in custom and in law, and he is protected in that status. The Negro's position as defined in law nowhere corresponds to his actual status as defined in custom, and custom is everywhere different.

I was eager to show Dr. Washington the condition of the European peasant as I had come to know it through my studies with Knapp in Strassburg. Besides that, while I was in Strassburg I had become intimately acquainted with the Black Forest. The result was that, in the late summer of 1910, we sailed for Europe. I went ahead, and spent a couple of weeks exploring East London, getting acquainted with a part of London I thought Dr. Washington would most like to see, and working out a plan for a journey across Europe, that would enable us to see in the shortest time possible, what it seemed to me was, for our purposes, most worth seeing. It was, as I look back upon it, a most remarkable journey. In six weeks we went from London to Skibo Castle, to visit Andrew Carnegie, then went from London as directly as possible to Prague, stopping only a few hours, to change trains in Berlin. From Prague we went to Vienna, from there as directly as possible, with a short stop-off in Rome, to Naples, then to Sicily, visiting the sulphur mines on our way to Catania. Thence returned to Rome, crossed the Adriatic, and went straight to Buda Pesth. We were interested in race problems and in peasants[,] and the Austrian Empire, with its mixed population, was the place to study both.

From there we went to Krakau, Poland, and in that region we spent some time, making excursions into outlying villages, everywhere meeting men who had lived in America and were delighted to talk with us.

Then we returned to Berlin. Dr. Washington went to Denmark, to get acquainted with the rural High Schools, for which Denmark is so famous. . . .

We made this journey in the incredibly short time of six weeks and, strange as it may seem, I learned more that was interesting and profitable there than I ever did in the same period before or since. I learned, perhaps more than Dr. Washington did, for I was well prepared by my previous studies and my four years in Europe, for what we were to see. Out of observations on that journey we made the book called *The Man Farthest Down*. This title was taken from a phrase that Ray Stannard Baker in his volume *Following the Color Line* had applied to the Negro.

If he had gone to Europe alone to study the condition of the lowest classes of Europe, Park would have gone directly to labor leaders and intellectuals already familiar with their condition. He saw to it that Washington met just such people, including members of various socialist parties. Since in America he was accustomed to consorting with top-level financiers and Republican politicians, this was a new experience for Washington. He said:

In Denmark and Italy . . . I met men of the very highest type who were members of the Socialist party. In Copenhagen, I was entertained by the editors of the Socialist paper, the *Politikin*, which is perhaps the most ably edited and influential paper in Denmark. In Italy, many of the most patriotic as well as the most brillant men in the country, writers, students and teachers are members of the party. In Poland, on the other hand, I met other Socialists who had taken an active part in the revolution in Russia and who, for aught I know, were members of that group of desperate men who are said even now to be plotting from Cracow, Austria, a new revolutionary move among the agricultural classes in Russia.

In the United States, Washington had been using all his energies to promote the economic rise of the blacks by urging them to buy land, to get an education, and to form economic organizations like the National Negro Business Men's League. He now realized that, pursuing similar goals, the lowest classes of Europe effectively used such methods as strikes, work stoppages, labor unions, cooperatives, and membership in radical political parties to gain their end. In an unpublished note, Washington says:

> The possibility that farm hands may be organized in labor unions and make use of that form of organization to compel land owners to raise wages *had never occurred to me*. [Italics added.] I found that where the masses of the people are oppressed, where the people at the bottom are being crushed by those above them, there Socialism means revolution. On the other hand, where governments have shown a liberal spirit, and especially where Socialists have had an opportunity to participate in government or have been able, by means of the cooperative societies I have described, to do constructive work for the benefit of the masses, they have ceased to be revolutionaries.

Washington and Park found that Denmark had done everything possible to ensure the security, dignity, and intellectual quality of the lives of her peasants. In Alabama almost all rural blacks were tenant farmers or cash tenants; in Denmark three-fourths of the peasants owned their own farms and they held seats in Parliament. Washington commented: "In Denmark, the peasant is not only free, he rules."

Both Washington and Park were fascinated by the contrast between the conditions of the peasants in Denmark and in Russia. Washington felt the most sympathy for those in Russia, because he believed their situation to be similar to that of American blacks. He commented: "In the little village of Barany, in Russian Poland, I had reached the point farthest removed, if not in distance at least in institutions and civilization from America, but as I stood on a little elevation of land at the edge of the village, I felt that I was merely at the entrance of a world in which . . . there was much the same life I had known and lived among the Negro farmers of Alabama."

To their great disappointment, the travelers were not permitted to cross the Polish-Russian border into Russia. On the edge of Barany, they stood, two Americans, Dr. Park and Dr. Washington—one Anglo-Saxon, the other half Anglo-Saxon, half African—peering wistfully at the land of the czars. An encounter they had near the border stirred in Washington memories of Negro slave revolts:

> . . . we came upon a foot passenger who was making his way toward the Russian border with great strides. He turned out to be a Jew, a tall erect figure, with the customary round flat hat, and the long black coat which distinguish the Polish Jew. Our driver informed us,

however, that he was a Russian Jew and pointed out the absence of side curls. . . . As we were obviously near the border, and he was obviously from Russia, I suggested that Dr. Park show him our passports and ask if they would let us into Russia. He stopped abruptly as we spoke to him and turned his piercing black eyes on us. "That is no passport," he said and then added, "It should be the visa of your counsel."

I was reminded of this strange figure a few months later when I noticed in one of the London papers a telegram from Vienna to the effect that some 30 persons had been arrested at Cracow who were suspected of being the ringleaders in "what was believed to be a widespread revolutionary organization of refugees." . . . It all recalled to my mind the stories I had heard from my mother's lips of the American Underground Railway. . . . It reminded me also of the wilder and more desperate struggles, of which we used to hear whispers in slavery times, when the slaves sought to gain their freedom by insurrection. . . . It is fatally true that no community can live without fear in which one portion of the people seeks to govern another by terror.

Once while they were in Eastern Europe, there was a shortage of accommodations and Park and Washington had to share a room. On getting up the next morning, Washington remarked that he had not liked sleeping with "a great big white man" and Park replied that he had not liked sleeping with "a great big black man, either." In London, Washington was entertained at two luncheons and spent much time with John Born, a labor member of Parliament. In Scotland the two men were entertained at Skibo Castle by Andrew Carnegie—one of Washington's staunchest supporters who in 1903 had given him $600,000 for his institute. The trip was so invigorating that Washington was eager to have Park plan another European tour for the next year. However, Park advised him that if he wanted the second tour to be as successful, he should find something new to talk about to European audiences. He suggested that a trip to the West Indies, before returning to Europe, might be just the thing.

This 1910 European tour was important to Washington's intellectual development. Although he was a patriot, believing or wishing to believe that everything in the United States was better than in Europe, he noted that the European lowest classes were exerting pressure on their governments to make changes and that the governments were not wholly unresponsive to it. In one of the manuscripts Washington dictated and gave to Park in the course of the 1910 trip, he said: "As one goes through Europe and studies the conditions of the poorer working classes, he is struck with the fact that much more is done in Europe to help the working classes than for the Negro in America. In England they have the old-age pension; in Austria the working man who gets sick is furnished for a period of 20 weeks by the State with free medical treatment and free medicines."

Some of Washington's biographers have observed that he took a stronger position on black civil rights during the later part of his life than he had taken in the 1890s. This undoubtedly had more than one cause, but the amount of instruction in European history that Park gave Washington on their European tour, combined with Washington's own powers of observation, probably contributed. If so, it may have been Park's most important service for Washington during the seven years they were together.

On 26 April 1911, when the manuscript of *The Man Farthest Down* was almost finished, Park wrote Washington a letter suggesting that they sign the book jointly:

My dear Mr. Washington:

Your letter of April 23rd referring to the way in which my name should appear in the final publication of *The Man Farthest Down* has just been received and while the matter is fresh in my mind I want to outline in a general way what I think about the matter. It seems to me the best thing to do would be to put my name on the book as a joint author. In case that is done a statement could be made in the preface or in the introduction as to what my part in the book was. In case that is done I should not like to be represented as a professional writer who had helped you to put together the book. Rather I should like it to appear that I had been working at Tuskegee, interested in the school as are others who are employed there. I would not want to be represented as engaged in any philanthropic or "unselfish" work. I should like the real fact stated that I was interested in you and in the work you are doing; that we had travelled about and gotten the same ideas; and it was because I understood you and we understood each other; were interested in the same things, that the book came to be written.

I think the matter can be presented in some such way as to add to the interest of the book rather than take away from it. I think the matter can be so presented that whatever I have added to the book has really been yours as well as mine. In that way it can not be said that you hired an outsider to write the book as I fear they are likely to say otherwise. I do not know as I have made myself very clear but if what I have said suggests anything to you I wish you would dictate something on which I can work.

You understand that it is not a desire to have you "do justice to me," but to put me in a position where I can talk about the book with some freedom and where I can continue to do the work I have been doing more comfortably. If people understand that whatever I write or may have written in the past is written by one who shares in, believes in, and is capable of interpreting what you think and mean that will be a great deal more satisfactory all around than it will if they believe my part in the book is that of a mere hired man.

As a matter of fact if the situation were not as I have stated I would never have been willing to do the work that I have done.

I am very truly
Robert E. Park

This letter was necessary because Washington was accustomed to publishing under his own name books that had been written in some part by a collaborator who was not acknowledged. John Hope Franklin notes that A. Liang Williams had done much of the work on Washington's biography of Frederick Douglass. In 1945 the black sociologist, Franklin Frazier, reviewing the massive collection of Washington papers in the Library of Congress, said: "It is generally known that the eminent sociologist, the late Dr. Robert E. Park of the University of Chicago, spent seven years in close association with Booker T. Washington. Moreover, it is now an open secret that Park was a co-author of some of Washington's books."

The Library of Congress papers show that Park assisted Washington in writing three books: *The Story of the Negro* (1909), *My Larger Education* (1911), and *The Man Farthest Down* (1912). The first two were signed by Washington alone. Park noted in a letter that he suggested the theme of *My Larger Education* to Washington. He also described amusingly how he edited both Washington's and his wife's writing, saying that he could "make Clara sound more like Clara and Washington sound more like Washington" than either could sound alone. Washington's secretary, Emmet Scott, who had some literary ability, also collaborated in this way.

Park's consenting to work anonymously on the first two books is understandable. Tuskegee always needed fresh financial contributions and, since Washington had an international reputation, his name on a book attracted donors. In addition, Washington was an extraordinarily busy man; he spent at least half the year away from the institute, lecturing and cultivating his political, social, and financial contacts. Such collaboration and editing as Park supplied for Washington were a small part of his work as a publicist for Tuskegee Institute. He supplied newspapers with a continuous stream of fresh news. He also wrote many newspaper and magazine articles under his own name.

Washington and Park returned from their European trip in fall 1910. On 1 December Park learned that his father was ill. He went to Watertown, South Dakota, and persuaded his father to come to Florida. On 11 February 1911, when Hiram Park died he left the bulk of the shares in the Park & Grant Mercantile Co. to his second wife, Anna, and to his two sons, Herbert and Robert.

That spring in New York City, Booker Washington was beaten severely on the head by a white man named Ulbrich. Washington charged Ulbrich with assault in a New York police court. Washington never fully recovered after this beating; he died four years later, at fifty-six.

During the last half of 1910 and spring of 1911, Park was so involved, first with the European trip and then with his father's illness, that he did not often get back to his family in Wollaston. The pleasures and difficulties of the Park family during the years of his preoccupation with the Tuskegee Institute have been described by his daughter Margaret.

According to Margaret,

Clara Park was never wholly reconciled to having her husband away from home so much. Nevertheless, she managed. The children were getting older and more helpful. She developed her own interests, and as she had an elderly Irishwoman, Mrs. Collins—commonly known as Colley—to help in the kitchen, she was not entirely housebound. And she had the new house in Wollaston.

In summer 1907 the Park family moved themselves up to the not quite finished new place. They were alone on Third Hill except for one neighbor who raised cows and chickens. The Park house was a good house for the family. It had a great deal of land and magnificent views—the Blue Hills, the lights of Boston and environs, and the picturesque castlelike water tower and reservoir. Although Park was gone much of the time, the new house was important to him. Interested in and committed as he was to his work in the South, he could not have tolerated—at least not cheerfully—his months away from his family if he had not felt secure in them and his home. "There are a lot of things I think that I do not speak about," he told Clara. "I should like for instance to do something first rate—something or other, not much matter which—but I don't and the time is slipping by with terrible swiftness. But I think my first real achievement was in marrying you. My second is in getting our little home, and as I have said before, I believe these are the most valuable and lasting achievements. . . . In short I believe the chief labor of man is to build a house and rear a family. It is also the most satisfying in the long run. I aim to be an ancestor." Later, in referring to this period, he said: "I guess maybe I neglected my family." He did not feel he was doing so at the time; in fact, it does not seem he did. His influence on and participation in the life of the family were so great when he was there that they continued in his absence. Clara once wrote him, "You have a sort of talent for being with the family, it's too bad you can't exercise it more."

He preferred to arrive home unexpectedly, or at least without planning too far ahead. But he was always home to take the children to the circus in the spring, always to celebrate Christmas with song, story, Yule logs, and presents. Park, although not a sportsman, was always a walker and country lover. He walked to the beach with the children and taught them to swim. They hiked to the more distant Blue Hills, where cast-off rattlesnake skins could be found. They picked berries in the woods. In two summers Park took his children and a neighbor's child on walking trips in a New Hampshire then untouched by motels and ski lodges, adventuresome trips in which they slept on pine boughs on the mountainsides or got shelter from a friendly farmer. He encouraged gardening—there was a large kitchen garden, and currant and raspberry bushes to be cared for as a money-earning project by Edward as chief and the two younger children as assistants. Park did not attempt to garden himself. He did, however, enjoy keeping up the wood supply for the two fireplaces. He went to cut apple wood in a deserted orchard over the hill, trundling the logs back in a wheelbarrow, a large man with a black beard and a gaggle of children following him.

He was fond of music, especially opera—*Tristan und Isolde* was his favorite. He also enjoyed family singing at the piano from the songbooks brought from Germany. His greatest pleasure was in books—buying books, mainly from secondhand bookshops, reading books, reading books aloud to his family. When he was away, Clara would read children's books aloud. But Robert would read Plato and Homer. *Les Miserables*, unabridged, was very popular—the youngest child, not quite eight, said it was "his favorite book." He read Scott, *Ivanhoe* and *The Talisman*. Somewhat later, he read glorious *War and Peace*, also Jane Austen, G. K. Chesterton, and George Bernard Shaw. He liked poetry by Whitman and Tennyson best, then Yeats, Robert Frost, and others. The children, encouraged to keep up their German, memorized some poems by Heine. Sometimes, especially after seeing a performance at the old Castle Square Repertory Theatre, they would read Shakespeare's plays aloud.

In a letter to his father-in-law, Judge Cahill, in spring 1910, Robert Park described his financial situation and his feelings toward it.

Clara has told you no doubt that I will go abroad this summer. I am sorry that I have to be away from home so much of the time and do not intend to spend as much time away from home in the future as I have in the past. I wish none of you would get the idea, however, that I am doing this work at Tuskegee merely for fun or for philanthropy. I have looked over the whole field and I find there is nothing that I could do that would keep me at home more, that would earn on the whole more money or that I could do so well in.

I am doing good work at Tuskegee, valuable, original first hand work. I am not getting any great reputation out of it, but I am doing the work. I am getting just as much pay for it as they can afford to give me or as I could expect or ask for. I am getting about what the average assistant professor in a college gets, not considering my traveling expenses which are heavy and which I do not have to pay. . . .

Of course we are poor. We try to live on two thousand a year and actually do live on twenty-three and twenty-five hundred. But poverty, mild poverty, such as we have endured all our lives is not such a bad thing. . . . I notice that everywhere around me there is the tacit understanding that money and comforts, security from dangers and all the rest which wealth brings, are very desirable things. My experience has convinced me that none of these things are true. My earnest wish for my children is that they will never have and never want to spend any more money than I do. I am trying to bring them up in the notion that our situation here is ideal, that it needs nothing to make it as perfect as life can tolerably be for human beings—it needs nothing but health, sunshine, contentment, work and joy, all of which we can contribute very largely ourselves.

I am telling you all this because it seemed to me that you may have had the idea that we had been living for the past few years under conditions of peculiar hardship. It is not really so. We have been living under conditions where life has had a peculiar zest for all of us. If you don't believe it just come down and see the way the children have grown; see what Clara has accomplished and see how proud she is of herself.

If we had had five hundred dollars more a year Clara would never have written the articles she did. She would never have become one of the distinguished women of America, she would have been less in touch than she is now with the great mass of mankind who have less than we do; she would have been less in touch with real life, more disposed to be peevish, discontented, dissatisfied. Our whole household would not have been the healthy, wholesome, toiling, aspiring place it is for our children. Five hundred dollars would not make much difference in this direction, but it would have made some.

It has sometimes occurred to me that it was barely possible we had too much money. If we had even less we might do more, and doing more we should enjoy life more. The deadening effect of wealth is that it teaches you you can not do things and so cuts off that much of the world from your experience.

Clara Park did not agree with her husband that "it was barely possible we had too much money." Her daughter Margaret notes that

although she never said anything to her parents or neighbors, she wrote to her husband about that "extra five hundred dollars we always fell behind in and had to get out of the atmosphere, somewhere, with *blood and tears*." The struggle was hardly a glorious challenge, but she accepted it as a part of a life which on the whole she felt to be right and admirable. To feed and clothe four growing children, to pay the insurance, the coal bill, and the mortgage, was a constant strain.

In the first days at Wollaston, she had earned some money by doing pastel portraits of children, but her contacts were too limited to make this practical for long. She had some facility in writing, and on occasion when they needed money she would sit down, in the evening when the children were all in bed, to write an article which one of the Sunday newspapers was willing to buy for the magazine section. These pieces were not, however, what made her the "distinguished woman" her husband mentioned; it was her work, quite nonprofessional, in social welfare, especially with women and children. It tended to involve expense—trips to conferences and so on—rather than additions to income, but was worth the trouble as a morale builder. Robert Park who, as a sociologist, was thought to be quite unsympathetic to social reformers, both admired and encouraged his wife in this field. Her most noteworthy case—which eventually led to a mother's pension, one of the first in the United States—resulted from her sympathy with a widowed mother of eight whose children were about to be taken from her and placed in various orphanages. Clara's first actions were to raise money by raffling a barrel of flour (which was illegal in Massachusetts; but no notice of it was taken) and to encourage a great deal of newspaper publicity. Through this she obtained the sympathy of the general public and the interest of the legislators, since it was demonstrated that it would be more humane to give money to the mother to maintain her family and it would save considerable governmental funds. Clara persisted in keeping the matter alive until a satisfactory bill was passed. Among others Theodore Roosevelt, then president, wrote to her about this, and they had a brief, pleasant correspondence.

Clara could not have done so much as she did if she had not had Mrs. Collins and children who were beginning to grow up and becoming able to help at home. Nevertheless, she was tired. Thus, when Hiram Park left her husband stock in the family business, dividends from which would guarantee a comfortable income, she anticipated not luxury but a loosening of financial stringencies. In March 1911 she wrote her husband:

> It makes me laugh the way you have to drag and haul me up Parnassus, I hanging back and balking all the way, but at last toddling after. Of course you know that to continue feeling at one with you I would do anything in reason. To do me justice, I feel that I would like, in the beginning, all that you say, if I did not feel that the "business" end of it, as they say of a bee, was stinging me more than it was you. I want to be an angel, but I do not feel that the angels have taken me by the hand and asked me to step up beside them. I feel that I have been imposed on, not intentionally, but carelessly, and veritably. It is impossible to feel virtuous while you are in debt unless you see a way out.
>
> One of the funniest things, I think, in the world, is the sight of me, this morning, sitting there with a dusty volume of Paulsen's *Ethik*, trying to console myself for owing Edward $18 plus for eggs. It makes me laugh, and that helps some, but doesn't help Edward.

She was not always able to laugh. On 6 August 1911 she wrote:

> I do not feel to blame that I do not like to go on living in debt, in parsimony, and in unceasing care. . . . I may take you at your word and tell you what I would like. I would like to have you take, from your dividends paid from the business, enough to raise our present income to about four thousand a year. I do not think we can be comfortable on less, unless it all comes out of me. . . .

[Margaret concludes that] although they adored their father, the children sympathized with their mother, especially the two elder ones, who knew the difficulties she had. For some time Robert was reluctant to enlarge the domestic budget by more than a very little, though always ready to spend money on education—for Edward at Harvard, for Theodosia at the Quincy Mansion School for Girls with art school to follow. He was planning that in 1915, when Edward would have graduated from college and the younger daughter from high school, all four children would go to study in Munich, a favorite spot.

During 1911 Park was preoccupied with plans for staging an International Conference on the Negro at Tuskegee Institute in spring 1912. Through an Associated Press report, he discovered that another conference—called The Friends of Africa—was to be held in London in 1911. Park wrote to Emmett Scott that the Tuskegee conference would in no sense be a rival to the London conference and, further, that the public should not be allowed to confuse the two.

The Tuskegee conference was to open on 19 April 1912. Just before this date Park was in his home in Wollaston, where one of his children had the measles and the rest were quarantined. Park, it would seem, had for some time been contemplating leaving Tuskegee. On 8 April 1912 while in Wollaston he started a new notebook labeled "Notes on Race Psychology." He dated it, an unusual procedure, since most of Park's notebooks are undated. Two days later he wrote Washington that he wished to leave Tuskegee.

My dear Mr. Washington:

After thinking the matter all over I have determined to leave Tuskegee. My reason for doing so is my desire to spend the next few years, while they are growing up, in closer contact with my children. I want to say, now that I am leaving here, that I have never been so happy in my life as I have since I became associated with you in this work. Some of the best friends I have in the world are at Tuskegee. I feel and shall always feel that I belong, in a sort of way, to the Negro race and shall continue to share, through good and evil, all its joys and sorrows.

I want to help you in the future as in the past in any way that I can and would gladly remain if I could persuade my family to come South to live. I am very grateful to you for the privilege of knowing you as intimately as I have. I feel that I am a better man for having been here.

I am sincerely,
Robert E. Park

P.S. I should like to leave Saturday night after the conference.

II. At the University of Chicago

Chapter 8. The Convergence of William I. Thomas and Robert Park

The International Conference on the Negro opened as planned on 19 April 1912 at Tuskegee Institute. William I. Thomas, a professor in the Department of Sociology at the University of Chicago, was a speaker.

The conference was entirely Park's idea. It concerned not only the blacks of the United States but also those of the West Indies and of Africa. Washington, though never much interested in Africa, was prepared to help Park do what he wanted to do. The conference had been widely publicized. Washington informed Park that 3,700 persons had been invited and that the Department of State had notified "all the governments that have Negro possessions" about the affair. Park himself was speaking, and so was the United States Commissioner of Education. Among the speakers were representatives from Jamaica and Sierra Leone. The theme of the conference was "the Education of Primitive Man." Park sounded the keynote of the conference by posing the question: "How far is it possible by means of education to abridge the apprenticeship of the younger to the older races, or at least to make it less cruel and inhuman than it now frequently is?"

Thomas's speech, "Education and Cultural Traits," was well received by the Tuskegee *Student* which said: "Professor Thomas revived the old question of the fitness of the Negro as a race to acquire the culture of the white man and participate in the white man's civilization, but he did it in a novel and a surprisingly witty manner."

When the conference ended, it was decided to have a second one three years later, in 1915. Washington himself, Emmett Scott, Washington's secretary, and Park were to serve on the committee.

Before the Tuskegee conference Park and William I. Thomas had never met. Thomas recalls that

> about the year 1910 I received a letter from Booker Washington which resulted in an important influence. Mr. Washington wrote inviting me to participate in a conference where Negroes from 21 countries were to be present. He further went into an analysis of my printed works. . . . As a result I attended the conference at Tuskegee and discovered that this letter was not written by Mr. Washington at

all but by a white man, Robert E. Park. This was the beginning of a long and profitable association. Park was not only ruminating all of the time but imposing his ruminations on me, with eventual great profit to myself.[1]

Four days after the conference ended, Thomas was writing the first of the following letters to Park from Chicago:

My dear brother in Christ:

I am amazed to find how ignorant I was before I met you and how wise I seem to be now. Truly it was a great experience to meet you, greater than to meet all the other colored persons present.

I have concluded that the negro question beats the peasant question, and am thinking of returning from Europe in time to spend January to April in the south, and possibly in the West Indies. What are your plans for the West Indies? Cannot I go along?

At the same time I think something is going to result from a comparison of the negro and the peasant. I think it will turn out that we shall want a volume based on the Tuskegee materials, one on the south in general, treating some topics which would not appropriately come in the Tuskegee vol. A vol. on the West Indies, one on West Africa, and one on the southern poor white. When we get through we shall have something. . . .

Good hunting
W. I. Thomas

He wrote again on April 24, 1912:

Dear Colleague:

I think you had better come here and teach eventually but I would not rob the negro of you just yet. I am sending you my paper on race prejudice. It was written before I attained my full powers (as our British Guiana friend would say) but I promised it. I also send a proof of my schedule.

Yours,
W. I. Thomas

And again on May 6, 1912:

My dear Park:

Your two letters reached me together. It has been the greatest thing that ever happened to me to meet you, and if we can pull this

1. "The Life Histories of W. I. Thomas and Robert E. Park," with an Introduction by Paul J. Baker, *American Journal of Sociology* 79 (September 1973), 249.

thing off, as we are going to, and eventually get together and teach alongside it will make life interesting.

As to the schedule, once for all, it is not my schedule but ours. It lacks the reality and depth of insight that you have gotten through your more intimate association with the negroes. I do not attach any great importance to it in its present shape. I think, of course, that it has some merit, but all that you say in your letters and that is in your head should go into it, and we shall surely find some things should be dropped out. Your point about the subconscious element in race-prejudice, for instance, is fine. Some of your points, as the study of individuals, I meant to include under "great men," in the section which I call imitation. But certainly your suggestions on this point and on the others lend life and an enlarged meaning to what had passed through my head. Certainly whatever you think worth going into the plan will go. I think it would be a good plan to take one copy of the schedules I am sending and insert notes on points as they occur to you which we can embody in our plan when we talk it over. I will come on for a week or five days and see you either in Wollaston, Boston, or New York, just as you say. I can leave here about the 10th of June, and sail the 18th. I want to talk to Robinson and Dewey, in New York. Would it suit you to meet me in New York at my expense? Or what do you propose?

As I said to you I see more now in the negro question than in the peasant, and am anxious to get around to that. At the same time the peasant has a comparative value which we must not give up. When we get around to it we shall probably want to include the yellow races (after we have gone together to Africa!) Up to this point golf has been my main interest, but I think I shall be pleased to work now in our vineyard.

I have told Small about my meeting with you and that we are going in together on this thing. He said right off that he got a very fine impression of you. He is a very fine fellow in his spirit, and will do almost anything I say within his power. It would strengthen our department greatly to have you here. We ought both to have six months teaching arrangement, as I have now, and could go into the field then together half the time. I will talk over the West Indies trip with you. We may decide that it is best for me to stay nine months in Europe and get that part of the business as advanced as possible at once. . . .

Write a line whenever you can to your blood-brother. We will perform the rite later. I am a bad one for writing.

More anon.
W. I. T.

Ten days later, on May 16, his enthusiasm had not diminished:

We are evidently going to have a good deal of fun out of this thing. It will be a lot more interesting to both of us to go double than single. I will come on to Boston just as you say, I think as early as June 8th, and we can beat about the town and see the mulattos.

As to the pathological side of the case, Freud of Vienna has something on all the psychiatrists. They also have something on him, for he sees nothing but sex in everything. But his cases and those of his school, especially Jung of Zurich, are most important for our business. I had a talk with Freud last year and read all his stuff. (Perhaps I spoke to you of it in Tuskegee.) Evidently this side of the case is a whole world in itself. I am sending you some of Freud's stuff. I have marked the best papers. The analysis of the phobias are particularly interesting in connection with race prejudice, as showing how the mind is prepossessed. You may have seen the stuff I am sending. I sent Dewey some of the best stuff, and he has it still, but I can get it in New York. What you say about the adjustment in connection with crisis is a fault in the schedule. I had "crisis" in mind to cover the whole process of disturbance and reaccommodation, we could call the missing link "accomodation." . . .

If convenient, we will go to New York together and have some talk with any men you want to see and some I would like you to know better, such as Dewey and Robinson—though I believe you are familiar with Dewey.

Don't get excited, son. We must make this a pleasure jaunt. I am preserving your letters, so that if you forget anything I will have it down in black and white.

More anon.
W. I. Thomas

The Frommigkeit of Graf Zinzendorf is just an interesting Geschichte from the Freud standpoint.

Thomas's earliest letters to Park were recently found in a file of old business letters in a built-in cupboard of the Wollaston house. With them was the draft of a letter by Park to Thomas about what he had "stewing in the think tank" in relation to isolation, crisis, and accommodation. The letter is unfinished and unsigned:

October 6, 1912

My dear W. I.:

Since I saw you last or rather wrote you last I have been away out in Oklahoma and have visited two negro towns and some other interesting places besides being among those present at a "baptiz-ing." This was way down in the "sticks" where the wild people live.

I wish that I could have taken down the sermon that was preached at the edge of the pool. It had many interesting details, mixture of learned language, with homely illustrations and withal inspired by some shrewd practical wisdom.

Also I have einfälle in regard to Isolation, Crisis and Accom-modation. I am going to present you some things that are stewing in the think tank as they come to the surface (we can find out what they are worth afterwards) when we come to apply them to the interpreta-tion of the stuff.

Isolation: mental characteristics of the isolated are naivete, preva-lence of custom (social habit), rule of authority, a disposition to interpret experience according to the rules of magic (i.e. by intuition and use of principles grounded in the subconsciousness and not clearly thought out).

Crisis: mental characteristics, exaggerated self consciousness (group consciousness), mobility (suggestibility), rule of abstract right; disposition to interpret experience scientifically (i.e. by abstract laws, skepticism, critical-mindedness).

Accommodation: mental characteristics, disposition to view per-sonal and group relations objectively, toleration, disposition to look at conditions from practical standpoint rather than sentimental; abstract principles embodying themselves in custom and habit gradually yield to practical and personal considerations. Disposition to take the historical common sense rather than the abstract scientific view.

It is necessary to define what we mean by *Naivete*.

When an individual speaks or otherwise behaves without con-sciousness of the comment which his behavior excites in other minds, that is a display of naivete.

What this naivete discloses is a character or point of view, a mental background that has got itself bedded in the back of his head, which is different from the character and point of view of the person to whom he appears naive. It is a symptom of isolation, a revelation of his individuality. Individuality in the narrow sense defines his place or position in a group to which he belongs. Individuality is, in other words, the product of social relationships. The person who had no individuality is the cosmopolitan.

I am a little mixed here because I am using individuality in two senses. The individuality which a man possesses because he has a definite place in a group is the individuality of which he is con-scious, more or less. It is the thing which marks him off from other

members of the group. The individuality which he possesses revealed in what we call his naivete is the individuality which he
possesses by reason of belonging to a group. It is the individuality of
the group.

What I mean is this: in every nation, race, class or other stable
group of individuals there are a great many points of view, habits of
thought, instinctive ways of interpreting experience which all use
but of which none are conscious. They are the suppressed premises
in all kinds of intercourse; the principles that no one calls in question; that have not even been formulated; the matters we cannot
discuss nor arbitrate, et cetera.

The fact that these notions are so uniform within the group is an
indication that they have been transmitted by unconscious imitation. The fact that similar notions, having a different form of expression, may be found in many different groups, living under similar
conditions, or in the same grade of culture, is an indication that the
same fundamental notions are bound to spring up under the same
environment—is an indication, therefore, that they are *not* racial.

With change in conditions there comes *crisis*. There is a question
whether crisis ever arises as a result of internal growth or development inside the group. I doubt it. I think crisis arises when the group
comes in contact with another group and there is a consequent
attempt to readjust their social relations and their conceptions of life.

In one of his autobiographical notes, Park says of his meeting with
Thomas:

By this time I had a good many notions about the Negro and about
race problems. I had a vast amount of information about the Negro
and a good deal of insight, but I had nothing, actually, to write. The
whole situation presented itself to me as a series of questions and
problems that needed to be investigated, and what was most needed
here, as in the case of the newspaper, was not so much facts as some
theoretical scheme in which these problems could be stated in their
more general bearings. I found in Thomas, almost for the first time, a
man who seemed to speak the same language as myself. When,
therefore, he invited me to come to Chicago and give a course on the
Negro, I was delighted to do so.

Park quit his job at Tuskegee in spring 1912 and gave his first course at
the University of Chicago in the winter quarter of 1914. During the
interim he made for the Stokes Foundation a three-month survey of
southern black schools. The Year 1913 marked the fiftieth anniversary of

the Emancipation Proclamation. The blacks Park met on the survey told him they were by no means happy about this anniversary:

> As I have travelled about the country I have had the opportunity to talk with colored people in all parts of the country and I have found the conviction very general that somehow, quietly, and without anything in particular to indicate it, a decided change has taken or is taking place in the situation of the Negro. . . .
>
> I have had my attention more than once called to the fact that in the year 1913, at the very time we are celebrating the 50th anniversary of our freedom, the Negro is exercising less influence and having less part in the governing of the country than at any time since the Civil War. . . .
>
> One other thing to which my attention has been called is the fact that while in 1913 there was probably less crime, fewer lynchings and more homes built among Negroes in proportion to the population than ever before, it was the year in which all that remained of the Civil Rights Bill, the law which attempted to secure for Negroes equal privileges with white men in hotels, theaters and public conveyances, was finally erased from the Federal Statute books.

It was also a time when black leadership was undergoing profound change. Two men, Booker T. Washington and W. E. B. Du Bois, had dominated the scene during the late 1890s and the first decade of the twentieth century. When Washington's friend Theodore Roosevelt was defeated in his try for a third term in 1912, Washington's great political power declined. Two organizations that have remained influential came into existence at this time: the National Association for the Advancement of Colored People in 1910, and the National Urban League in 1911. Park chose to identify himself with the latter:

> I was present at the first meeting of the Urban League when it was organized in New York at the time of Mrs. William H. Baldwin. I recall that among the other persons who attended that meeting was Ray Stannard Baker. I was the first president of the League in Chicago and I have followed its history with interest ever since. As we conceived the League at that time it was to devote itself largely to improving race relations; to making possible the cooperation of different agencies of both races, not merely for the benefit of the Negro, but for the common good. One of the things that we regarded as important was that the League should be source of knowledge and insight as to what actual conditions were. It was for this reason that we established, in connection with the League in Chicago, a bureau of research of which Charles Johnson was put in charge.

In making the transition from Tuskegee to Chicago, from the South to the North, Park set down some of his sociological musings in his letters to W. I. Thomas. But he also dashed off—strictly for himself—some colorful impressionistic notes summing up his emotional reactions to the scenes and persons he had been involved with for seven years:

> Primitive peoples are not necessarily inferior peoples. . . . The Negro is the finest primitive in the world. . . . There is no evidence of which I know that proves the Negro is racially inferior to the white man. . . . There is no evidence to prove that the mulatto is the superior of the black man. . . . The Negro has had the fortune to have met the white man and lived. No other primitive people have done so.
>
> The Civil War did away with slavery in the South. It did not do away . . . with the domination of the black man by the white man. This domination was founded in wealth, education, in the ownership of land, in the solidarity of the white race. . . . This domination of the white by the black exists today in the South. . . . The most violent and dangerous expression of this system is the notion that the only way to maintain this domination is by spreading general terror among the colored people. This is the idea that was back of the Atlanta riot. It is the idea that is back of the lynchings. It is the idea that gives support to every iniquity that is peculiar to the South today.
>
> 1. The Catholic South—instance of temperament breaking through. The Protestant North—the stolid, silent, brooding North, its ferocious appetites and passion. Its capacity for sentiment and ideals.
> 2. The facile, graceful, formal South. The South gay, polite, superficial. Set of agile-minded men, mobile, ready sympathy—Faith in ceremonies and bureaucracy.
>
> Among Negroes in the South the notion is inculcated directly or indirectly that the white man is a superior being, that he is dangerous, not to be resisted, but kindly disposed if properly placated.
>
> In the North the idea is inculcated that the white man individually is a powerful and cruel rival, that he is to be resisted wherever possible, but that it is not impossible to get on with him. The sentiments are those of one who regards himself as unjustly shut out from opportunities, companionship, etc.

In this series of notes, Park also comments on the characteristics of two great black leaders: Washington, whom he knew intimately, and Du Bois whom he had never met:

Du Bois, sensitive, refined, educated at Fisk and Harvard, started to be an historian and sociologist. Became a literary man, poet and agitator. . . .

Du Bois had a very high ideal of the white man, that is the reason he thought of him as a blonde beast. He hated him as he actually found him. The white man held the world in his hands, God-like in his power, no explanation for him except that he was evil. Du Bois did not expect so much of the Negro—that was the reason he was proud of him—the beauty of his genre, the sweetness of his soul, the strength of his meekness by which he was to inherit the Earth. . . .

The Du Bois movement represented the talented South—the free Negro in the North, the educated Negro in the South. . . . Washington represented the masses of freed men. . . .

Washington, born a slave, tells somewhere how as a child he used to fight with the pigs for the corn thrown out to them. . . .

Washington, like Benjamin Franklin, Andrew Carnegie, a self-made man. Vigorous common sense . . .

Du Bois, handsome, graceful, elegant, aristocratic in every instinct and ambition, except that of generosity to his opponents and graciousness toward those he regarded as inferior to himself. . . .

These two men have divided the white and dark world between them. Du Bois has defined the relation as one of radical and irreconcilable opposition. Washington is cooperative despite divergences and differences, not, however, minimizing the conflict of interest where it exists.

Du Bois and Washington were of mixed ancestry. In one of his undated notes on matters connected with black history, Park referred to the phenomenon of mixed racial strains: "The free Negro . . . He was an anomaly. He was the marginal man. He was characteristically a mixed-blood." And in some later notes: "The man on the racial margin . . . The racial borderland . . . *The Marginal Man—A Study of the Mulatto Mind.*"

Park was in time to develop the concept of the marginal man much further, but his original use of the phrase clearly applied to Americans of black and white ancestry. During his seven years at Tuskegee Institute, he had come to know a number of them rather well—one, Washington himself.

When Thomas asked Dean Albion W. Small, chairman of Department of Sociology of the University of Chicago, to make Park a member of the department, he found that, although Small was quite willing to do this, the matter was not simple. Everett Hughes says: "The records of the University show that Park was first appointed in the Divinity School, as there was no position in the Department of Sociology and Anthropology. Small had been given to understand that sociology was not to be expanded at the University of Chicago. . . . Small, a college president before he came to Chicago, became a power in the administration. . . . I heard it said he aspired to the presidency when Harper died. But lost out to a conservative man who was going to balance the budget. . . . Park thus came at a time when the current had been running against sociology."

Small, powerful in University affairs, managed to take Park on anyway by employing him as a professorial lecturer. The salary for this in 1914 was $500 for a single course. Obviously it would not support a family, and Park decided to use some of the money he had inherited to supplement his income. Until then he had been willing to use the inheritance only for his children's education.

Park's ideas about money and its use were striking. His daughter Theodosia says:

> My father had ideas, perhaps from Karl Marx, about money. He said wealth was produced by labor and that capitalists who lived on inherited wealth were taking it away from those who had earned it. He felt some guilt at having accepted so much from his father. However he had no real taste for making money. When he came back from Germany, he took a position at Harvard which paid very little, because he found it so inspiring to work under William James. He had a little motto which he put up somewhere: "God don't care for money; look who He gives it to." The other things he did, working for the Congo Reform Association and for Booker T. Washington could not be called well paying jobs, but they were intensely interesting to him.

Chapter 9. Sociology—the Youngest Branch of Learning

In fall 1913 Robert Park delivered an address at the University of Chicago on "Racial Assimilation in Reference to the Negro." In 1914 he gave his first course in the university's Department of Sociology and Anthropology:

> *The Negro in America*: Directed especially to the effects, in slavery and freedom, of the contacts of the white and black race, an attempt will be made to characterize the nature of the present tensions and tendencies and to estimate the character of the changes which race relations are likely to bring about in the American system.

He thus pursued, in a new setting and with new colleagues, the subject of his work in the South. He was also breaking ground. This course was certainly one of the first dealing exclusively with black Americans to be given in any predominantly white university in the United States and may, indeed, have been the first such course.

He found his association with his colleagues in the various social science departments stimulating. On 22 August 1914 he wrote his twelve-year-old son, Robert: "Chicago is not a nice place to live (compared to Wollaston), although it is very interesting because so much is going on here and then it is fine to be in the University where you get a lot of clever and interesting people. Perhaps, next year, we will be living here. If I am really going to be a 'professor,' this is the best place for me."

By 1916 Park was giving four courses: "The Negro in America," "The Newspaper," "Crowd and Public," and "The Survey." Lincoln Steffens said: "What a reporter knows and doesn't write becomes either literature or sociology." The sociological baggage Park had from his eleven years as a reporter was rich. He had later spent seven years preparing for "The Negro in America." His course "The Survey" was based on his knowledge of five American cities. Summing up his early days in Chicago in a biographical note, he said: "I gave my first course on the Negro in Chicago in 1913. I found Chicago a congenial place to work and I conceived the notion that the thing for me to do was to stick around and see if I could work out in the classroom the more general theoretical problems which had arisen, as far as I was concerned, out of my own encounters with life."

Park's children longed to be with him in Chicago, but this was not immediately feasible. Park and his wife agreed that it was better, at the moment, for her to stay in Wollaston and for the children to continue their schooling in the east. Edward was to graduate from Harvard in 1915 at the age of twenty; Theodosia was studying at the Art Students League in New York; Margaret was to be a freshman at Wellesley; and Robert was in public school. Park spent as much time as possible with his family, either in Wollaston or in the summers at Roaring Brook, but some of the time he was living alone in Chicago.

The family came to Chicago gradually. Edward came first in fall 1915 and began graduate work in sociology. Theodosia and her friend, Fentress Kerlin, also an artist, came next and kept house for Park. Mrs. Park was for a long time detained by her mother's last illness and the whole family was not completely reassembled until spring 1916.

The years between 1913, when he learned that Dean Small was prepared to hire him as a professional lecturer, and the spring of 1916, when his family was finally all in Chicago, were among the most important in Park's life. He had a good deal of leisure. He was consciously preparing to be a teacher of sociology. These were the years for reading, dreaming, and thinking, with a minimum of obligation and a maximum of freedom.

As a student at the University of Michigan from 1883 to 1887, Park said he had never heard the word "sociology." No university in the United States was giving a course in this field. Having studied philosophy in five universities, Park now had to equip himself to be not a philosopher but a sociologist. He was greatly assisted by William I. Thomas who in 1914 was one of the country's outstanding sociologists. They were nearly the same age, Thomas had been born in 1863, Park in 1864. Thomas graduated from the University of Tennessee in 1884, taught Greek and modern languages there, did graduate work at Goettingen and Berlin and became professor of English at Oberlin in 1889. Feeling that the teaching of languages did not make enough use of the abilities he felt he had, Thomas got a Ph.D. in sociology from the University of Chicago in 1896. This was one of the earliest degrees granted by the University of Chicago's Department of Sociology.

In this, Thomas was exceptional. Almost all the great sociologists born in the nineteenth century took their degrees in some field other than sociology and were only later recognized as doing thinking that was essentially sociological. Le Play (1806–82) was an engineer and Pareto (1848–1923) had studied engineering. Tarde (1834–1904) and Durkheim (1858–1917) had studied law. Max Weber (1864–1920) and Charles

Cooley (1864–1929) were economists. Lester Ward (1841–1913) was a biologist. Herbert Spencer (1820–1903), Georg Simmel (1858–1918), who wrote a dissertation on Kant, and Robert Park (1864–1944) were philosophers. Scholars who cross boundary lines between disciplines and are among the first to explore a new field tend to have original minds. Everett Hughes calls these nineteenth-century men the pioneer generation.

In addition to his paper on "Racial Assimilation in Secondary Groups," Park wrote a 60-page booklet, *Principles of Human Behavior*, the sixth in a series of social studies published by the Silasz Corporation in 1916. When Jesse F. Steiner, a graduate student from the state of Washington, wrote a Ph.D. thesis on the Japanese of the Pacific coast in 1913 and published a book called *The Japanese Invasion*, Park wrote the Foreword. However, by far his most important piece of writing during the 1914–16 period was a 50-page paper, "The City: Suggestions for the Investigation of Human Behaviour in the Urban Environment," based on what he had learned as reporter and editor. Characteristically, he wrote not as one who knew the answers but as a thinker who was aware of the problems that existed and who was interested in the questions that needed to be asked so that further investigations would be possible.

During his early years in Chicago, Park was mainly occupied with preparing his courses, getting acquainted with his students, and reading. He had all the sociological works with which he was not already familiar to absorb. However, his habit when looking up a subject in the library was to avoid standard texts, to explore books with odd and interesting titles, and, when he found a good one, to plunge into reading like a swimmer diving into a refreshing lake. In his explorations he ignored the boundaries supposed to confine a scholar to his own terrain. In this way he discovered ecology years before other sociologists did. He was so fascinated that he tried to persuade his youngest son, Robert Hiram Park, to study ecology. In "Memoir of My Father," Robert says: "Whether it was in 1915 or 1917, I recall that Pop stopped off at Lansing with the idea that he would try to interest me in studying plant and insect ecology, which he explained was simpler than human ecology but would be valuable to me if I ever decided to study human society. . . . I understood his point but didn't follow through as I was already spending all my spare time studying electricity and mechanics. . . . It was not that I had no interest in what he had in mind, but the point was that I had developed the impression that the world of my age was going to be highly technological, and this being the case, I wanted to prepare myself to be a part of it."

Because of his habit of exploratory reading, Park probably discovered certain early writings on ecology shortly after they were published. Four books to which he frequently referred are: Eugenius Warming's *Oecology of Plants*, which first appeared in English translation in 1909; W. M. Wheeler's *The Ant-Colony as an Organism*; Charles C. Adams' *Guide to the Study of Animal Ecology*; and C. J. Galpin's *The Social Anatomy of an Agricultural Community*, which appeared in 1915. Certain similarities between the cycles observable in plant, insect, animal, and human communities teased his mind and he was—in the course of time—to develop a concept which he called human ecology.

World War I began the first year Park was teaching in Chicago and was much on his mind. He had already studied the military for his excellent article on "The German Army" for *Munsey's Magazine* in 1900. His work on it had made him aware of how long ago plans for a possible war had probably been considered by that army's strategists. On 23 February 1916 he wrote his seventeen-year-old daughter Margaret, a freshman at Wellesley, that he wanted to study war as a sociological phenomenon:

Dear Datyschen:

That was a very lovely present you sent me on my birthday. . . . I have not been reading any poetry or anything much but books on sociology for several years past now and all the sap is drying up in my veins. . . .

Do you remember last year . . . when I was in Wollaston that I was digging away on a paper for Prof. Thomas? Well, I had a terrible time completing that paper. I always have a terrible time completing papers. . . . After that was published I felt so buoyant and light-hearted that I determined to take up something else right away.

Then an idea occurred to me. I said the simplest problems after all are world problems, the problems of the contacts and the frictions and the interactions of nations and races.

Does that strike you as simple? Probably not. However, they are. Any way I made up my mind to study the problem, the problem from the point of view of psychology is the problem of "War and Peace."

Why do we, irrespective of specific causes, have wars? Why do men fight? What is the function of war? Is war one way, one necessary way, of getting on in the world? Is it part of the cosmic process of evolution, part of the struggle for existence? Are human beings so made that the world would be worse off if these tremendous struggles did not exist? In short, is war founded in the nature of human beings?

This is what constitutes the problem. Now about this time Edward came along and after talking the matter over, he finally has settled down to make himself a sociologist and he has gone to work with me to help me to put together this book.

However, by fall 1916 Park was launched on a writing enterprise triggered by an external incident. A young man of thirty, Ernest W. Burgess, who had received a Ph.D. in sociology at the University of Chicago in 1913, in 1916 was asked to return as an instructor. Everett Hughes describes how Burgess happened to ask Park for help: "Burgess was expected to teach an introductory course. He asked a Professor Bedford, who was teaching such a course for his outline. Bedford refused to give it, saying that he would have to get up his own course. Thereupon the older Park and the young Burgess worked out a set of readings and outlines which, after use in classes, became the famous Park and Burgess *Introduction to the Science of Sociology.*"

A good writer himself, in 1916 Park was aware that beginning sociology textbooks were usually mediocre and extraordinarily dull. Park and Burgess planned to produce a book that would be exciting and attract able students. They put together mimeographed sheets for each sociological theme, including bibliographies, questions for discussion, and topics to be written about. They saw how students responded and revised their materials accordingly. In the preface to the first edition of *The Introduction to the Science of Sociology,* Park says:

> An experience of some years . . . has demonstrated the value . . . of a body of materials that are interesting in themselves and that appeal to the experience of the student. If students are invited to take an active part in the task of interpretation of the text, if they are encouraged to use the references in order to extend their knowledge of the subject matter and to check and supplement classroom discussion by their personal observation, their whole attitude becomes active rather than passive. Students gain in this way a sense of dealing at first-hand with a subject matter that is alive and with a science that is in the making.

The *Introduction* is a 1,000-page book organized around fourteen sociological themes illustrated by 196 readings. The index lists over 1,700 writers. Biologists, philosophers, and men of letters, as well as sociologists, are quoted. There are extracts from diaries and private journals. Of the ten writers most frequently cited one is German, Simmel; two are English, Darwin and Spencer; three French, Durkheim, Tarde, Le Bon; and four American, William Graham Sumner, Charles Cooley, Park himself, and William I. Thomas. The objective Park and

Burgess had in compiling this massive *Introduction to the Science of Sociology* was not merely to entertain or intrigue the student. The authors say that it "is not conceived as a mere collection of materials, but as a systematic treatise."

In the first chapter, "Sociology and the Social Sciences," which Park originally wrote as a paper for the *American Journal of Sociology*, Park seeks to define sociology:

> Sociology, so far as it can be regarded as a fundamental science and not a mere congeries of social-welfare programs and practices, may be described as the science of collective behaviour. With this definition it is possible to indicate in a general and schematic way its relation to the other social sciences. . . .
>
> Historically, sociology has had its origin in history. History has been and is the great mother of all the social sciences. . . . In history and the sciences associated with it . . . we have the concrete records of that human nature and experience which sociology has sought to explain. In the same sense that history is the concrete, sociology is the abstract science of human experience and human nature.
>
> On the other hand the technical (applied) social sciences, that is, politics, education, social service, and economics—so far as economics may be regarded as the science of business—are related to sociology in a different way. They are . . . applications of principles which it is the business of sociology and psychology to deal with explicitly.
>
> Sociology has to do with those modifications in human beings that are due to the human environment.
>
> The same social forces which are found organized in public opinion, in religious symbols, in social convention, in fashion, and in science . . . are constantly recreating the old order, making new heroes, overthrowing old gods, creating new myths, and imposing new ideals. And this is the nature of the cultural process of which sociology is a description and an explanation.

There are a number of passages in the *Introduction* which refer to the relative immaturity of the science of sociology. Edward Westermarck is quoted as saying in 1901 that sociology is "the youngest of the principal branches of learning." Park and Burgess also refer to sociology as "a science that is in the making." The following comment is especially sharp:

> Sociological research is at present [in 1921] in about the same situation in which psychology was before the introduction of laboratory methods, in which medicine was before Pasteur and the germ

theory of disease. . . . Social problems have been defined in terms of common sense. . . . In very few instances have investigations been made disinterestedly to determine the validity of an hypothesis. . . . Sociology seems, however, in a way to become, in some fashion or other, an experimental science. . . . We have, if it is permitted to make a distinction between them, investigation rather than research.

In the Preface, Park and Burgess express "their indebtedness to Dr. W. I. Thomas for the point of view and the scheme of organization of materials which have been largely adopted in this book" and refer in a footnote to Thomas's well-known *Source Book for Social Origins.* Everett Hughes feels, however, that the outstanding influence in the book is that of Park's mentor, Georg Simmel, and notes how strongly Park's reading in the field of biology and ecology influenced his treatment of sociology:

The basic framework of the Park and Burgess *Sociology* is that of Simmel. . . . Even in using Simmel, however, [Park] was very thoughtful and original. As I think of it, he seems to have built his system out of these basic ingredients (perhaps more): (1) the very abstract but infinitely flexible conception of interaction which he got from Simmel, and (2) the notion of collective behavior (crowd, public, social unrest, social movements) which he got in part from Windelband, Tarde, et al. But he also worked a new concept of evolution into it—evolution as itself a product of interaction. This idea is the leading one of the new school of evolutionary biologists.

Introduction to the Science of Sociology, begun in 1916, was published in 1921. The distinguished sociologist, Edward A. Ross, said in the *American Journal of Sociology*: "This ripe and scholarly volume is the last word in perfection in source books for the classroom and no teacher of sociology can afford to be without it."

The *Introduction* was soon widely used. Some teachers complained that the book was too difficult for students taking a first course in sociology. However, since both Park and Burgess had for several years prior to its publication been successfully teaching students taking a first course in sociology with the materials that appeared in the book, they were not overly impressed by this objection. In the Preface to the Second Edition (1924) they therefore refused to yield an inch and said:

There has been some criticism of this volume, on the ground that it is too difficult for students beginning the study of sociology, and for that reason not a good introduction. On the other hand, the criticism has been made by students in other sciences that sociology, as at present taught, is not an "intellectual discipline." How far that criticism is justified is not necessary for us to discuss here, except to say, in our own defense, that only a book that compels the student to take the science of sociology seriously, can meet this criticism.

Introduction to the Science of Sociology was republished in 1970. Its permanent importance lies in the largeness of Park's mind, the quality and diversity of the readings, and its comprehensiveness. Before its publication, sociology was presented to the beginner as a continent only haphazardly mapped. After the Park and Burgess book, the entire continent had been, as it were, surveyed from the air and the relationships of its various regions to each other were clearly discernible. Robert E. L. Faris, one of Park's students, said in *Chicago Sociology: 1920–1932*:

> *Introduction to the Science of Sociology,* the famous textbook written by Park and Burgess, has been thought by many sociologists to have been one of the most influential works ever written in sociology. . . . This contention is based partly on the observation that before its publication in 1921, general treatises on sociology were so variable in content that they had little in common. . . . Thus sociology today has a recognizable connection with this book in a way that it did not have with the works of the earlier American writers, Small, Ross, Giddings and Ward. . . . The direction and content of American sociology after 1921 was mainly set by the Park and Burgess text. . . .
>
> The existence of this work in the hands of young research students gave meaning and a possible place in a broad unified theory for proposed research topics of a great many kinds. The book provided a sense of proper territory for sociology so that one could work with some degree of confidence that his interests belonged in the field and that his findings would be cumulative and organized.

Chapter 10. World War I: Problems It Revealed

On 6 April 1917 the United States entered the war. On 7 April Park's son Edward married Fentress Kerlin, an artist and dancer. Assigned to a Texas cavalry regiment, he decided it was not a cavalry war; he attended Officers Training School and as a second lieutenant was sent overseas with a black regiment, the 803rd Pioneer Outfit. The father-son book on the nature of war was thereby indefinitely postponed.

When, immediately after America entered the war, the *American Journal of Sociology* asked 130 persons what social scientists could do to assist the government, Park wrote about how the social sciences might cope with the phase of history which lay ahead:

> The social sciences will not come unscathed out of the world-war. Much of their inherited ideology is already shattered. More is crumbling. It is perhaps a small matter, but it seems to me quite likely that what still remains of the classic distinction between the different social sciences, i.e., economics, politics, history and sociology, will have been pretty thoroughly broken down and obliterated by spring of 1918.
>
> . . . Scholars in the different sciences studying the same problems from different points of view, may eventually acquire a common language in which they can speak and be understood.
>
> The traditional division of the social sciences is, after all, English and not Continental. It is inherited from a period when the dominant English political theory was individualism: when the state was regarded as a sort of umpire whose function was to preserve the peace between mutually competing and antagonistic individuals.
>
> . . . With the rise of the industrial state, organized politically and economically for international competition and international war, the scene changes. The exigencies of the new situation demand of the state not merely freedom but efficiency. The radicals want not merely individual liberty, but social justice. These demands conflict and the reconciliation is at once an economic and a political problem. It is a nest of problems.
>
> After this war we shall perhaps no longer think of social problems as exclusively economic, political, or social-welfare problems, these

will rather present aspects, points of view, from which almost any social problem may be viewed.

. . . In his introduction to the second edition of *Law and Opinion in England* Mr. Dicey points out that for a century and more there has been a constant steady trend in English legislation and opinion from an individualistic to a collectivistic conception of society.

The present war has served merely to expedite . . . it would seem, a change already in process. This change, as he points out, is not the result of argument or of agitation. It must be regarded rather as the relatively unreflecting response and adaptation of a social institution to fundamental changes in its environment. The agitation and the social reformers are less a cause than an effect.

This does not mean that in political life we are any more under the control of blind forces than we are in the realm of physical nature. It does mean that, in order to control the historical forces working in and through us, we must understand them. Thus only do we become masters of our political destinies.[1]

Park then suggested that "what sociologists might do in the present crisis . . . is to make a survey of the problems that are now actual." With one of these problems—the possible disloyalty of America's immigrants—Park soon became considerably involved.

During World War I, Americans were surprised to learn that European immigrants were living institutional and cultural lives that had little or nothing to do with America. For example, there were twenty million German-Americans, the Deutsch-Amerikanischer Bund had 6,500 local societies. The Sons of Italy had 887 lodges in 24 states; a Polish organization had 1,000 branches. Americans demanded that immigrants be instantly "Americanized." The superintendent of New York's public schools insisted on "absolute forgetfulness of all obligations or connections with other countries." The hysteria of the times centered on German-Americans and also, after the Russian Revolution, on radicals of all kinds, culminating in the Palmer raids of 1919.

Recognizing that this could endanger America's traditional civil liberties, the Carnegie Corporation decided to make ten studies of immigrants and asked Park to be director of the study of the foreign-language press. Out of consideration for American public opinion, the Carnegie studies were called "Americanization Studies," a term many immigrant intellectuals disliked. The studies were scheduled to begin in January

1. Robert E. Park, "The Social Sciences and the War" in "Symposium: What May Sociologists Do Toward Solving the Problems of the Present War Situation," *American Journal of Sociology* 23 (July 1917), 64–65.

1918 and to be concluded by July 1919. Park agreed to the proposal and arranged to take some time off from his teaching.

He was strongly opposed to the school superintendent's demand for "absolute forgetfulness of all obligations or connections with other countries." In *The Immigrant Press and Its Control*, he said:

> The present immigrant organizations represent a separateness of the immigrant groups from America, but these organizations exist precisely because they enable the immigrants to overcome this separateness.
>
> It is an interesting fact that as a first step in Americanization the immigrant does not become in the least American. He simply ceases to be a provincial foreigner. Würtenbergers and Westphalians become in America first of all Germans; Sicilians and Neapolitans become Italians and Jews become Zionists. . . .
>
> The ambition of the immigrant to gain recognition in the American community, to represent the national name well in America, as Agaton Giller says, is one of the first characteristic manifestations of national consciousness and it is because he has been unable to get recognition in America as an individual that he seeks it as a member of a nationality. . . .

Instead of being alarmed by the existence of immigrant organizations and the foreign-language press, Park recognized that they constituted a bridge which helped the immigrant to get to that promised land he had hoped to find:

> A survey, both in this country and abroad, of the press supported by the language groups that supply the majority of our immigrants, shows these groups to be everywhere involved in a struggle for existence as distinct racial and cultural groups. Formally, this is a struggle to preserve the racial mother tongues, and to make the speech of the common man a written as well as a spoken language. Intrinsically it is a struggle of peoples, culturally isolated, to preserve their own cultural inheritances and at the same time, through the medium of the language they know best, to gain access to the cosmopolitan culture of Europe and the world. It is, to state it generally, a struggle to get into the great society, to enter into and participate in the conscious life of the race. The most important instrument of this movement is the press.

Since the foreign-language press was printed in over forty different languages and dialects, it seemed that studying it would be a formidable task. Actually, it proved comparatively easy; two government agencies, the Post Office and the wartime Committee on Public Information, were already involved. During the spring and summer of 1918, Park's research staff covered the foreign-language papers of Chicago, which was—after New York—the largest center for their publication. In fall 1918 Park shifted his headquarters to the Post Office in Washington, which had since 1914 been translating much of the foreign-language press with particular attention to radical papers. Shortly before the Armistice, Park went to New York. The Committee on Public Information had a branch office there that sent releases to the foreign-language press. Park found it convenient to employ the committee's staff members as translators.

At some point before the Armistice, Park found himself directing not one but two of the ten Americanization studies. Herbert Adolphus Miller, head of the Sociology Department at Oberlin and director of the study of immigrant heritages, informed the corporation that he would be unable to continue. The November 1918 *American Journal of Sociology* announced that Miller, after handling the Immigrant Heritages study for ten months, had asked Oberlin for a leave of absence, explaining that he wished "to devote his time to the organizing of the League of Central European Nations. . . . His work in promoting this movement . . . has had remarkable success and has contributed in no small measure to the disintegration of the Austro-Hungarian Empire."

Park was a natural choice to succeed Miller. He was the only other sociologist among the ten study directors, and his approach to the problems of the immigrant was essentially the same as his friend Miller's.

In accepting the new assignment, Park knew that there would be difficulties. Miller had employed a large staff, started many projects, and spent a considerable share of his $14,700 budget. Since Park was teaching part of the time, he probably would not have taken on the study of immigrant heritages if it had not been possible for him to employ his friend William I. Thomas, then living in New York City to assist him. Thomas had had to resign from the University of Chicago because he had been involved in behavior then considered scandalous in many academic circles.[2] The Carnegie Corporation had no desire to be associated in the mind of the public with a man having this kind of a

2. See Donald R. Young's introduction to *Old World Traits Transplanted* by William Isaac Thomas together with Robert E. Park and Herbert Miller, Americanization Studies, Patterson Smith Series in Criminology, Law Enforcement, and Social Studies, 1971, pp. vii–viii. Young quotes from the "Biographical Note" in *Social Behavior and Personality: Contributions of W. I. Thomas to Theory and Social Research*, Edmund Howell Volkart, ed., where Volkart says: "The association of W. I. Thomas with the Department of Sociology at the University of Chicago continued unbroken until 1918, shortly after he was arrested on a charge involving violations of the Mann Act and of an act forbidding false registration at hotels. Although the charge was thrown out of court, the extensive publishing of the arrest, particularly in the Chicago press, resulted in the termination of his appointment at the

reputation. However the Board of the Corporation had a high regard for Park and Park persuaded them to employ Thomas since due to his justly famous studies of the Polish peasant in Europe and America, Thomas was the country's outstanding authority on the immigrant.

Park was keenly aware how much he owed to Thomas. The two men who had done the most for him were his father, who had financed his excellent education and Thomas who had engineered his teaching at the University of Chicago. In allocating funds for the two studies he was directing, Park paid Thomas as liberally as possible and later spent $1,200 of his own money to finish the book on the immigrant press. To make things agreeable for Thomas and himself he also rented the floor above Strunsky's restaurant on the Lower East Side. Recalling the surroundings in which *The Immigrant Press and Its Control* was completed, Park notes the "very vivid and highly stimulated bohemian life, centering in the numerous restaurants and teahouses of the East Side. On Second Avenue, the Broadway and Fifth Avenue of the Lower East Side, generally spoken of as 'up-town,' there is Strunsky's where poets and writers and artists and their hangers-on are to be found every night around the little tables."

In addition to the Strunsky clientele, Park and Thomas enjoyed the lively street life of Second Avenue and the proximity of five Yiddish theaters, all but one within walking distance of Strunsky's. Park's initial idea had been to write a book entitled "The Foreign Language Press and Theater." He therefore gave Renée Darmstadter, a gifted writer and one of Miller's research assistants, the job of covering New York's foreign-language theaters. Park himself was especially pleased with Ossip Dimoff's Yiddish play, *Bronx Express*, which he called "a very clever satire on Americanization."

If Park had been handling the immigrant heritage study from the beginning, he would have broadened it into a study of America's immigrant communities, of which their heritage from the old country is a part. What such a survey would have covered he indicated in an article he wrote about the two books. It appeared in the *American Review* in 1925, and was called "The Immigrant Community and the Immigrant Press."

He had learned that the immigrant was, on arriving in the United States, extraordinarily dependent not only on the immigrant community but also on its leaders. If they were intelligent and concerned, his Americanization was rapid; if indifferent, the immigrant remained in a backwater. Eugene Bagger, an editor of the Cleveland Hungarian *Szabadsag*, wrote a brilliant paper for Park about the Hungarian commu-

---

University." The obvious inference is that the sponsors of the Carnegie Studies were as sensitive as the University of Chicago concerning possible adverse reactions if Thomas's name were carried on the title page.

nity in which he commented on this flaw in the Americanization process: "This is the paradox of the immigrant colony—that it is constantly losing its best element, which manifests itself just by being able to detach itself and merge into the larger American life." Of the editors of his own paper, Bagger said, "The editors of the *Szabadsag* have a curious theory which shocked me a great deal when I first joined the paper . . . It is usually summed up in the motto: 'Anything is good enough for the buddy.'"

The "buddy" was the ordinary Hungarian reader of the *Szabadsag*. Because the editors seemed to him so very indifferent to their readers, Bagger felt that the influence of Cleveland's two Hungarian papers—the *Szabadsag* and the *Nepzeva*—was "evil."

Park found that the editors of a famous radical paper, the New York Russian-language *Novy Mir*, were equally indifferent. He said:

> Up to the fall of 1915 there were no Bolshevist papers in the United States. . . . When Trotzky came to New York, the Bolshevik wing got together a lot of Lettish sympathizers, ousted the Menshiviki from the editorial board and made Trotzky editor of *Novy Mir*. The United States, therefore, had a Bolshevik paper two seasons before the Russian revolution occurred.
>
> The business manager of the *Novy Mir* (New World), a Russian Socialist paper, said the paper was running a deficit, but none of the editors were obliging enough to write so they could be understood. Letters came in from readers who were peasants, saying "Please send me a dictionary. I cannot read your paper"; or sending in an underlined copy of the paper with a note attached, which read: "Please tell me what this means and send the paper back to me. I paid for it and I have a right to know what it means."
>
> Many of the younger men who were writers for the *Novy Mir* re-emigrated to Russia at the expense of the Kerensky government in the Spring of 1917. These journalists are now writing for the official Bolshevist newspapers—the *Izvestia* and the *Pravda*—and they are writing just as they did in New York City, for the intellectuals rather than for the people. Only Volodarsky, who was the "Question and Answer" man on the *Novy Mir* and who became "Commissaire of the Press" for the Soviet government, had discovered how to write a Socialist paper for the people.

Among the immigrant groups who handled the process of becoming acclimatized to America in a spirited fashion, Park especially admired the Jews and the Japanese. He discovered a gold mine in the New York *Jewish Daily Forward*, an outstandingly successful Yiddish newspaper edited by Abraham Cahan, who, prior to becoming its editor, had written a successful English novel, *The Rise of David Levinsky*. The *Forward* contained a now famous column known as "Bintel Brief" (A Bunch of Letters)[3] in which readers described their personal dilemmas often with great verve and style. Park promptly acquired copies and had them translated. Thomas, who had spent years painfully acquiring letters for his famous five-volume study, *The Polish Peasant in Europe and America*, was delighted by the accessibility of this material and asked Park's permission to use the "Bintel Brief" translations in the book on immigrant heritages. About these letters, Park says:

> I know from my own experience in the ten years I was in the South and from my further experience in studying the immigrant how important these intimate autobiographical sketches can be . . . It is knowledge of this sort and not statistical knowledge that gives one the insight one needs to understand race relations and to understand human beings. I recall in my own case that my attitude toward the Jewish immigrants was revolutionized in the course of a few months by the autobiographies of Jewish immigrants which I discovered and read while we were making Americanization studies in New York City.

Both Park and Abraham Cahan, editor of the *Forward*, had been New York city police court reporters; both had been part of the "take the roofs off the houses" school of journalism of the 1890s. Park admired Cahan for his achievement in taking the often barely literate sweat-shop workers of New York's East Side and making them into citizens of the world. He quotes Joel Enteen as saying:

> Through the medium of the popular press the learning which had been the privilege of the few became the common possession of the many . . . The younger generation, particularly the most ardent and intellectual among them, went over to Socialism *en masse*. Socialism gave the common man a point of view at any rate, from which he could think about actual life. It made the sweat shop an intellectual problem. . . . It should always be borne in mind that Yiddish literature in America is purely proletarian. It was never stimulated by wealthy patronage, it never had an academy to guide it, and never had a literary salon to advise it. . . .
>
> It is true that while rocking in its leaden cradle it often also had Turgenev, Tolstoi, Zola, Dostoyevski, Chekhov and Andreiev for its fellows. . . . Yet it was Yiddish literature that paved the way for the best in the world's literature to the receptive mind of the Yiddish reader. The Jewish sweat shop worker would have no appreciation

3. Isaac Metzker, ed., *A Bintel Brief: Sixty Years of Letters From the Lower East Side to the* Jewish Daily Forward (New York: Doubleday, 1971).

of Maupassant or Gorky if he had not previously been trained by Libin, Korbin, Gordin, Finski or Raisin.[4]

The Carnegie Corporation's Americanization studies have proved to be extremely valuable and are all today available in hard cover or paperback. Nevertheless, these studies were a headache for the Corporation. They were begun in January 1918 and were slated to end in July 1919, but when the studies were only half completed, World War I ended and the public's interest in the loyalty or disloyalty of America's immigrants quickly faded. Moreover, not all the studies proved satisfactory to the Board of the Carnegie Corporation. A review committee was appointed which, as Allen T. Burns, director of the 10 studies, has noted, "carefully examined the 10 volumes . . . and have in some cases required extensive alteration and revision." Because the Americanization series was proving to be an embarrassment to the Corporation, the situation became uncomfortable for a number of the people working on these studies. On one occasion the research assistants working on the ten studies were lectured by a young man whom they had never seen before about what they could and *could not* do. Young Max Ravage, a Roumanian-American educated in a middle-western university then rose and said: "I have written a book on *The Making of an American*. I could now write a book on the Unmaking of an American." In 1923 the publisher, Harpers, notified the Corporation that interest in the series was declining. Burns was then told there would be no money for his summary volume which angered him a good deal. In 1924 Harpers informed the Corporation that it was losing money on the series and in 1925 it scrapped the plates.

The immigrant heritages study to which Miller, Park, and Thomas had all contributed was published in 1921 under the title *Old World Traits Transplanted*, the authors being listed as Park and Miller. Thomas was nowhere mentioned, although it is likely that he did most of the writing. All the studies except the *Old World Traits Transplanted* study had a foreword written by the director of a particular study. Park, for instance, wrote a foreword for the book on the immigrant press. However, he was *not* asked to write a foreword for the *Old World Traits Transplanted* study. If he had been asked, he would have mentioned Thomas's excellent contributions to this book.

When Thomas realized what was happening, he was enraged. A scholar of outstanding reputation, he had already suffered one body blow when he was asked to resign from his Chicago professorship. He was not prepared to take a second blow tamely. The situation created a short

4. Joel Enteen, *Jewish Communal Register*, 1917–18, pp. 592, 594, 595.

temporary strain in the Thomas-Park friendship, which both men were careful to conceal. Why could Park not have done more? Park was distressed, but powerless to alter the situation.

The strain between Thomas and Park did not last. As noted in the epilogue Park was successful a few years later in helping to restore Thomas to his proper place in the academic community. The two friends continued in touch with each other throughout their lives and ten years later on January 1, 1931, Thomas wrote Park:

Dear Robert:

On the train and just now I have read your paper with great attention. It is probably the best paper we have ever had and very important to me . . .

I want to thank you also for your very generous and superintelligent handling of The Polish Peasant in Chase's book . . .

With all good wishes for the New Year and deep appreciation to yourself,

W. I. Thomas.

Twenty years later, in 1951, when the copyright on the original edition of *Old World Traits Transplanted* had expired, the book was republished with an introduction by the sociologist, Donald R. Young. In the introduction Young reprints a letter from Allen T. Burns, director of the 10 Americanization studies, to Professor Ernest W. Burgess. Burns says:

The volume, *Old World Traits Transplanted*, of the Americanization Studies was written primarily by W. I. Thomas though at the time it was considered by all concerned best to have it appear under the authorship of Park and Miller who also worked on the volume. I am very glad that Professor Thomas is to receive credit for his invaluable contribution.

The new edition of *Old Worlds Traits Transplanted* listed Thomas as the main author. The title page reads "By WILLIAM ISAAC THOMAS together with Robert E. Park and Herbert A. Miller."

The acknowledgement by Donald R. Young that three men had something to do with this book is a proper one. However, it remains true that there is a curious flavor of anonymity about both the 1921 and the 1951 versions of *Old World Traits Transplanted*. In the 1921 text Thomas is not mentioned, and in the 1951 text Park is not mentioned. Miller appears in the 1951 version only in a footnote. It is not entirely clear what went on behind the scenes. However, the one conclusion that can safely be drawn is that three men—Miller, Park, and Thomas—contributed to its contents and that Thomas is the major author.

The Immigrant Press and Its Control was published in 1922. Park had found it impossible to make it a more inclusive book to be called "The Immigrant Press and Theater," although he was convinced that the theater provided the best way for Americans to participate in and thus understand the dilemmas, tragedies, and humor of immigrants' lives. The author Mary Austin and many of the people working on the 10 Americanization studies agreed with him.

When the ten studies were completed, the Carnegie Corporation's editorial committee appropriated $700 to distribute these studies to libraries and an extra $1,000 to distribute Park's book on the press. Of *The Immigrant Press and Its Control* a member of the Review Committee remarked that "no history of the United States covering the early part of the 20th century could be written . . . without covering this report."

In summer of 1919, while Park was studying the immigrant, Chicago had a race riot. The United States had had three major race riots in 1917 and one in 1918; there were three more in 1919. The Illinois Commission on Race Relations decided the Chicago riot should be studied. From the beginning the study staff was biracial from top to bottom. There were an equal number of black and white stenographers, and the study was directed by Graham Romeyn Taylor, a white man, and Charles Johnson, a black man.

Charles Johnson was one of Park's ablest students. After a year of graduate work in the Department of Sociology of the University of Chicago in 1916–17, Johnson worked under Park's direction, in the Chicago Urban League's Department of Investigation and Research on a study of wartime black migrations. On 21 January 1918, in a letter to Emmett Scott, Park noted that Johnson had collected 1,200 letters in the course of the study of wartime black migration, and that he and Johnson were planning to edit and publish these letters "with the purpose of reflecting the naive reactions of the colored people to the whole situation."

Because of Johnson's thoroughness in these migration researches, Park recommended him as very well qualified to serve as a director of the study of the 1919 Chicago race riot. In one of three articles on the blacks written for the English publishers of *Nelson's Perpetual Lease-Lend Encyclopedia* in 1924, Park said:

A still more serious riot [than the one in Washington] occurred in Chicago from July 27 to August 4 of the same year. The disorder began along a bathing beach where individuals of both races congregated and resulted in the death of 16 whites and 22 Negroes, the injury of 537 of both races, and the arrest of 229 persons. . . . The first dispassionate study of one of these riots and the underlying causes, was that of the Chicago Commission on Race Relations, published in 1922 under the title "The Negro in Chicago." This will for some time serve as a model for subsequent surveys.

The Commission report is still respected. In a 1971 booklet of the University of Chicago Center for Policy Study called "Social Control and Escalated Riots," Professor Morris Janowitz, chairman of the university's Department of Sociology, notes that:

The most adequate and comprehensive study of a race riot still remains the one prepared by the Chicago Commission on Race Relations on the Chicago rioting of 1919—the result of the careful work of the late Charles S. Johnson, which was done under the supervision of Robert Park of the University of Chicago.

Park's confidence in Johnson was justified.

Chapter 11. Interaction: Students with Teacher

Park gave his first course at the University of Chicago in 1914, and in his first seven years there as a teacher of sociology, he gave seven different courses. He lectured on "The Negro in America," and then added courses on "The Newspaper," "Crowd and Public," "The Survey," "Research in the Field of Social Psychology," "Field Studies," and "Race and Nationality." In 1919–20, Ernest Burgess and Ellsworth Faris joined Park in giving the course in social psychology. The course in field studies proved so popular that it was given every year throughout the 1920s, not by Park alone but by a group of faculty members.

During the early period, Park had a number of interesting students: Erle Fisk Young and his wife Pauline V. Young, Frederic Milton Thrasher, Kimball Young, Nels Anderson, Charles Johnson, George S. H. Rossouw, Edward Byron Reuter, and Roderick Duncan McKenzie. Park's principal difficulty in these early years at Chicago arose because he regarded sociology as a science, while some undergraduate students thought of it as a series of social problems to be cured by political and social reforms. One of Park's students, Nels Anderson, had a name for it: "The previous approach had been reformistic, fighting evils, Many-D-Sociology (Drink, Drugs, Disease, Desertion, Delinquency, Disorganization). The sociologist was supposed to be in there, fighting for all good causes. . . . Crusading had no place in the new approach."[1] Park's battle to keep students from confusing sociology with "do-goodism" was also being fought by other members of the sociology department. Robert E. L. Faris says, in *Chicago Sociology, 1920–1932*: "The emphasis on objectivity became firmly established in Chicago in the early 1920s. . . . Small was partly responsible for this stress, and Thomas as well. Park was probably the only one who directly attacked the humanitarian attitude when it appeared among sociologists. More than once he drove his students to anger or tears by growling such reproofs as 'You're another one of those damn do-gooders.'"

Park's behavior when he had a reformer in his class has been described by Theodore K. Noss:

1. Unless otherwise indicated, quotations from Park's students in this chapter are taken either from letters written by them to the author or from papers formerly in the author's possession and later donated to various university archives and special collections.

One day he attacked the Quakers for their self-righteous meddling in the abolition movement and had a few things to say about all reformers in general, that the greatest damage done to the city of Chicago was not the product of corrupt politicians or criminals but of women reformers. . . .

The class was not large, some male and female graduate students. . . . One of the elderly women was an aggressive reformer. She angered Park to the point where he strode into class one day with a book by William James. Then he began reading "On a Certain Blindness in Human Beings". . . . It was about our failure to understand the inner world of the people around us.

In notes and personal letters, Park expressed himself forthrightly about this matter:

Sociology, insofar as it can be regarded as a fundamental science and not a mere congeries of social-welfare programs and practices, may be described as the science of human behavior.

In developing the techniques of sociology we must escape both *history* and *practical application*. . . . The first thing you have to do with a student who enters sociology is to show him that he can make a contribution if he doesn't try to improve anybody. . . . The trouble with our sociology in America is that it has had so much to do with churches and preachers. . . . The sociologist cannot condemn some people and praise others.

Sociology cannot be mixed with welfare and religion. "A moral man cannot be a sociologist." Sociology should not help to build up reform programs, but it should help those who have to build these programs to do it more intelligently.

In 1937 Howard W. Odum asked Park about his main contributions to sociology. Park said that he felt he had been useful to Chicago students in two fields, the city and race: "As a reporter I had learned a good deal about the city and I had used my position as city and Sunday editor to make systematic studies of the urban community. During my connection with Booker Washington and Tuskegee, I learned a great deal about the Negro. It was from these two sources mainly that graduate students found materials for the researches which I directed after I went to Chicago."

Students agreed that Park's courses dealing with the city and with race were fascinating. Robert Faris reports:

In my senior year I took Park's course on The Crowd and the Public. . . . To my surprise I found it extremely interesting. Park was full of enthusiasm, rich in ideas, and made each hour a very fast-moving one. I did a term paper on the mayoralty campaign of William Hale Thompson. There was plenty of material, and I enjoyed doing it and was given a part, or maybe all, of a class period to report it to the class. Park was highly enthusiastic, and I was walking on air, for I had a poor opinion of my scholarly ability. I soon received a letter from Kimball Young in Wisconsin, a big name to me, asking for a copy of the paper, and was immensely flattered.

Harold F. Gosnell, of the University's political science faculty, was collecting material for his book *Negro Politicians*. He reported:

> On the urging of Miss Williams, I visited Professor Park's class on race relations. I found him to be a marvelous teacher. He spoke with great conviction and held his classes spellbound. I had many conferences with Dr. Park. . . . I was greatly impressed with his emphasis on the usefulness of life history cases, the value of contemporary newspaper accounts, the place of the participant observer, the need for defining fundamental concepts, and the proper role of statistics. He had an unearthly horror of the use of statistics for trivial or unproductive purposes.

City life was not a new field of study when Park came to Chicago. Many of his courses touched on this theme, but he added a dimension with his knowledge of seven major American cities. He had done city reporting for eleven years. Studying the city was as interesting to him as studying the brain is to the biologist. When a student was beginning to examine some aspect of city life, Park frequently accompanied him on at least one trip. He was a tireless walker. One student recollects: "Once we walked through a shabby warehouse district on the edge of the Italian section. He talked out loud—not so much to me as to himself—about its past, its present status, its probable future." Proud of his knowledge, Park once said, "I have probably walked more miles of city street than anyone in America." And, at another time: "The city is, finally, the habitat of civilized man. . . . It is a quite certain, but never fully recognized fact, says Spengler, that all great cultures are city-born. . . . This is the actual criterion of world history as distinguished from the history of mankind: world history is the history of city men."

Between 1921 and 1931 fifteen research studies of city life were done by Chicago graduate students. Seven were published and Park wrote introductions to three. The studies often had intriguing titles: *The Gang: A Study of 1,313 Gangs in Chicago* (a Ph.D. thesis by Frederic Milton Thrasher); and *The Hobo* (an M.A. thesis by Nels Anderson). Henry L. Mencken, editor of *American Mercury*, reviewed *The Hobo* and thereafter kept track of other books in the Chicago city series. A number of these books are still being published. *The Hobo* has not been out of print for fifty years.

The forty-two theses or books written about race, culture, and ethnic relations by students while Park was teaching at Chicago (some were written after the students had left the university) constitute a special chapter in the history of American sociology. Twenty-three dealt with the United States, fourteen with foreign cultures. George S. Rossouw and William O. Brown wrote about South Africa; Romanzo Adams, Andrew Lind, and Clarence Glick about Hawaii; Donald Pierson about Brazil, Tai Chang Wang and Maurice T. Price about China; and Everett C. Hughes about French Canada.

Park wrote an introduction or a foreword for Jesse F. Steiner, *The Japanese Invasion*, 1917; Maurice T. Price, *Protestant Missions as Culture Contact*, 1924; Louis Wirth, *The Ghetto: A Study in Isolation*, 1926; Pauline V. Young, *The Pilgrims of Russian Town*, 1932; Charles S. Johnson, *Shadow of the Plantation*, 1934; Romanzo Adams, *Interracial Marriage in Hawaii*, 1937; Bertram Doyle, *Etiquette of Race Relations*, 1937; Everett V. Stonequist, *The Marginal Man*, 1937; Donald Pierson, *The Negro in Brazil*, 1938; and Andrew Lind, *Island Community*, 1939.

When Bracey, Maier, and Rudwick published *The Black Sociologists* in 1971, they called one section "In the Parkian Tradition." They named, as the greatest black sociologists the United States had to date, W. E. B. Du Bois, Charles S. Johnson, and Franklin E. Frazier. Johnson and Frazier were University of Chicago men; both studied with Park.

In *Commentary* in 1950, reviewing *Race and Culture*, a series of papers by Park, Seymour Lipset said:

> If the climate of opinion about race has changed in the last forty years in America, certainly a large share of the credit must go to the approach developed by Park and his students. . . . Much of the work in the field of race relations in the twenties and early thirties that now forms one of the most imposing monuments of American empirical sociology was a result of Park's encouragement to his students to study the background of various racial and ethnic groups. . . . And the more technical empirical sociology of the last fifteen years has time and again verified many of the hypotheses developed in his works.

Not all Park's students wrote about the city or about race. There were seven theses on the newspaper, including Carol DeWitt Clark's 1931 Ph.D. thesis, "News: A Sociological Study," and Helen MacGill Hughes's 1940 Ph.D. thesis, "The Human Interest Story."

Park's course on "Crowd and Public" dealt with collective behavior, which, as his student Herbert Blumer has noted, covers such diverse matters as "crowds, mobs, panics, manias, dancing crazes, stampedes, mass behavior, public opinion, fashion, fads, social movements, reforms and revolutions." One thesis in this field was Lyford P. Edwards's *The Natural History of Revolutions*, published in 1927. After reading an early paper by Edwards, Park expressed the hope that revolutions might turn out to be "like earthquakes, measurably predictable." However, in his introduction to Edwards's book, Park admitted that this was "perhaps an impossible task, demanding a precision that is quite beyond the limits of the social sciences." He also noted that he was not in "perfect and complete agreement with its conclusion that all revolutions have and will continue to be economic in their origin." In his introduction to Hiller's *The Strike*, he wrote of "the slow burn of revolution."

Another study of collective behavior is Pauline V. Young's Ph.D. thesis, "The Pilgrims of Russian Town," about the Los Angeles Molokan sect. Park believed that revolutions tend to begin with sects. Of sects, he said at one point: "I study the different sects as one studies botanical specimens, and find these external characteristics have a functional relation. Then I find out what each particular sect gets out of it. . . . When I began to study sects I found they mostly wore long hair and curious clothes. . . . Those that were lively and vigorous, those were the sects that were persecuted. . . ."

Park's last years of teaching at Chicago, 1925–32, helped produce many able students. Louis Wirth completed his Ph.D. thesis in 1926; Herbert Blumer, Everett Cherrington Hughes, and Robert Redfield, in 1928; Everett Verner Stonequist, in 1930; Franklin Frazier and Andrew Lind, in 1931; and Edgar Thompson in 1932. The *International Encyclopedia of the Social Sciences* says of Park's influence on his anthropologist son-in-law Redfield:

> His career . . . spanned a period of rapid growth in anthropological research and in the maturation of the social sciences. The University of Chicago was a center of such developments. Redfield's father-in-law, Robert Park . . . helped to give his career its direction. . . . Following a suggestion of Park's, he developed an ideal-type construct of folk society as a way of making a more systematic analysis of the transition from folk to urban communities.

Because Park was an interesting teacher who influenced many students, Louis Wirth asked him to write about his teaching experience at the close of his Chicago career. Park produced a paper called "Methods of Teaching,"[2] but it told nothing about his own methods. Instead it described the methods of his favorite professors in five different universities.

His students have been less reticent. They say that, on first being alone with them, he was likely to interview them about their life histories. In this way he got acquainted with them very early. They say that he had the brusquerie as well as the charm of an ex-newspaperman and that, while lecturing, he often made rather shocking statements. His zest while accompanying them on their researches into Chicago city life was contagious. He could be very demanding about the quality of their work, and he used his skill as an editor to advise his graduate students about the structure of their theses. What his students liked especially was that he respected them and tended to treat them as his equals.

Charles S. Johnson, who came to the university in 1915 and knew Park over three decades, describes how his relation with Park evolved:

> I met Dr. Robert E. Park in my first quarter of study. His course on "Crowd and Public" seemed challenging and I signed up for it with no prior intimation of his personality as a teacher. It was not long before he was on a basis of easy and stimulating exchange with individual members of the class and I was one of a great many who . . . had an opportunity to follow him to his office . . . as he continued . . . to explore, with insightful clarity, the murky channels of our thinking.
>
> A first personal revelation came, when I discovered through one of his excursions that it was possible to identify my own experience and thinking with a large and respectable fund . . . of social knowledge, thus providing some realism for the university experience. A second came when it dawned on me that I was being taken seriously and without the usual condescension or oily paternalism of which I had already seen too much. The relation of teacher and student grew into a friendship.

Edgar T. Thompson, a Southerner, came to Chicago in 1924 and took Park's course on the black in America. Given the choice of six topics for his first class paper, he chose "The Plantation: The Physical Basis of Slavery," since he had grown up on a plantation. Park later persuaded him to make this the subject of his Ph.D. thesis. When working for a time in Park's office, Thompson listened to Park interview students about their life histories: "A student would come in to see him about a thesis problem. . . . Dr. Park would question him about his background, his life,

---

2. "Methods of Teaching" is in the Louis Wirth file of Special Collections in the University of Chicago Archives.

his experiences. He would probe and probe until finally some experience, which had never seemed important perhaps until that day, would emerge, burn itself into the student's consciousness and set him on fire."

Although Park generally got on with his students in a relaxed way, from time to time he startled or offended them. This was sometimes a matter of principle—his unwillingness to have sociology confused with reform; at other times it was a matter of temperament. Horace Cayton, the grandson of Hiram Revels, the first black U.S. Senator, tells how Park upset him when they met:

> I first met Park on the Pacific Coast when I was an undergraduate at the University of Washington. One of the professors had arranged an interview for me with Park during which I told him that I was interested in Negro history. He replied that Negroes didn't have a history, which angered me a great deal, and I replied that everyone had a history, even the chair I was sitting in. . . . I had decided that I'd never look him up again, but, when I ventured into his office at the University of Chicago a few years later, he welcomed me with open arms. He had only been trying to feel me out, to get a rise out of me.

Cayton had many dealings with Park and, later, with St. Clair Drake, wrote a book about Chicago called *Black Metropolis*.

If a student did something really stupid, Park never hesitated to say so. When a woman student writing about an isolated European minority referred to their lives as being "castor-colored," Park said coldly, "If I ever catch you writing like the *Atlantic Monthly* again, I will personally drown you in the nearest well."

His particular kind of scoffing was especially in evidence during his early teaching years. Fentress Kerlin, an actress and Park's daughter-in-law, describes the Park she met in 1916, two years after he had begun teaching at Chicago, and she says that he "had very little toleration for stupidity. . . . " To her it seemed that "he hated pettiness more than anything else. People found it hard to understand his manner of scoffing. . . . His intention was to shock them into thinking about the point he was making. He was like George Bernard Shaw. . . . I think they would have gotten on well together, Park and Shaw."

Although Park sometimes shocked a student, the graduate students who were able to get acquainted with him usually liked him. One such student was Theodore Noss, son of a missionary in Japan, who discovered that he could walk home with Park if he waited at the entrance to the social science building at about five. They would then stroll together down the Midway discussing points in Noss's M.A. thesis on "The

Awakening of the Quaker Movement against Negro Slavery in Colonial Pennsylvania and West New Jersey." Noss says: "When we arrived at his apartment . . . he turned to say goodnight, giving me his full attention. . . . There were several of these occasions. . . . I liked them because of his respect for conversation but primarily because of the sense of warm companionship he always gave me."

William Oscar Brown, a Texan whose Ph.D. thesis was on "Race Prejudice: A Sociological Study" (1930), was for many years head of the Center for African Studies at Boston University. According to Brown, "Park was the greatest intellectual influence in my life. . . . All of us . . . had great respect for him, coupled with a kind of pride in being his students. . . . I sometimes found him irascible but never mean. . . . He was never familiar with his students, but he respected them, he understood them, above all he was interested in them. He always respected you as a person."

Everett V. Stonequist came to Chicago from Oxford, and in 1930 he wrote his Ph.D. thesis, "The Marginal Man: A Study in the Subjective Aspects of Cultural Conflict," a topic of great interest to Park. According to Stonequist, "I spoke to him of my interest in the deracine. . . . His response surprised me in its immediate enthusiasm, stating, 'Here we call such individuals marginal men.'" Stonequist commented later: "In our early discussions he did not offer advice on procedure, scope, or specific references but preferred discussing ideas. Occasionally an author would be mentioned. Usually he would wait for a question, then turn it over in his mind and give his comments. He had the gift of making me feel like a collaborator rather than a student."

Park enjoyed companionship with his brighter students. One of his prolonged and close relations was with Helen MacGill Hughes and her husband, Everett Hughes. He saw them through their theses. When he went on exploratory sociological trips, they sometimes served as his drivers. If he woke up in the morning wanting to begin a new book, they cooperated—they were his favorite playmates. "They know how to enjoy life; they have a genius for it," he said. Describing her complex professional and personal relations with Park, Helen Hughes says:

> It seems to me now that I did my doctor's work under very old-fashioned circumstances that have a special advantage and a special charm. I mean a situation that may be likened to that of apprentice and master, entailing long association not only on the job but in other matters. This long association with my professor of course developed my subject and . . . it developed me. When the association is long-lasting and personal, as well as professional . . . it comes to have

a special nature that is hard to find otherwise. . . . The pedagogical relationship when it becomes personal is made tolerable by careful checks and balances: to honor and respect above loving; to be close but a little timid, deferential yet endlessly laying claims and having them admitted. Year after year I was going gladly, joyfully into my teacher's debt, with no hope or expectation of repayment unless it were in the way prescribed by the Hippocratic oath, which considers a like situation.

Although a genial man, Park could be extremely demanding about the standards he expected his students to meet in writing their theses. Earle Young says:

> Park had in unusual measure the ability to attract young energetic students into research work. . . . For him there was only one way to deal with an unanswered social question: study it. . . . He had an uncanny ability to formulate the specific questions to be studied. . . . He cut squarely through current preconceptions, conventional cliches, and closed systems of thinking. . . . Students were frequently shocked to learn from him that an elaborately developed thesis, which had painstakingly followed a line of reasoning as demonstrated by the data in hand, was to be challenged and unhesitatingly discarded if further reflection or newer data demanded such action.

Park was demanding but correspondingly helpful, as Edgar Thompson shows:

> One summer when I was living in Bob Redfield's house . . . I was having considerable difficulty getting my thesis . . . into focus. I had read everything I could get my hands on . . . but I had no frame within which to connect the facts. Dr. Park appeared at my door one Sunday afternoon. He had been thinking about me and my problem, he said, and he thought he might be able to suggest a plan for organizing my material and giving it a point of view. The afternoon cleared up my difficulties. I started all over again, and this time I made it.

Park was fortunate in having many able students but he also had mediocre ones. Herbert Blumer refers to this in an appraisal of Park's teaching abilities:

> Dr. Park had a remarkable ability to attract students and to bring out from them a level of achievement which, paradoxically, exceeded what one would think to be the limit of their abilities. He attracted a

wide variety of students, some of the greatest ability, others of average talent, and some less than mediocre. He worked patiently, persistently, and hard with each. . . . He succeeded in getting a large number of them to develop an unflagging interest in concentrated work on their topics, resulting, it should be noted, in a very impressive series of publications. These publications were, by and large, excellent; they frequently represented achievements which the individual students would, under other conditions, never have been able to realize. It is of some interest to observe that in the case of a number of such students their subsequent intellectual careers were not impressive. . . . In the course of my more than 30 years of observations in the field of graduate work I have never seen any teacher who could be as successful as Park in awakening, mobilizing, and directing the talents of students and bringing them to their highest potentiality.

I suspect that in the history of American sociology there has been no sociologist on the graduate level who has attracted and retained a larger coterie of devoted students or exerted a more powerful influence on them. In my judgment Dr. Park's impact on American sociology was much greater through his training and guidance of graduate students than through a reading of his sociological writings. In making this observation I in no sense denigrate his writings but only call attention to the powerful influence which he exerted on graduate students.

Park privately agreed with Blumer's opinion that some of his students were "of average talent, and some less than mediocre." Visiting the political science section of a conference at another university in the late 1920s, he said to an associate, "Their students are so much brighter than ours." Everett Hughes has noted that "Park remarked more than once that sociology would only get ahead by making the most of the people it got, not by waiting for a better class of people."

But it is even more notable how many of the graduate students of Park's era were able. Ernest Burgess, Park's colleague and close associate, said: "Park's investment of time in his students produced high dividends in a score or more of first-class research men who took as their special field a problem which he had defined and often had developed in its main conceptual outlines." Writing of Park in his *Masters of Sociological Thought*, Lewis Coser says: "There is no better testimony to the impact of Park's teaching than the imposing roster of his students. Everett C. Hughes, Herbert Blumer, Stuart Queen, Leonard Cottrell, Edward Reuter, Robert Faris, Louis Wirth, and E. Franklin Frazier all became presidents of the American Sociological Society. Helen MacGill

Hughes, John Dollard, Robert Redfield, Ernest Hiller, Clifford Shaw, Willard Waller, Walter C. Reckless, Joseph Lohman, and many other students of Park were leading social scientists. It is hard to imagine the field of sociology without the contribution of the cohort of brilliant men whom Park trained at Chicago."

In the final paragraph of "Methods of Teaching" that Park wrote for Louis Wirth in 1937, he described the qualities an ideal teacher should have. One of these is imagination: "There is always likely to be too much routine and too little imagination in our educational procedures. . . . I am convinced that the influence which an uninhibited teacher with insight and understanding can exert on a pupil . . . has rarely been overestimated." This description comes close to being a portrait of Park himself. As Everett Hughes has noted, what his students got from Park was "the dialectic between the reporter and the philosopher." He knew the Chicago slums intimately, but he also knew "the Main Street of the world . . . the great ocean highway that connects London, New York and San Francisco with Yokahama, Shanghai, Hong Kong, Calcutta, Bombay, and the Mediterranean." He wrote his daughter in 1916 "that the simplest problems are after all world problems." He could move from a discussion of urban geography to the reflections of philosophers on the phenomenon of civilization, which began with the existence of cities.

Chapter 12. Race Relations on the Pacific Coast

During summer 1923 the Institute of Social and Religious Research, a foundation in New York, approached Park about the possibility of his directing a survey of race relations on the Pacific Coast. The director of the institute, Galen S. Fisher, formerly a missionary in Japan, was concerned about tensions between the Japanese and the Americans on the Coast, where the Asiatic Exclusion League and other organizations were demanding that the federal government restrict Japanese immigration. Park undertook the survey. At the time he noted, "race relations was a political issue."

> The people were all excited about it. They were worried about the fecundity of the Japanese race. Japanese people on the Pacific Coast had a high birth rate. This was very distressing. Statistical studies seemed to indicate that in a short time the country would be overrun by Japanese because their birth rate was so much higher than the native stock. They were afraid that in a short time there would not be any room for us on the Pacific Coast or in America. When we undertook this study, therefore, they wanted us to answer questions of this sort, questions that were then the subject of discussion in the newspapers and in individual groups of people interested in social politics all over the state. However, I was convinced in my own mind, no matter how these questions were answered, it would not alter very greatly the existing relations between the Oriental and the Occidental population.

Before deciding to make the survey, the Institute of Social and Religious Research asked J. Merle Davis, a historian familiar with the Orient, to find out how white people living on the Pacific Coast felt about such a study. Davis interviewed 225 leading citizens, found that sixty percent approved of the idea, and organized those who did into five regional committees. Ray Lyman Wilbur, president of Stanford University, who later served as Secretary of the Interior under President Hoover, became chairman of the Northern California Committee.

In the process of interviewing people, Davis learned much about the pro-Oriental and anti-Oriental factions of the Pacific Coast. "It was soon apparent," he noted, "even to a new-comer on the Pacific Coast, what groups were pro- and what groups were anti-Oriental and why this was so. The politician, the legionnaire, and native son, the working man, the small farmer, the shop keeper were usually against the Oriental, or, at least, opposed to the Japanese. On the other hand, the president of the Chamber of Commerce, the financier and banker, the importer and exporter, the absentee land-owner, the large rancher, the mission secretary and the church worker, the social worker and many school teachers and university professors were friendly to the Asiatic."

Davis encountered hostility toward Orientals and even toward a survey. Since it was to be financed by the Institute of Social and Religious Research, many people assumed that it would necessarily be pro-Oriental. Davis was told: "I know who you are and where you come from. You are from Japan and a spy of the Mikado. . . . This Survey is loaded with religion and capital. Who's going to pay for it anyway? Capital. The capitalists will pay for it and the church will run it and either way labor will get flimflammed."

The survey was to begin 21 January 1924 and to last nine months. During fall 1923 Park made a preliminary trip to the Coast to explore the situation. Although he had never lived there he was familiar with its problems. In 1918, while making studies of immigrants, he had spent a month on the Coast interviewing Orientals, and in 1914 had written an introduction to Jesse Steiner's *The Japanese Invasion*, where he said, "Race prejudice may be regarded as a spontaneous, more or less instinctive defense reaction, the practical effect of which is to restrict free competition among races."

In investigating race relations on the Coast, Park proposed to use the same cycle he had used in studying immigrants—competition, conflict, accommodation, and assimilation. Competition between Oriental and white workers, farmers, and businessmen was the crux of the problem in 1924. Park felt that once there was competition and it was recognized, there would always be conflict. He wanted to find out what kinds of more or less successful accommodations between Orientals and whites had been worked out and how rapidly the young American-born Orientals were being assimilated.

How competition with the Japanese affected white working-class Americans is illustrated by a statement the survey got from a white clerk in Portland, Oregon:

> I worked in orchards and in the sugar beet fields with the Japanese. I got to know them quite well and learned to like them personally. They were thoughtful and hospitable. I found many things about their characters that I liked; *while I admire the Japanese for many*

things, I am afraid of them. First, I fear their power as a race.
Second, I think they offer too keen competition for Americans.
Japanese will work all day from early dawn until late at night and I
cannot, nor can other Americans with our ideas of hours of labor,
compete with them as individuals. They just work too many
hours. . . . Given the same amount of ground they produce more;
they save more. They take no vacations. . . . The Japanese seem to
have an uncanny gift for getting into those lines of work at which
they excel Americans. I fear the military power of the race. . . . All in
all, I think we should exclude them.

Feeling against the Japanese in the United States and against both the
Japanese and the Chinese in British Columbia was intense and sometimes irrational. A Tacoma, Washington, woman wrote an editor a letter
entitled "Exterminate the Japanese." It was reported to Park that a group
of American women had decided that "the Japanese have no souls."
Writing to Bogardus, Park said: "The outstanding fact in connection with
race relations on the coast, when this race relations survey was begun,
was an inflamed public opinion."

Park's opinion was confirmed by a letter from J. W. Gilmore of the
University of California at Berkeley, who had once founded a college in
China:

It has been my experience that surveys of this sort are extremely
difficult of interpretation largely because of sentiment interwoven
with fact. . . . As I see it, based upon fact, there is really very little [of
an] Oriental problem on this coast, but based on sentiment and
psychic factors the problem is really of considerable magnitude.

Park replied:

I am greatly interested in what you say. . . . I note particularly your
statement, "There is always a psychic aspect to all such questions
and it is extremely difficult to eliminate this factor or to separate it
from those statistical and physical facts that bear on the subject."
That is, of course, precisely the point. So far as our study is able to
justify itself at all, it will do so just to the extent that we are able to
disentangle the psychic aspects from the statistical and physical
facts that bear upon the subject.

On a 1923 trip to the Coast which preceded the survey, Park interviewed many people. On 12 September 1923 he was entertained at
dinner by Mr. Ohashi, the Japanese consul in Seattle, and Park, in one of
his notebooks, described the occasion in detail:

The restaurant is upstairs in a frame building . . . located in a rather messy street in the Japanese quarter which is adjoining and indeed a part of the homeless man area. The dining room was handsomely fitted up in Japanese style. Everything was managed in a very precise and decorous fashion and one had the feeling that underneath this order and neatness there was a rigorous social ritual which only generations of social discipline could have established. . . .

We talked about Japanese American life, we talked familiarly, almost like Americans. There was a certain amount of reserve, but a great deal of candour, and none of the ordinary Japanese stiffness. I explained the importance of getting life history materials, intimate personal records which show how life in America looks from the standpoint of a Japanese immigrant. There is, I explained, only one way of combatting prejudice and that is by getting the American people interested in the actual problem of living as it presents itself to the Japanese. We do not want to determine in this study who is right and who is wrong. . . . It is not likely, even after we have all the facts that it is practical or possible to get, that the different parties having different interests will not interpret these facts differently, but the issues will at any rate be defined. . . .

The Japanese problem is to a certain extent a product of Japanese reserve. The reason the Negro—in spite of the differences in his physical appearance and the inferiority of his culture—is able to accommodate himself as no other colored people has been able to do to American life is . . . that he has a sense of humour that permits him to look at himself impersonally. . . .

Ohashi is a wise little man. He stated what seemed to him to be the trouble with the world quite simply. He said the spiritual organization of the world has not kept up with the material. There is too much individualism. He thinks, therefore, the present civilization will not last. This is interesting as coming from an Americanized Japanese.

On 31 January 1924, Park's notebook reported a visit to a 700-acre California ranch and an instance of prejudice against the Japanese:

Visited Kate Vosberg's ranch at Azuza. This is a fine old estate. Kate Vosberg is a vigorous, intelligent, high bred woman of pioneer stock. Her father . . . was a lawyer in Nevada. She grew up with the Chinese, whom she regards affectionately. Her father was really a lordly, but generous and genial grand seigneur of the peculiarly American type. He appreciated Indians, Chinese and Mexicans and retained their loyalties even after they had got out from the control center of the intimate family affections. . . .

She has had experience necessarily with Chinese, Japanese and Mexican labor. She does not like the Japanese. One of her Japanese servants abandoned her without explanation, took his vacation with pay and never returned. When he took his trunk she asked him why. He replied he wanted to go to the beach. He returned later and worked on a neighbor's plantation, and then it came out that his wife was lonesome on the ranch. . . .

On another occasion Mrs. Vosberg expressed herself more sharply about the Japanese. "There are certain races to which you have a natural antipathy. I like Frank and Maria, but I never liked the race. I like Chinese, Mexicans and Negroes, but I abhor the Japanese as a race." . . .

Keith Vosberg—typical outdoor, highbred intellectual, educated at Harvard and Oxford in history, says as long as they were employing Japanese his mother had no prejudice and they were the most efficient laborers they ever had. He thinks it is all "just prejudice," which, of course, it is. The question is what is the situation which calls out this kind of prejudice?

Park filled 22 pages of his notebook with details about the Vosberg ranch and its Oriental and Mexican farmhands: "Problem is related to geography and climate. Imperial Valley and Sacramento Valley very rich, but very hot. White people won't work in such heat. . . . Imperial Valley not suited to small farms, but to large corporations controlling irrigation, etc. Owners of Imperial Valley favorable to Japs."

The most important thing Park did during his 1923 trip to the Coast was to recruit a research staff of professors, mostly sociologists, teaching in the leading Pacific Coast universities. It included Theodore H. Boggs of the University of British Columbia, Roderick D. McKenzie of the University of Washington, Philip A. Parsons of the University of Oregon, Elliot G. Mears of Stanford University, and William Carlos Smith and Emory S. Bogardus of the University of Southern California. Park wanted this research group to make a united attack on the problems of the Coast. To further this end, he supplied the group with six documents about intermarriage, the Oriental population, Oriental communities, vice and crime, and race consciousness. Each document included a questionnaire to be used exclusively by members of Park's research staff. None were to be publicized. However, the curiosity of the white public about intermarriage was so great that Park finally gave permission to release that particular questionnaire.

From the beginning the survey had two elements: the research staff headed by Park; and the public opinion element, consisting of five regional committees with some 250 members, organized by Merle J. Davis. These regional committees included members of both anti-Oriental and pro-Oriental organizations and members of the public interested in race relations. V. S. McClatchey, an editor and head of the Japanese Exclusion League, was a member of one of the committees. There was a San Francisco office, out of which operated Park, Davis, and Winifred Raushenbush—Park's research assistant who had worked with him earlier during the Carnegie Americanization study.

Park considered the life history to be the most important sociological tool the survey could use. "Friendly relations," he said, "seem to rest not so much on the clearing up of mutual misunderstandings, as on intimate and personal understandings between individuals. If we can get an interesting body of stories concerning the lives, experiences and hopes of Oriental immigrants . . . they will reveal the mind of the Oriental to the American."

Because he believed in the importance of life histories, Park asked the professors on his research staff to get students—"preferably graduate students"—to collect them. The University of Washington and the University of Southern California were the main centers for this activity. In his constant traveling up and down the Pacific Coast, Park often conferred with students who were collecting life histories. Bogardus of the University of Southern California preserved some notes about these meetings: "Dr. Park explained to the assembled graduate students that he was not particularly interested in statistical data . . . he wanted interviews and life history materials that would be obtained from the second generation Japanese living in southern California (the Nisei)."

Of Park's second meeting with eight students, Bogardus said:

> Perhaps because of suggestions from me they stressed descriptions of what had happened and did not obtain an account of reactions to happenings. They stressed "facts" but Dr. Park was irritated, and startled us all by declaring that sociology is not interested in facts, not even in social facts as they are commonly understood in their objective aspects. Sociology wants to know how people re-act to so-called facts, to what is happening to them. How do they accommodate themselves to what is taking place in the work-a-day world around them? Have the Japanese in any place or connection worked out a satisfactory (to them) accommodation with Americans? [During his third meeting with these students Dr. Park wanted the interviewers to find out] how the Nisei's experiences had changed their outlook on life. . . . What was happening to their philosophy of life as a result of being treated with deep-seated prejudice by Americans?

How one American-born Chinese girl eighteen years old responded to this Park discovered through his acquaintance with Flora Belle Jan. Writing to W. I. Thomas, he said: "I wish . . . that you could have met a girl I had dinner with the other evening. Her name is Flora Belle Jan, and she lives when she is at home at 100 ½ China Alley, Fresno. . . . She is the most emancipated girl I have ever met. Clever, sophisticated, Americanized. She has been writing for the local papers in Fresno and now comes to San Francisco to write for the *Examiner.*"

While in Fresno, Davis learned that Miss Jan's parents felt their daughter "had been ruined by Western civilization" and therefore refused to pay tuition for her studies at the University of California. Davis reported to Park that "Flora Belle is the only Oriental in town . . . who has the charm, wit and nerve to enter good white society. . . . She has become accepted (some say with reservations)." In a letter to Park, Miss Jan described the reservations:

> The more I learn about American men and boys, and some girls, the more I think that friendly relations, at least in California, are for the most part impossible. I know that I have penetrated more American homes than any other Chinese girl, and I have found many people cordial. . . . But some one some time must make comments, and these do not fall gently on my ears. . . . Of late, the only sincere friendship I have had was with an intelligent American boy of good family. . . . I have always liked him and he has liked me, but he said several times (to others) that he hesitated to accept my invitations to parties, because he knew he could not return them; his sisters, moving in their select circle, could not include me. . . .
>
> Sometimes I think I am very impertinent to step out of my bounds and see the Western world through Western field glasses—. But then, it was not my fault that I opened my eyes one morning eighteen years ago and found myself "stranded in a foreign land."

Like Miss Jan, most Chinese in British Columbia were aware that there was prejudice against them. Young Chinese-Canadians back after graduating from one of the great Eastern universities of the United States found no entree into Canadian society. "Our friends are very charming," one of them remarked, "but there are so few of us. It is like living in a ghetto."

The furious editor of a Vancouver Chinese newspaper recounted to a survey staff member all the insults the Chinese had received since first arriving in Canada and said: "We have been writing editorials against you (the Canadians, the North Americans, the whites) for thirty years and *you have never answered once.* . . . I have studied the history of the Jews and especially the careers of Brandeis and Disraeli. It will come eventually; we too will have such a man as Disraeli in the Canadian Parliament. But it will not happen in my life time."

When he was asked to study race relations on the West Coast, Park was like the physician who understands in advance the inflamed and feverish condition he is going to deal with and who also understands by what means the condition can be alleviated. The anti-Orientalists of the Coast had often made exaggerated claims about the number of Orientals there and the number engaged in various occupations. Park's initial attempt at alleviation of the conflict was, therefore, to get anti-Orientalists and pro-Orientalists to agree on the statistical facts. The public readily accepted the survey's statistical findings, because so many distinguished university personnel were involved. Here, Park's efforts to get anti-Orientals and pro-Orientals into the same universe of discourse succeeded.

His second step was to try to get white people interested in the Orientals as human beings. To most people the Orientals were strangers about whose lives they knew nothing. Park would tell his audiences fascinating stories about particular Orientals, based on interviews he had had and on the life histories which the survey had collected.

He noted in his speeches that the Orientals of the Pacific Coast also had prejudices: the Chinese, mostly from southern China discriminated against the Hakkas from northern China and the Japanese ostracized Japan's lowest class, the Etas. In a few instances these prejudices were crumbling. When this happened it was usually among the second generation of Oriental-Americans, and usually the member of the hitherto despised group who was being accepted was especially attractive and female. In a small California town a club consisting exclusively of American-born Japanese High School boys invited an ambitious Eta girl who wanted to be a musician to become a member. When she accepted they elected her president. A Chinese-Canadian graduate of a famous American university, after waiting years, was finally permitted by his parents to marry an exceptionally beautiful Hakka girl of a good and well-to-do family.

In talking to Pacific Coast audiences, Park and other members of the survey staff also described situations in which the relations between whites and Orientals were good. In Livingston, California, a small grape-growing town, all the Japanese were Christians. The town had two able leaders, one an agricultural scientist. These leaders had helped the Japanese farmers of Livingston handle relations with the whites so intelligently that their second-generation children in elementary school and high school were encountering no perceptible white prejudice.

On 26 May 1924, when the survey's work was about half done, the Japanese in the United States and those in Japan were profoundly affected by Congress's passage of a Japanese Exclusion Act limiting future Japanese migration to the United States. In July 1924 Professor Anezaki of Tokyo University wrote a letter to an American friend which was forwarded to Park:

> The immigration bill passed by the House of American Congress is a severe blow, almost mortal, to the cause of international amity and justice. This I say not for the cause of the Japanese but for the sake of humanity.

In his article "Behind Our Masks" in the May 1926 *Survey Graphic*, Park said that the Japanese people were

> undoubtedly less shocked by the Act than by the gesture with which it was performed. And what was their reply? An unknown man committed suicide on the steps of the American Embassy. Something like an epidemic of suicides ensued. America . . . missed the significance, as well as the pathos of Japan's tragic gesture. . . . It was in this way that the Japanese sought to appeal their case to a higher court; to the future, to the conscience of mankind, to whatever gods there be that rule the destinies of nations. The whole incident is illuminating since it indicates to what an extent, for the Orientals, this whole matter lies in the region of the so-called imponderables, in the realm of the spirit.

The Exclusion Act affected not only the Japanese but also the survey which Park was directing. The enthusiasm which had so far supported the survey disappeared. Wilbur, chairman of the central executive committee of the regional committees of the Coast, said in a letter to Fisher, the director of the Institute of Social and Religious Research: "Confusing the fundamental purpose of the investigation with political issues, the average man said, 'These exclusion laws make the whole survey project a *dead issue.*' Some of the most intelligent men on the Coast told us that the task of the Survey had now become an 'autopsy' instead of a 'diagnosis,' that there was no longer need of it, and that the best thing to do was to close up."

The survey had been assured of $55,000. Of this, $25,000 was to come from the institute. The five regional committees had pledged themselves to raise $30,000. They had raised only $7,200 before the passage of the Exclusion Act. Afterward only about $2,000 more was raised, leaving Park and his research staff $20,000 short.

Although Park and Wilbur tried hard to obtain further money from the institute and from other foundations, they did not succeed. A month after the passage of the Exclusion Act Park wired Fisher asking for $7,000 for six of his university staff. The institute was not interested but said it would pay Park's salary and running expenses. Park replied that if the institute would not pay his staff, he would accept no salary for himself.

Park left the Coast in August 1924, after telling W. I. Thomas that he had had "a strenuous year." Before leaving, he initiated a correspondence course in Americanization for high school teachers and wrote a letter of farewell and encouragement to the young second-generation Orientals of the Coast.

Davis, the administrative director of the survey, closed the San Francisco office on October 31, 1924. In a 14-page pamphlet issued on 1 September 1924, he noted that: "Research councils representing twelve universities from British Columbia to Los Angeles are assisting in the survey and directing the studies of seventy students and workers on specific projects. . . . Two hundred and ten persons . . . are serving on regional and local committees from Vancouver to the Mexican border. Six hundred documents, comprising 3,500 typewritten pages . . . have been filed and will be used in the reports of the survey findings."

During the fall and winter of 1924–25, Park was teaching at Chicago and organizing his survey materials so he could write a book. However, the drama between the institute and the survey was to have a final act.

Early in 1925 Wilbur persuaded Park that a conference should be held at Stanford University to persuade the Institute of Social and Religious Research to support the survey for another three years at $15,000 a year. Eleven members of Park's research staff agreed on their findings and a 24-page pamphlet called "Tentative Findings of the Survey of Race Relations" was prepared by Davis and Louis Bloch, a statistician. The *San Francisco Bulletin* for 26 March reported: "Educators here believe that the race relations survey meeting has been one of the most important gatherings in many ways that the Coast has ever seen." However, Fisher of the Institute of Social and Religious Research was not impressed. Two weeks after the Stanford conference, Fisher wired Mears of Stanford to say:

> Further grants doubtful until have seen Park's manuscript. Institute thinks first paragraph of findings on public opinion dubious and misleading. Desire statements from Wilbur and Rowell concerning value of survey already completed and its indirect, uncontroversial, factual approach.

Wilbur replied rather sternly to Fisher's telegram:

It is my firm conviction that the work already started should be documented on its present lines and expanded throughout the colleges and universities of the Pacific Coast. . . .

My opinion of the intrinsic value of this Survey is unchanged, except that my belief is stronger than ever that facts are cheap at any price. An excellent start has been made as noted in our Tentative Findings, but this is merely a beginning. Research work cannot be made to order—it requires time, and its final results cannot be foretold. Should the Survey be cut off entirely now or hampered seriously by lack of funds, we would present a spectacle which would be a credit to no individual or institution.

In April 1925, about a month after the Stanford conference ended, Park made a final attempt to reconcile his point of view about the survey with that of the institute. He wrote to Fisher. (The earlier relations between the two men had been cordial. Davis claimed that the difficulties the survey had with the institute were due not to Fisher but to a board member.)

This Survey, as I conceive it, has not been organized primarily for the purpose of promoting academic studies in RACE RELATIONS; it is organized primarily for the purpose of improving RACE RELATIONS. This has been my conception of the study, and I think it is important that, in the future as in the past, the idea that these studies are being made for this definite, practical purpose should be kept before the men in the Universities, who are continuing the work of the Survey.

It has been very clear to me that the only thing which could lift a study of this sort above the level of propaganda is that it should be such a study as would elicit the interest of academic men and be accepted by them as scientific. The fact that we have been able to secure the interest of many of the best minds in all the Universities up and down the Coast is an evidence that this end has been achieved.

To any one who is interested in the long future of the RACE RELATIONS between the Orient and the Occident, therefore, whose interests are really permanent instead of being exhausted by the success or failure of any immediate program, the fact that there are certain fundamental changes in RACE RELATIONS that have been, that are and that will continue to go on in RACE RELATIONS is a very fundamental conception.

As a student of American history and a scholar in the race relations field, Park knew that race relations cannot be improved overnight but that they do change with time. During the fifty years since the survey ended, Japanese-Americans and Chinese-Americans have held distinguished posts in Pacific Coast universities. Although the feeling against intermarriage was strong in 1924, sociologists have recently noted that the rate of Japanese-American marriages is high in certain sections of California. In Canada, a Chinese-Canadian boy born in 1924, the year the survey took place, served in the air force during World War II and was later elected to the Canadian Parliament. It is true that no Chinese-Canadian has yet become a prime minister like Disraeli, but the doors to political office can no longer be considered closed.

No book on the survey of race relations on the Pacific Coast ever appeared. Park arranged that its findings should be reported in a special May 1926 East-West issue of the *Survey Graphic* magazine. The issue contained poems by Flora Belle Jan and an article by Kazue Kawai, a student at Stanford University, who said: "My desire is to choose as my life work some profession which will allow me to utilize my peculiar characteristics as a member of the second-generation Japanese in America . . . in making a distinctive contribution to American life. In a general sort of a way I believe that I have found such a life work. I think of the fact of race conflict. . . . To prepare myself . . . I am studying the history of the Orient and especially the history of the relations between the Occident and the Orient." The issue also contained articles by members of Park's research staff—R. D. McKenzie, Emory S. Bogardus, William C. Smith, Elliot G. Mears, Winifred Raushenbush, and Merle J. Davis. Park contributed two articles: "Our Racial Frontier on the Pacific" and "Behind our Masks, a Psychological Study of Self-Consciousness and Race Consciousness."

In undertaking to direct the survey, Park had specified that he wanted something from it for himself. He succeeded; he found himself fascinated by Japanese civilization. On leaving San Francisco, he said to an associate: "The civilization of Japan is quite as extraordinary as that of Athens. I want to get there as fast as I can and see it before it disappears."

Park made his first trip to the Orient in 1925.

Chapter 13. A Sociological Generation

Park, during his nineteen years at the University of Chicago, learned a great deal from his students, and they in turn studied him. Herbert Blumer, who got his Ph.D. from the university in 1928, compares Park's mind to Darwin's:

> Dr. Park was indeed a very remarkable and outstanding person. He had an excellent mind, one that was marked by great imagination and a persistent restless searching for the posing of proper questions and seeking meaningful solutions to them. He was ever pondering on problems and in doing so was ever alert to suggestions and hints from any source. I have always felt that his mind was very much like that of Charles Darwin. I suspect that the two of them would have found each other very congenial in the way in which they approached the study of their respective areas of interest. . . .
>
> Dr. Park had enormous insight into human beings and their conduct; he was indeed a rare and gifted person in this respect. I have always regarded him as one of the great students of human nature; in the sense that we use that term when we think of great playwrights and scholars such as Shakespeare. Presented with accounts of human conduct, he would ever so frequently make judicious observations showing that he grasped the significance of the accounts in a profound way that escaped the detection of others, however intelligent or learned they might be. I have never encountered in my own range of human association anyone who could approach him in this respect. Others were also aware of his rare gift along this line. I recall hearing Professor Edward Scribner Ames, a renowned scholar in his own right, say that he learned more about human nature through an hour's conversation with Dr. Park than through spending a half year reading allegedly scientific works in the social and psychological sciences. I think that this was a legitimate and accurate testimony to Dr. Park's remarkable penetration into human understanding. . . . Of the great contributions made by Dr. Park, I would say, first of all, that one of his great achievements was the stress which he placed on the naturalistic study of human group life. . . . This is the way in which he conceived the scientific task of sociology. This is why I liken him

to Charles Darwin. This type of approach has unfortunately been pushed into the background by developments in our discipline over the last two decades [1944–66]. But I believe that it will re-emerge with vigor. At that time I believe that sociologists will develop a proper, profound regard for the work of Dr. Park. . . .

Edgar Thompson, who delighted Park with his persistent explorations of plantation life, likewise comments on Park's understanding of human nature:

As I think about it, it seems to me, that in my own case at least, Park was the man who transformed human nature from a psychological or biological into a sociological concept. He made human nature, the nature that is in all people, into a sort of absolute. . . . Like the giant in the fairy tale, wherever Park caught the scent of human nature, there his quarry was. I do not recall Park ever talking about "Man" or "Humanity." He talked about people, the people behind tools and machinery, behind the written documents, behind institutions. If people were not there, he did not seem interested.

The range of Park's firsthand acquaintance with Americans in all social and economic groups was extraordinary, but he was, primarily, continuously engaged in thought. Everett Hughes says: "He thought sitting down, lying down, and standing up." Park once apologized to his class because he was so often preoccupied, explaining that his need to go on with whatever thinking he was currently doing was responsible.

All his students were familiar with his notion about the two kinds of knowledge a sociologist needs, "knowledge about" and "acquaintance with." In Park neither kind of knowledge outweighed or dominated the other: they coexisted in balance. Everett Hughes has described some aspects of this phenomenon:

It has been the peculiar cachet of American sociology to combine curiosity about what is going on in the world and about the news behind the news, with a more theoretical interest. Park, more than anyone before or during his time, brought these two interests together.

Outstanding about Park was what one might call the dialectic between the reporter and the philosopher. No human event was too small to start going in his mind a philosophical speculation of the most abstruse sort.

In his ecological work Park spoke of centers of dominance, a phrase which he used very much. In an early seminar . . . I did a paper in which I listed the great cities of the world according to the number of commodities in which they were great central markets. London was the central market for more things than anywhere else, with New York second. Park was a bit romantic about this and carried it over into talk about the family business in the northwest, speaking of the central towns out there as small centers of dominance for a hinterland which lay behind. Dominance and hinterland were very important concepts for him. He tied up the distribution of groceries in the West with his consideration of the great markets of the world. He saw them as forming a network. . . . In fact he wanted me to take as my Ph.D. thesis the study of credit, meaning by credit all this complex of buying and selling and trusting one another in terms of symbols without any goods present. . . . Perhaps that was where his greatness lay—that the small things, the small events and his own experiences were somehow or other seen in his mind as connected with the great world. The concrete was always something to be retold in abstract and general terms. Park's was a slow-moving, fertile kind of thinking with its head in the philosophical clouds but with its feet always down to earth in the human mess. As a matter of fact, he seemed always to be trying to bring these two things together, philosophical thought and the human mess.

One of the most illuminating comments Park ever made on the two kinds of knowledge appears in a letter of advice he wrote in 1930 to Bernard Hormann, who was studying a Chinese village:

Civilization develops by the growth of knowledge that can be transmitted because it can be checked up. It can become funded, a part of the general knowledge of the world. Our ideal is to have a scientist in each social institution—a person who isn't interested in improving any particular case a bit, but is interested in *cases of that kind*. This demands accuracy, definiteness, precision. The scientist ought to have a conscience about that. The people who are talking about techniques are applying conventional methods to facts, theories and hypotheses. But if a person has no acquaintance with things outside the laboratory, he is not likely to have so many fruitful hypotheses to check up. So the men who contribute most to science are those who have had a wide experience. There is no scientific method for getting "hunches." These must arise out of experience. . . . Edison was never a scientist. He wasn't capable of doing scientific work in a strict sense, but he had 240 scientists working for him. Edison was trying to create things. . . . You cannot learn to generate new ideas. New ideas arise, whether in the individual or in the group, from the contact and ferment of the people who are moved to act—moved with the urge, the desire and aim to achieve something or other.

In this letter, Park revealed a good deal about himself. Although affectionate and sociable, he enjoyed nothing more than he did thinking. He had discovered that he did his most joyous and creative thinking by exposing himself to new situations and people and thus getting insights, having hunches, evolving fresh hypotheses. At this point the process which might lead to "knowledge about" could begin.

As a teacher and as a student of the human condition, he dedicated himself to the many forms the process of education could take. Hughes, one of the principal authorities on Park's work as a sociologist, recalls some of the aspects of this dedication:

> When he was teaching at Chicago, he did not simply teach a subject and then liquidate it and the students when he sent in their grades. He tended to get students involved in a sort of movement and many of us were drawn into that movement.
>
> He was not a man who, after a long practical career, got curious; he was a restless, curious man whose ideas and questions followed and plagued him throughout his career.
>
> In his belief in news, experience, free enterprise, education as the way to reform, Park was practically a 19th century man. In his practice, much ahead of the 1970 reality. . . .
>
> He was greatly interested in experiments of the Indian Bureau to replace the Indian boarding school. . . . Park's sympathy was always with the Negro doing it on his own, or with support—and not with the missionary school teacher type. . . . He also took part in meetings got up by the U. S. Department of Agriculture on improving farming and social life in marginal agricultural areas. When he went again to the city to live—to Chicago—he studied the city with the same drive, speculative detachment and curiosity as he had studied Macon County in Alabama.
>
> He never went anywhere or looked at anything simply because he—or other people—had never been there or seen it before. I have heard him say, "Why go to the North Pole or climb Everest for adventure when we have Chicago?"

What Hughes got out of Park for himself was the sense that society is interaction. Describing his first contact with Park, he says:

It took me the better part of a term to begin to sense what Park was talking about. Then it turned out to be theories and ideas. One moment he talked in a newsy way: next, in a very abstract way. Whatever his course in a given term, I took it. . . . While the substance of the courses was new and interesting, it was the point of view that took hold of me. Society is interaction. Interaction involves sensitivity to others, but to some others more than to other others. Sects control their young by isolating them from interaction with dangerous others. "Even that which appears solid and fixed, such as the table on which my hands are resting, is a product of the mad interaction of particles. It could blow up." So said Park in class one morning.

Park became intimate with Louis Wirth, first as a student and later as a colleague. In 1930 Park recommended Wirth for a teaching position in Chicago, and after Louis and his wife, Mary, of whom Park was fond, had settled in Chicago, he was a frequent visitor in their home. In August 1930, when Wirth was studying in Germany, Park wrote to him:

I have just finished reading your very interesting article on Clinical Sociology. . . . I think the point you make that delinquency is only delinquency because of social definition of the group in which the delinquency occurs is the core of the whole thesis. If that is given prominence it at once emphasizes the fact . . . that a psychiatrist who bases his diagnosis upon the analysis of the behavior of the individual and upon his supposed biological or mental deficiency still seeks to effect a cure by putting the individual in a favorable sociological environment and leaves the real task of dealing with the patient to the social worker. If stated in this way it really raises the question of what business has a medical man dealing with behavior problems of this kind at all.

On 9 August 1930, Wirth, in a letter from Germany, replied:

Thank you for your letter and your efforts on my behalf in Chicago. The prospect of being among the three million unemployed in America was none too cheering. . . . In the last few months I have made the acquaintance of most of the German sociologists. . . . Almost all of the men I have met are intensely interested in American sociology. . . .

Much excitement is expected in view of the general elections. The progress of the German fascist movement has been enormous.

Of Park as a sociologist, Wirth says:

Few of the phrases that we ordinarily use to describe our fellow-men apply to Robert E. Park. He was not an ordinary man. Even on first acquaintance he stood out and, by his very presence, dominated a group. As a teacher, as a scholar, as a friend, as a personality he was what newspapermen—with whom he felt a lifelong kinship—call a phenomenon.

He found it useful to distinguish between three fundamental types of knowledge (1) philosophy and logic, which are concerned primarily with ideas; (2) history which is concerned primarily with events; (3) the natural or classifying sciences which are concerned primarily with things. . . .

He sought to cultivate social science as if it were a natural science, as far as possible recognizing that as one labored on that assumption one would soon enough encounter the values, morals and preferences of men before which the methods of natural sciences would prove inadequate.

In one of his . . . brilliant articles analyzing the similarities and differences between the human community and the plant and animal community, he said, in what those who knew him could identify as the spirit of Whitman, "I should like to add, if the comment were not wholly irrelevant, that it is a comfort in these days of turmoil and strife to realize that society and human beings, when in repose, do retain and exhibit some of the dignity and serenity of plants." He conceived of society as a set of reciprocal claims and expectations and mutual understandings. He knew that we acquire the stature of men through communication with others and through participation in a common life. He was fond of saying that "what a man belongs to constitutes most of his life career and all of his obituary."

He described man's socialization in these words: "One begins life as an individual organism involved in a struggle with other organisms for mere existence. . . . One becomes involved later in personal and moral, eventually economic and occupational, and ultimately political associations; in short, with all the forms of association we call social. In this way society and the person or the socialized individual, come into existence and as a result of the same cycle or succession of events."

This conception of the epic of the human career, we might add, was also his conception of the essential task of social science. To understand it was the calling of the sociologist. Colossal as his scholarly output was, no man in my acquaintance has ever left behind so much unfinished business. This unfinished business of his will be the theme of many books to be finished by others.

One of the pieces of unfinished business that Park eventually handed on was the subject of collective behavior, which he passed on to Herbert Blumer, persuading him to do some writing in this area. Blumer not only did the writing but continued to think about and develop the concept. He says: "Park laid the foundation for this area of sociological concern and should be regarded as its source. My own indebtedness to him in the area of collective behavior is enormous."

Of Park as a sociologist, Blumer says:

> Dr. Park had wide and persistent interests in human group life and thus must be placed in the very center of sociological areas of concern. What is distinctive of his orientation, in my judgment, is that he saw human society as consisting of human beings meeting the conditions and requirements of their life situations. He definitely felt that to analyze and understand human society or human group life the entree had to be made through the experiences of the people themselves. This emphasis on getting into the world of experience of people making up any group is, I think, the mark par excellence of Park's position as a sociologist.

> He was tremendously interested in analytical theory. . . . It would be a serious mistake . . . to think of him as merely trying to provide a higher level of journalistic description. Instead he was always seeking to extract from the down-to-earth descriptive accounts meaningful characterizations and generalizations. Moreover, he tended to view this theory pragmatically. . . . This was both the strength as well as the weakness of his concern with theory. His theory was always empirically grounded. And this is to his great merit.

> However, in not working out the logical presuppositions of his concepts and propositions he did not work in the direction of developing systematic theories. Any lack in this respect cannot be advanced as any serious criticism of him. . . . The significance of my observation is that Park was not a systematizer in the area of theory. . . . I have always felt that a contribution of the first order might be made in our discipline if someone with the proper talents were to assemble the incisive theoretical observations made by Park and work out their logical premises and presuppositions. . . .

> In my confirmed judgment, Dr. Park ranks along with William Graham Sumner and W. I. Thomas as one of the three great American sociologists we have had down to date.

Everett Hughes once remarked that a university is a place where you have an occasional genius and many charismatic personalities. The word "genius" has customarily been applied to natural rather than to social scientists. However, during the period from 1914 to 1933 at the University of Chicago, there were many extremely able and some brilliant students and there was a touch of genius in the air: George Herbert Mead, William Isaac Thomas, Robert Ezra Park. Robert E. Lee Faris, who took his Ph.D. at Chicago in 1931, has described in his *Chicago Sociology: 1920–1932* the intense energy and the spirit of achievement which characterized the sociology department during the latter part of Park's teaching career:

> Throughout the twenties, at Chicago, success built on success. The large student enrollment, the prominence of the faculty and the pride in being independent of doctrine all combined to produce the high morale that characterized the department until well into the 1930s. . . .
>
> The period of interest (1920–1932) has no precise beginning or ending, but the temporal focus of the inquiry is on the few years in which the sociology department achieved a strong momentum and held a sort of temporary performance championship in the United States, which in that time meant the world championship of sociology.

To have lived through a period when a young discipline—sociology —was first achieving some degree of maturity was exhilarating for Chicago students of Parks' era and for Park himself. Recalling this period of his youth many years later, Robert Faris said in a letter to a fellow student: "I remember Park as a mountain—from which I am receding."

Chapter 14. Travels

A year after the Survey of Race Relations on the Pacific Coast ended, Park was invited to participate in the newly created Institute of Pacific Relations, which was to meet in July 1925. Honolulu was chosen as a central location; one hundred and eleven participants were coming from nine countries. William Allen White, in his report on the conference, "The Last of the Magic Isles" wrote, "anywhere else in the world such a group would represent somebody, but in Honolulu they didn't. They represented themselves"—that is, they did not represent any pressure groups but were chosen as individuals. Park, however, perceived in the round table discussions that there were three informal divisions based on points of view. He noted down: (1) The Williamsburg crowd—Education of Public Opinion; (2) The Anthropologists and Sociologists—Race Problems and Immigration; (3) Goodwill Organizations, Missionaries, Y.M.C.A. wanted a Resolution, something expressive, the Golden Rule.

As a social occasion the conference was a complete success. The IPR was very generous in paying the expenses not only of each guest but also of "one other," so, as always, Park took his wife with him.

The trip to Honolulu by luxury steamer was itself pleasant and relaxing, the hospitable reception and sense of racial goodwill in Hawaii noteworthy. Park sensed possibilities for intensive research in this melange of races, but at this time his "Notes of a Traveler" did not delve deeply. The Parks stayed in Hawaii after the close of the conference and visited some other areas, including Maui. Wherever he went, Park noted the names and backgrounds of the many individuals he met and his impressions of the institutions visited. He also jotted down "Topics for Investigation."

   I. The Mormon Colony. History—What type of Hawaiian joins etc.
  II. The Birth of Christianity among Japanese in Hawaii.
 III. Interracial Personalities.
 IV. Prestige of the American Haole Community.
  V. Interracial Relations and Devices for Carrying them on.
 VI. The Organization of the Racial Communities. The role of the "patrons" in foreign language schools.
     The role of the teacher.

In 1926 the American Group of the Institute of Pacific Relations was organized. Park was a member of the research committee, with Clark Wissler, Quincy Wright, and others and was on a subcommittee on information and publicity with Bruce Bliven, William Allen White, and Henry Luce. However, he did not participate in group meetings and did not interrupt his summer teaching to attend.

The next IPR conference he attended was held in Kyoto in November 1929. Clara Park commented in a family letter:

> Now we have been in Kyoto since October 22nd, and the meeting has been formally opened since the 28th. Pop has been more than pleasantly surprised, even enthusiastic about the whole affair. You may remember that he never was cheered by the Honolulu Conference, as I was, but this time it seems to be right after his own heart: that is, there are people here who actually are going at the thing as he would like to see it done, and there certainly are lots of people here who know their jobs.

When they arrived in Kyoto the Parks had been traveling since 23 March. Their first goal was the 4th Pacific Science Congress to be held in the middle of May at Bandung, Indonesia. They arrived several weeks before the opening of the Congress and so were able to visit a number of nearby areas.

At the Congress Park's paper on "Mentality of Racial Hybrids" was well received. A week later he acted as chairman, then was chosen as permanent chairman, of the Anthropology Section.

Along with the lectures and discussions, participants in the congress had many relaxations—views of the countryside, a grand ball at Sultan Sunan's palace, and a trip with archaeologists to the cave where Pithecanthropus erectus had been found. Early in June, after the Congress, the Parks spent a delightful week at Bali. Then they went to Soneabaya, Djakarta, and Singapore, and spent about a month in the Philippines, much of it at the University of Manila. By September they were in China. At Shanghai College, Robert gave a short course on social science research; in China, as Clara said in a family letter, he was "booked to lecture all over the place, especially in Peking, which seems to have a dozen mouths waiting to gobble him up." He did not get to

Peking at this time, however. He was scheduled to speak at the University in Nanking in October, but he became ill and was hospitalized there.

By 22 October he had recovered and so was able to get to Japan ahead of the opening of the IPR conference on 28 October. Park's extensive notes for this period began in Kyoto, 2 November 1929. As he wrote later, "When I first came out I collected a great many interesting anecdotes," but, "by the time I got back I had forgotten them, and had become interested in things not anecdotal."

He was stimulated to do a great deal of rethinking and enlarging of ideas by contacts with radically different cultures and civilizations. The discussions of the IPR conferees—Chinese, Japanese, British, American, Canadian, and one Russian—were about news in the machine age, censorship (defended only by the Chinese), telegraph tolls, and, in general, the practical difficulties of communication. The newsmen felt that lowering telegraph rates would not immediately affect the flow of news, since the barriers to communication were psychological and cultural rather than technical—the trouble was not obtaining news but getting people to read and understand it. This was illustrated by the difficulties that foreigners in Japan had—for example, theatrical performances were admired but largely incomprehensible and the role of the geisha was misunderstood. A motto hanging in a hotel dining room said, translated literally, "In the fumes and fragrance of wine, peace, fraternity, and praise"; it was translated by a waiter as "It just says all kinds of drinks here." Park noted the prejudices in Japan about the Eta caste. He continued his interest in cultural encounters, in the results of mixed marriage, and in the religious sects springing up, Christian and Buddhist. He felt that "we must assume that in the long run and when we know the facts there is nothing human that is foreign to us, so we are bound to recognize in every individual in any situation whatever what, but for the grace of God, is ourself." So he was particularly concerned to explore what he called "the Japanese temperament":

> The meticulous way in which it seeks to regulate life, the extent to which etiquette rules and controls their lives as manifest in the tea ceremony and in the regulations under which an individual is permitted to protect himself against burglars. Under these laws the sort of weapon one may use under different circumstances is all so regulated and controlled that unless every citizen was not only familiar with their regulations but has drilled and schooled himself in the movements in quick action they could not possibly be carried out as prescribed.[1]

1. Park commenting on a clipping from the *Japan Advertiser*, date unknown.

Regarding the constraints on conduct in Japan, Park noted, "the law as defined in custom and on the statute books and as embodied in the habits and conscience of the individual man is identical or nearly so. . . . It was true of Anglo-Saxon people once. It will probably not last and is very likely in process of decay in Japan."

He perceived marked differences between Japanese and Chinese. While in Tokyo he had been told about the Chinese

> that one must not go home after visiting China for a few weeks and write a book. As a rule it is recommended that one would do best to live 20 years in China before forming an opinion for publication. This is discouraging in itself but what is more discouraging is the statement so often heard that the longer they have remained the less they know and understand the people about them. I think that except for missionaries and students, who make an effort to understand, this is literally true. On the other hand the long stayers know a great deal about the external aspects of life here and of the people, they know how, as they say, to deal with them. But in the meantime there has grown up a caste feeling which cannot be overcome. How this caste feeling grows up out of a multitude of annoyances due to misunderstandings and mistrust is one of the problems that needs to be studied more in detail.

The 1929 notebook takes us from Tokyo to Seoul, then briefly to Shanghai, Nanking, and Yenching University outside Peking, where Robert delivered an address and both Parks began friendships that would continue. By 3 January they were back in Honolulu for a few weeks.

Park's days at Honolulu at the beginning of 1930 are recalled by Andrew Lind, then a graduate student assisting in the Department of Sociology, as showing a Robert Park quite different from the teacher whose crowded office in Chicago he had dreaded to visit. Park was no longer "gruff, unpredictable, intense, and frequently angry." He was helpful, warm, enthusiastic about student projects for research; persons at the University of Hawaii looked forward to visits from him. On this visit Lind introduced Park to Bernard Hormann, then a young teacher in a Honolulu junior high school. Hormann recollects that he heard Park deliver a public lecture which did not impress him much but he was impressed by firsthand contact. Asked about a career as a sociologist, Park "gave no advice, but it was obvious that he believed that prospective Ph.D. students needed to have familiarity with a variety of social stituations before undertaking advanced study. It was on the basis of this interview that I looked for a way to get to the Far East, and was able to get the one year appointment to Lingnan University, which was renewed every year, through 1933–34."

From the spring quarter of 1930 until September 1931, Park taught at Chicago and spent summers in northern Michigan. He wrote what he called a preliminary paper on "The Problem of Cultural Differences" for the IPR conference in Hangchow, China, but did not attend the meetings.

On 12 September 1931 the Parks sailed from Vancouver to Honolulu where they became comfortably established in a house of their own, Park being visiting professor for the academic year. He had no formal teaching responsibilities but was expected to consult on teaching and research problems in race relations with the sociology staff. Romanzo Adams, head of the department, was only five years younger than Park and a University of Chicago man—he obtained his Ph.D. in 1904—and knowledgeable about the racial situation in Hawaii. He shared Park's interests. The assistants, Andrew Lind and Clarence Glick, had both worked under Park at Chicago. It was a good year for all. As Lind recalls:

> We persuaded Park to conduct an informal seminar on race relations, but I think it was chiefly in the informal conversations and bull-sessions throughout that year that I derived from him the insights and understanding which have remained with me most permanently and vividly. At one point Park suggested that we take out memberships in one of the swimming clubs at Waikiki and for several months we would plan to meet at the beach at Waikiki about 11:30, go in the water for a short swim and then lie on the beach or go for our lunch, while discussing matters of common, chiefly sociological interest.

There were also occasional long expeditions on foot, when, according to Lind, Park surprised the younger members by coming through "with little evidence of wear and tear, apparently refreshed by his own observations on all sorts of matters relating to human life and society, as well as the new knowledge he had obtained in answer to his questions about the island community."

There were a number of interesting people to become acquainted with. Peter Henry Buck was outstanding, as was Te Rangi Hiroa, the distinguished Maori ethnographer connected with the museum. Clara did his portrait in pastels while Theodosia Park Breed completed the portrait of Robert commissioned by the University of Chicago, which now hangs in the Social Science building. In June Park delivered a commencement address, "The University and the Community of Race." He spoke of the critical change which he felt was now beginning in the relations of East and West—the Occident already having become in a very real sense the old world; the Orient, now stirring, the new. Hawaii had certain advantages that correctly directed education would enable her to use. These advantages lay not just in her advanced agriculture but in her human element. "The study of human nature," Park observed, "by direct methods which anthropologists employ, need not and should not be confined either to primitive or non-European peoples. Political policy and political administration can be improved by a more intimate acquaintance with people—even with those people we are supposed to know, because we see them and jostle them every day in the streets."

The formidable quality of Hawaii as a melting pot was recognized and accepted but had hardly been studied. A young woman, Margaret Lam, herself part Hawaiian, had been stimulated by Park to begin working on the genealogical records of the old Hawaiian families, many of them a fantastic intermixture of races. And Park, with Romanzo Adams and others, proposed the creation of a thorough study of race relations in the future, a Honolulu institute, to meet first in summer 1934. The Parks left Hawaii the last week of August 1932 and made a brief stopover in Japan before going on to Yenching University in China. Notes on 8 to 10 September made by Bernard Hormann, gave these definite plans for the institute:

> We hope to bring together here people from different parts of the world, from places where race problems are real and have had to be considered. We hope to organize to study these things cooperatively, with one center in Honolulu and another in South Africa. . . . I am going to India, S. Africa, S. America, etc. to see what people are thinking, and who would want to cooperate—who have a disposition to study.
>
> We shall begin with the biological aspects and go on to race relations, finding in the Statesman Yearbook the places where a mixed population is recognized, etc., in Honolulu, in the Reunion Island off the coast of Africa in Mombasa, etc. We want to study the problem intimately to see what the cultural process is that results from such racial mixture, and to seek the life stories of people who have mixed in Honolulu,—what language they speak, etc., what motives to intermarry, etc.
>
> We find it is the individual who intermarries. The family does not encourage it unless the group is disorganized. So the motive is rather personal, largely romantic, particularly if the person married is a stranger. . . . You get a problem if you do, and if you don't, intermarry in such mixed societies. Such study cannot be done quickly. We

shall spend six weeks browsing around and talking with one another, and see what happens.

Yenching University had been founded by missionaries. It had an excellent reputation in the field of education and, under the presidency of Leighton Stuart, himself born in China of missionary parents, good relations between the student body and the faculty—half Chinese, half largely English-speaking Westerners. Yenching profited also from the interchange of ideas with the faculty of Tsing Hua University, whose campus adjoined. There were many capable individuals eager to work with Park. Two at least were outstanding, Fei Hsiao-tung and C. K. Yang. Fei, who was also a student of Malinowski's, wrote later of this time:

> It was at the end of the 1920's that China entered a period of political stability and reconstruction. Young students, after having participated in the previous revolution, began to settle down and think about more fundamental issues. It was clear that political enthusiasm by itself would be futile if it were not to be followed by a period of practical reconstruction of the country. . . . It was at this time . . . that Professor Robert E. Park of the University of Chicago visited Yenching University. He met the need of the students by inspiring them in how to carry on field studies. He himself visited the prisons and the Heaven Bridge, the red-light area in Peiping, to demonstrate that useful knowledge can be derived from the life of even the lowliest people.

C. K. Yang, who was later frequently published in the United States, gives a more graphic account of Parks' teaching:

> He gave a course to the juniors, seniors and graduates in Sociology under the title, I believe, of "Methods of Social Research." It certainly proved to be the most exciting course to most of the class members in their entire college career. I still remember vividly the first statement he made to the class: "In this course I am not going to teach you how to read books, but I am going to tell you how to write a book." This fired our imagination immediately because quite a few of us had the urge to write.
>
> His instructions following this remark lived up fully to the intention he set forth. He taught us the value and the technique of classification as a central task in scientific research. He taught us the ways to derive conclusions from classified facts, to formulate hypotheses, and to test them. Tradition of Chinese scholarship has committed the error of excessive reliance on book learning, which

resulted in repeating what people have said before, thus blocking discovery of new knowledge. Park pointed out strongly this weakness and inspired the class to seek new knowledge from facts through scientific methods. But he also taught us how to treat book knowledge as scientific data, and showed us the systematic accumulation of knowledge by proper reference notations.

He brought to each class-hour an independent topic of social research, and laboriously put on the board a series of questions for us to answer. In answering these questions, members of the class really had their curiosity aroused. We looked up books and went into the field on these small projects which gave us the first taste of sociological research and led us constantly to checking back and forth between facts and books.

One result of this was a collective volume edited by the advanced members of the class under the title of *Sociological Theories of Robert E. Park*. It was a volume written in Chinese by various members of the class, consisting mostly of field report and reflections of Park's own written works.

Even some of the older students who had studied abroad could profit from this guided research. Park commented later on his experiences in China:

At Yenching University I found many students who had earlier studied in America and were now attempting to use the ideas and conceptions we had given them to understand and study their own society and civilization. I also noted that many of the notions they had picked up in America were of no particular use or value in China.

For instance, recently we had a student who was studying crime in China as compared with crime in America. The Nanking government has adopted the categories of crime, most of them, that we have in this country, and they have added a few of their own, and they have got in their list crimes that actually do not exist in China at all and never did exist.[2]

Park was committed to only one quarter's teaching at Yenching. He and Clara left the University on Christmas eve, and he then began to gather materials on the social situation of the Eurasians, a decidedly marginal group there as in India. However, before reaching Hong Kong, he decided to visit briefly Canton and the University of Lingnan nearby. Park had been corresponding with Bernard Hormann who for two years

2. From a November 1934 lecture at the University of Chicago.

had been teaching English and German on the campus and studying a nearby village. Lingnan, the wealthiest missionary institution of learning in China and one of the more conservative, had not bothered to make itself popular with the local people and as a result Hormann's work had gone rather slowly. However, he had been persistent, had gradually been accepted by the villagers, and when Dr. and Mrs. Park arrived, he was able to introduce them to some of his acquaintances.

Park used the three days he spent with Hormann to teach the young sociologist how to do first-rate research. Hormann was so impressed with Park's advice that he set it down on paper. The first step, Park said, was to continue to study the village as a whole: "speak to everyone, use everyone"; the second was to be sensitive to people's feelings; the third, to focus, eventually on whatever had proved to be most significant. Park told Hormann:

Now, regarding your own research, you seem to be succeeding in getting acquainted with the people: Writing down your immediate impressions is also valuable. Later on many of these first thoughts will undoubtedly seem very immature to you. You should mull over your impressions and you will occasionally get at something bigger, a question of a possible generalization or some sort of an explanation. Write these things down separately. You should use all of Honan island as a setting for your study. Get a good map of the island. Then locate all the villages and plot other interesting information. Make the map graphic. Somehow or other you must make your village real to yourself and to your readers. Conventionalize what you plot. For instance, you have described the semi-circular shape of the villages. Make use of the semi-circle as a symbol. Put the masts of the salt junks in the river. Show the location of the boat-people. Then, coming to your particular village, make a map of it, showing in some graphic way how the houses are clustered together, how the narrow lanes cut across the semi-circle, so that from above it may look almost like a pie. In a third map locate all the temples, gods, shrines, and other objects around which there is or has been sentiment. Start with the public objects. Later get those in the homes. Then in the coming year you must get all kinds of information. Speak to everyone. Use everyone. Find out everything you can about the history of Honan, the boat people and this particular village. In the village you will have a difficult task. But you must try to discover what exactly are the sentiments of the various groups of people toward the objects of worship. You will find that their sentiments vary according to the groups, the time, and the occasion. From your books find out the various festivals and how they are celebrated. Then find out if and how these festivals are actually celebrated in the village. You should concentrate thoroughly on one such thing as "the expressive culture" of the village. Extend your study to the whole island. But concentrate on one phase. Do not neglect any information you may get on the other phases and include them briefly in your final thesis. But if you do one phase well, you will find you have actually gotten at the core of the village. You will be able to make a real contribution. One phase is so closely connected up with all other phases. What Mr. Brownell said regarding the god of eleven villages, who is annually in a procession passed on from one village to the next is very interesting. Find out more about that. Find out about land owning. How is land actually transferred? Is there a ceremony at the time of transfer? You must live with the people. You must put yourself on their level. Only thus will you be able to understand them. Then the next state in your thesis will be to write it as if meant for the final form. When you have written the complete thesis once, you will find that you have acquired an entirely different slant on it. You will have new interpretations. Only then will you be capable of actually writing the final draft in any adequate manner. Read some books on religion and on Chinese culture now, but do not bother about sociological theory until you come to Chicago. You will find several courses there extremely valuable, partly because they represent years of experience and have never been written up. You should take Dr. Faris' course in social psychology, my course in collective behavior, a good course in statistics, and the course in "Park and Burgess." My course will probably be my last at the University, but I shall initiate Blumer into it. After spending a year at Chicago you could go to Germany. Attend lectures here and there. Visit round. Get the German atmosphere. Then a year or more in Germany will be of great benefit to you. After that you could probably finish up at Chicago in six months.

Let me give you a few concepts which I have found helpful in thinking about culture. I started out by studying the institutions in society. Now I study collective behavior, a term which I think very useful. How people act together is something which can be studied objectively. Then I make room for the term "expressive" behavior. Art, religion, magic, play are all expressive behavior. In magic we have ritual with the expectation of a definite result. If we find a better way of getting the same result, we give up the magic. Thus magic leads to science. In religion we beseech a higher power for some sort of aid and hope for an answer. Art and play are related. They are an expression for relaxation—for the pure fun of it. In studying a ritual you should try to determine which form of expression is present. Sometimes several elements may be present. Then you must determine the attitude of the persons toward the ritual. Do they do it in order not to lose face? Do they do it with a sentiment of fear? It may also be possible to trace the sentiment at the time the ritual or ceremony started, through various stages.

Park wrote, between 12 January and 29 March 1933, three long letters to Romanzo Adams in Honolulu as reports on his impressions of the many varied aspects of race relations and culture patterns encountered along what he liked to call "the mainstreet of the world." Everywhere he sought, in spite of the limited time he had, relevant literature and representative individuals. Earlier in Japan he had found that the Eta were not receiving the "systematic study and research" he had hoped, although both Christian missions and government officials, the latter not solely for scientific reasons, were paying some attention to them. In China, before leaving Peking, Park became interested in Manchuria and inner Mongolia, two frontier areas into which Chinese civilization was expanding and which he would have liked to visit. His interest had been further stimulated by a dinner with a varied group. He wrote to Adams:

One of these men was a scholar of the old school, who reflected the traditional views of Chinese scholars, only slightly modified by the trend of current events. He was from Honan province. Another member of the group was the publisher of an agricultural paper at Peiping. A third was a reformed general, who has a large tract of land somewhere beyond the Great Wall, now in process of settlement. A fourth was a vice minister of education who had travelled a good deal . . . in Europe and elsewhere, and seemed to possess a surprising amount of detailed information in regard to agricultural conditions in the countries he had visited. The Vice Minister of Education was the only one of the group who spoke English, but I was able to converse with some of the others through the medium of Professor Cato Young of Yenching University who has a special interest in the Chinese peasant and in rural life and institutions generally.

What I learned from these men was not much, but was enough to give me a keen interest and understanding of Owen Lattimore's book on Manchuria, *Manchuria, Cradle of Conflict* which I read later. In fact that was the most enlightening book I have read on China. . . .

China has never achieved a sovereignty over the territory over which Chinese culture prevails such as is characteristic of, and essential to, the existence of a State in the European sense. India, with its caste system, seems to have been arrested midway . . . in the process of unification, racially and culturally. . . .

I shall have something to say about Indo-China and India later on, but with regard to China the picture is relatively clear. China, in the past at any rate, has behaved like some vast octopus which extends its tentacles in every direction, drawing into itself and absorbing the more primitive peoples with which it comes into contact.

The second letter to Adams began:

Since I wrote you last I have visited, in addition to Hong Kong, four port cities, Saigon, Singapore, Rangoon, and Calcutta.

All of these cities, with the exception of Saigon, have in addition to the native and aboriginal populations, considerable colonies of Chinese and Indians. . . . In all of these cities, in addition to other race mixtures, there is a well recognized Eurasian community, but the social status of the Eurasian population is different in every city. In Hong Kong, in Rangoon and Singapore, as well as in Calcutta and India generally, the term Eurasian is not in good repute, and is not ordinarily used in conversation. In Hong Kong the Eurasians have no generally recognized association, and seek to avoid the use of any distinctive racial name. They have, as I was told in confidence, a kind of secret and fraternal organization, by means of which they are enabled to cooperate, in order to promote, in unostentatious ways, their mutual welfare as individuals and as a class. In Saigon the term Eurasian is applied, without offense, to the mixed European and native population, and the Eurasian is not, so far as I could learn, regarded as in any sense a problem. . . .

Elsewhere the Eurasian is neither a native nor a European, but something distinct from both. In Saigon and Indo-China he is regarded merely as an interesting indigenous variety of Frenchman. He is a creole in the original sense of that term.

The third letter, mailed on arrival at South Africa in Durban, said:

We left Bombay March 8, sailing South. Since that time we have stopped at Mombasa, Zanzibar, Dar Es Salaam, Mozambique, Beira, and Lorenco Marques. . . . I did not see as much of India as I expected I would, but I have at least seen enough to convince me that it is undoubtedly the most interesting place in the world to study human nature, and particularly the thing we are just now most interested in—race relations.

I had assumed that India, because it is so vast and complicated, would not lend itself to any sort of comprehensive view; that in fact I would not learn very much either of the country or its people in the brief time at my disposal. I found however, that India had, in spite of the numbers and variety of its peoples, and of the diversity of cultures represented in its wide territories, an individuality as distinctive as either China or Japan. . . .

I am impressed with the fact that India, China and Japan represent different stages in the racial amalgamation and cultural integration of the different racial stocks of which they are composed. In other words, they are alike in so far as they represent the fundamental processes of racial and cultural fusion which we have been studying in Hawaii. At any rate with this as a working hypothesis, it seems possible to conceive that studies of Chinese expansion, of the caste system in India and of the experiments in stabilizing race relations in S. Africa, are to such an extent related that they may be discussed in the same universe of discourse, and ultimately brought within the limits of a single "frame of reference."

The letter went on to treat the differences between Muhammadans and Hindus, hypergamy as a development in the Indian caste system, and the social situation of the Anglo-Indians. There were no later letters to Adams about South Africa, but other correspondence shows that the Parks got in touch with some individuals and organizations interested and at that time able to function in objectively examining the racial situation. Years later, in a speech at Tuskegee, Park spoke about some of what had impressed him during his visit to South Africa:

I was more interested in what I saw in Johannesburg where, in the so-called "Bantu Night clubs," the native markets and in the Rand gold mines, the process of civilizing the natives was going on at a furious rate, and in the crudest possible manner.

There were, as I recall, some 200,000 natives employed in the mines when I was there. They were men without women. They lived in barracks in great enclosures or compounds where they are practically prisoners. Their amusements were tribal dances on Sunday and American movies, under the stars at night, on certain other days of the week.

I was indebted to Ray Phillips, a local Missionary, for showing me about Johannesburg and the mines. One night we drove for something like fifty miles along the Great Gold Reef, where the Rand gold mines are located. He was distributing cinema films. This was a work of compassion he had taken upon himself as part of his work as a missionary.

In the course of this excursion I made a little speech to a group of natives who seemed to be a little more sophisticated than more recent recruits, some of them from as far away as the tribal Kraals of Portuguese East Africa. I told them among other things something about the great school at Tuskegee. I found there were at least two Americans whose names these men knew well. One was Charlie Chaplin and the other was Booker Washington.

As a result of his world travels, Park saw "races and peoples coming out of their isolation, whether it be geographical, economic or political." But he was also aware that people were becoming race conscious and he commented: "The fact is that for the first time in history the world has become race conscious. We have in the past sought immortality in different ways, in our family and our clan, in our tribe and in our nation. Now we are seeking it in that somewhat mythical entity known as race."

III. Final Experiments

Chapter 15. Return to Chicago

Robert and Clara Park returned from their trip around the world in spring 1933. That summer, Park—who would be seventy on 4 April 1934—was formally retired from the University of Chicago and the University of Hawaii. He had, however, no thought of really retiring. From Johannesburg, he wrote to his friend and former student Roderick D. McKenzie, with whom he was planning to write a book on human ecology: "I want to get into this volume as many of my ideas as I possibly can. Otherwise I am afraid that I will die with a lot of stuff on my inside that I ought to get out before I quit. . . . You will be glad to know that in spite of my 69 years I seem to be in the best of health and I expect to do a lot of work still before I quit altogether." During the summer of 1933, McKenzie came to Roaring Brook and the two outlined the proposed book.

After his return to Chicago Park enjoyed a light-hearted period. He had good health, few set obligations, no family troubles, and a sufficient income for travel. In 1933 and 1934 his daimon was very much alive and he was filled with creative energy. On 22 February 1934, Louis Wirth, now teaching in the Department of Sociology, asked Park to write about the newspaper. Park replied:

> I'd be happy to write the paper on the newspaper that you suggest; I am bursting with notions on the subject. . . .
>
> P.S. Do you think that you could take time off in September to join a group of us who are planning to review some problems on a conceptual organization of our beloved science, but particularly the conceptual order best suited for the study of collective behavior?

On being shown this letter, Donald Schlesinger wrote a footnote to Wirth: "Louis: Why don't you go to Ann Arbor (at our expense) when Park is in a curiosity mood. Donald."

One project Park brought back from his travels was a plan to revise the 1,000-page *Introduction to the Science of Sociology*. On 5 September 1932, while on board the *Chechako Maru*, Park wrote to Wirth:

> My dear Louis:
>
> I should like to reconsider with you, and with Burgess of course, the future of the *Introduction to the Science of Sociology*. . . . My notion

is to make it a textbook which, after setting forth the concepts and the history, should review the research that has been carried on within the fields covered by the different concepts. . . .

Under this scheme the textbook might go on forever, restating in each new edition . . . the old concepts and reviewing the new literature. This would tend to make of it an institution. Eventually each of the grand divisions would have a special editor. In form it would have something [of] the character of Wagner's "Geographie."

In recasting the shape of sociology in his mind, Park was moving in the direction of greater simplicity rather than elaboration. Whereas the Park and Burgess *Introduction* had fourteen grand divisions, the revised book was to have four: Human Nature, Ecology, Socialization, and Collective Behavior and Institutions. Each was to be the subject of a separate volume.

The University of Chicago welcomed Park back. On 2 April 1934, Robert Redfield, his son-in-law, now dean of the Division of the Social Sciences, wrote to Park:

The Social Science Research Committee is just now engaged in reviewing the research interests . . . of the Division. . . . I should like very much to have studies in racial and cultural relations represented on its program, if set within such a frame of reference as you are working out. . . . Wirth, Schlesinger and the other members of the Committee look forward to learning your views with respect to this field of research.

As a result of Redfield's suggestion and Park's cooperation, a seminar was organized whose 1935 report said:

The Divisional Seminar in Race and Culture Contacts was held at the University of Chicago for the first time during the academic year 1934–35. It met weekly under the direction of Professors Robert E. Park, Herbert Blumer, Robert Redfield and Louis Wirth and had the cooperation of about thirty graduate students from various departments of the university. . . . [On 23 October 1934] Professor R. E. Park discussed the use of the life history and autobiographical documents in race and culture contacts stressing particularly its value for understanding motives and values.

During the winter of 1933–34, Park learned that a young Harvard anthropologist, Lloyd Warner, was studying not a primitive tribe but an American city—Newburyport, Massachusetts. Park asked his friend of Strasbourg days, biologist L. J. Henderson, to introduce him to Warner. Although Warner had never had a course in sociology and knew about

Park only at second hand, the two quickly discovered they were akin. Warner describes Park at seventy:

> I went over and met Robert Park. L. J. Henderson was there and so was Mayo.... He [Park] had a tremendous effect on me immediately.
>
> We all talked a bit, and after a little while it was clear that Park and I were carrying on a discourse. He must have been approaching old age even though his appearance and behavior were those of a very much younger man. He was full of interest and questions about what I was doing and very quickly drew me out.... I felt that I had someone who himself cared about and looked at the world and the problems of social science, very much as I did.... I called my secretary and asked her to cancel all my apppointments. Park and I went over to the faculty club, had lunch there, and talked well into the afternoon....
>
> On the whole I thoroughly disapprove of most of the conversation that takes place under the guise of professional interest. I felt about this one as if it were as exciting as having a good Scotch and soda and far more interesting and, of course, significant....
>
> I had read several of the books that came out of Chicago and Chicago had become an exciting place for me, not so much because of anthropology ... but because of the books that showed up under such titles as *The Gold Coast and the Slum*, *The Gang*, *The Ghetto*, *Suicide* and others.... They said some of the sort of things that I hoped to say when I reported on my study of Newburyport, which became the *Yankee City* series.

Some sociologists were displeased with Warner's study of Newburyport, since cities were a bit of academic territory which had been preempted by sociologists. Park, of course, did not agree. Anthropology had for a long time interested him very much, in part because his daughter Margaret and her husband, Robert Redfield, were anthropologists. On 5 October 1942 he remarked that "Social anthropology is really the kind of sociology I am interested in."

Between summer 1933 and fall 1936 Park wrote and published ten papers, encouraged and helped former students still struggling with their theses; he traveled a good deal, and engaged in a number of small enterprises. In 1933 he became a board member of a newly organized youth center, called Park House because it was near a North Side Chicago park; in fall 1934 he gave five lectures in the University of Chicago's "Race and Culture" series. In winter 1935 he studied the Acadians of Louisiana and that summer explored French Canada with Helen and Everett Hughes.

While living in Chicago, he continued to associate with such socio-logical colleagues as Ernest Burgess, Ellsworth Faris, Herbert Blumer, and Louis Wirth. Park's son-in-law Robert Redfield, Edward Scribner Ames of the Department of Philosophy, and Harold Lasswell of the Department of Political Science were close friends. Park's fecundity when it came to ideas was appreciated by everyone who knew him. In spring 1934 James Rorty was collecting material in Chicago for his book on depression America, *Where Life Is Better*; he interviewed both Park and Lasswell. Lasswell urged him to spend time with Park because Park was "a very creative fellow." Rorty agreed and reported: "Park gave me several good hunches. Best was the tactic of dictatorship; never commit yourself to anything. Nobody can put his finger on Roosevelt; hence difficult to fight. He keeps his freedom; in order to fight him the opposi-tion has to commit itself to something."[1]

On his travels Park often visited his children. His daughter Theodosia, a portrait painter who had twice painted his portrait, lived in Freeport, Illinois. Her husband, Donald Breed, was publisher and editor of the *Freeport Journal-Standard*. Park encouraged Breed to write a play and it won a prize. With his son Robert, a civil engineer working for the General Electric Company in Schenectady, Park explored Connecticut cemeteries looking for gravestones of his family. When in Boston, he stayed with his son Edward, now a member of a law firm. Whenever possible, he saw his old friend William I. Thomas. He also visited a number of former students, among them Edgar Thompson and Charles S. Johnson. In New York, he called on a *Fortune* magazine editor and explained to him how admirably *Time* and *Fortune* were carrying out the ideas which he, Park, and a newspaper editor named Franklin Ford had formulated in the 1890s.

The Park House youth center involved a number of University of Chicago people. In 1929 a sociology student, William R. Ireland, had been studying the young people of the Near North Side, Chicago's Left Bank or Greenwich Village, many of whom were aspiring writers or artists. Once the depression set in, they were in serious trouble. Ireland persuaded a member of the Smith Pepsodent family to set up a Smith Aid Fund. It was administered by a committee which included Park, Edward Scribner Ames, Samuel C. Kincheloe, and Herbert Blumer. In 1933 the committee acquired a three-story, twenty-five-room house on the Near North Side and engaged James D. Nobel, a graduate student in the University of Chicago Divinity School, to be its director. On 14 April 1934 Park's seventieth birthday was celebrated at the center and Clara

---

1. Letter to the author, fall 1935.

Park exhibited her paintings there. Park House continued for ten years and so did Park's connection with it.

His interest in the youth center mystified some of his friends. Had he, who detested do-goodism, himself become a do-gooder? They were also baffled by his attitude toward the religious tone of the enterprise. Park balked at having the center labeled. When pressed to explain what was going on, he said: "If Park House is to be tagged and catalogued, let it be classified as a religious rather than a social agency. . . . Park House is less an institution than an experiment. I suppose we might describe it as an experiment in religious education." He disliked the approach of social workers. He preferred not to use questionnaires and refused to have them used at Park House.

He knew what he and the Park House Committee were doing but he did not want to talk about it. He had lived through the panic of 1893 and the years that followed it—one of the worst depressions of the nineteenth century. Like it, the depression of the 1930s was a national crisis. Young people were repudiating the ideas they had been brought up with. Since change was the essence of what interested Park as a sociologist, he wanted to see what form their repudiation would take, and Park House provided him with material.

Director Nobel, in a book in progress (1974) has recounted the center's history and Park's involvement. He says:

> In this young adult "world" with its rebellion against convention and its fierce desire "to make all things new" Park glimpsed the emergent social patterns. Here was an ecological phenomenon which fascinated him. . . .
>
> In point of time we were perhaps a little ahead of the "God is dead controversy," but clearly we were dealing with the same problem of social psychology. . . . We were looking at these fundamental life experiences from which theologies are largely made. Furthermore we were looking at the marginal areas, the areas of questioning and conflict, doubt and disintegration (the Near North Side) rather than at the areas of institutional stability or normalcy.

After Park House had been in existence for five years, Park was ready to define what he found interesting about the center as a sociological phenomenon, and he wrote Louis Wirth about this on 12 October 1938:

My dear Prof. Wirth:

I have just received a questionnaire from Lloyd Warner, Chairman, Committee on Personality in Relation to Culture. In answer to the question "What problems do you find basic to personality research?" I am making the reply: Investigation of the moral and personal social world in which the individual lives and to which he is responsive. The gang, family, etc." In reply to the question "What do you believe our Committee could do to help you most in developing your studies on personality?" I am making the reply: "I am interested in two types of 'world,' the Bohemia on the Lower North Side in Chicago where Park House is located, and Cedar Street in Nashville, Tennessee. The first is an area like Greenwich Village, the other is an underworld of Negroes. I am interested in exploring these underworlds, which are characteristically cultural and racial melting pots, in every part of the world. When this survey is a little along and I have found a person equipped to do the work, I should like some funds to make a more systematic study of one of these areas. My studies of personality are mainly based upon life histories of a generally closed moral and personal order to which the individual person is most responsive, and they throw light also on the processes of acculturation which take place within the limits of such a minor cultural unit."

I am sending you this statement so that you will know what my interests are. . . . I want to emphasize the studies that have to do with the processes where the greatest amount of cultural changes are in progress.

The year 1936 was important in Park's life. During the spring he worked with McKenzie on the human ecology book and simultaneously did some teaching at the University of Michigan. During the summer he taught in the Harvard summer school.

On 18 July 1936 Park wrote to Hughes from Cambridge: "You have probably had the bad news from Chicago. Clara has had a severe heart attack and has been in the hospital." After his wife's illness, Park agreed to the urging of Charles S. Johnson, then head of the Social Sciences Department at Fisk University, that he come to Fisk as a visiting lecturer. Although retaining their apartment in Chicago, the Parks moved to Nashville in fall 1936 and settled in a small house at 1809 Morena Street near the Fisk University campus.

Chapter 16. Headquarters: Fisk University

Park first taught at Fisk University in the fall semester of 1936. Although he continued to teach there intermittently for eight years, he was not confined to regular courses and he remained a free spirit and a traveler, doing a great deal of commuting between Nashville and Chicago, Wollaston, Cambridge, and New York City. He spent his summers in Roaring Brook, he made trips to Europe and Brazil, and he frequently visited other colleges and universities in the south.

In 1936 Fisk was the only black college that had received an A rating from the Association of American Universities, but the quality of education that most students had received before coming to Fisk was poor. In 1936 two young sociologists at Fisk, Lewis Jones and Buford Junker, made a study of rural black schools. Park in 1937 wrote "A Memorandum on Rote Learning" based partly on their study:

> In reflecting on the subject of rote learning, my attention has been directed to folk schools like the Jewish Cheder, or the Moslem schools, where education consists almost entirely of learning verses . . . much as, when I was a boy, we used to learn to recite verses from the Bible. . . .
>
> Rote learning seems to be learning without, or with a minimum of insight. . . . I have found it difficult, in some of my classes, to induce students to ask questions. . . . On the other hand, they are often eager to learn the correct authoritative answers to questions they are likely to meet on examination. . . . This is not, under the conditions which the ordinary classroom imposes, conduct that is either unusual or unexpected. I encountered the same thing at Harvard years ago, when . . . I had to read papers in the introductory courses. But . . . what I encountered in my classes at Fisk last fall was an inveterate disposition—a tradition in fact . . . that had its sources in the historic condition under which education has grown up in the South. . . .
>
> Few people pursue knowledge anymore . . . and if they do there is nothing very exciting about the pursuit. This seems, however, more or less inevitable, where rote learning prevails. Fisk University probably stands at the peak of the Negro education structure, but it is

a structure erected on a system of rote learning. The trouble with Fisk as well as with all other Negro colleges begins, I suspect, in the common school.[1]

Since rote learning implies, by definition, a minimum of insight, the problem which Park and Johnson faced was to provide Fisk students with maximum compensatory insight. One of Park's favorite ways to do this was to get students to consider the circumstances of their own lives, or to send them into the field to study current situations. This process has been described in detail by Samuel C. Adams, who graduated from Fisk in 1940:

> Attempting to learn how to be perceptive about the world was really an art for Dr. Park. I recall that once, much to my chagrin, I was sent to the Mississippi Delta to collect folk tales and folk songs in a rural plantation community. It was in the same locale that reputedly had given birth to the Blues. On my first trip to the area following a stay of about two weeks, I recall reporting to Dr. Park that no one sang spirituals or folk songs any more or told folk tales in this community. He asked me had it ever occured to me what this meant? My answer was "no." He asked me what I had seen. My reply was that I had noticed a man leaning on a shovel, a WPA crew. I had noticed juke boxes in cotton fields; I listened to people say that it was better to belong to the burial society than to the church. But it had never occurred to me that any of this had anything to do with the fact that people no longer told folk tales or sang folk songs.

Adams sums up his indebtedness to Park by saying that Park made his world, as a black American, intelligible to him—"in making things, worlds, books, and people intelligible." He describes himself as he was at the time:

> I was a student; confused, more than was perhaps outwardly apparent—on the verge at times of revolt or falling apart, or just being very hungry; possessing nevertheless a determination that I would rather die than fail. . . . When I graduated from High School, I was 15 years of age. The years were those of the depression. The self or me that entered the University was a curious mixed-up pattern of emotions. . . . There was a sense that I was always running. I had grown up not understanding the intensity of the family pressure that we succeed, that we be extra-socially moral and Christian, that we lived in a hostile world of other Negroes, "who presumably were

1. Robert Park, "A Memorandum on Rote Learning," *American Journal of Sociology* 43 (July 1937), 24, 26.

like crabs in a basket," i.e., "every time one starts up another pulls him back," as well as an even more hostile world of white people "who were always out to get you" and though one prayed to an all powerful God, attempted to be good, saved one's pennies, more things on earth depended on the white man than heaven could possibly take account of.

One way Park found to make Samuel Adams's world intelligible was to read with him the letters the young man exchanged with his mother, who had been a teacher:

> We read my mother's letter to me together. I would in turn write my mother about the insights I had gained. . . . I recall discussing with him the strangeness my mother felt when she first came to Houston and had to live in a rooming house, in the poor district of one of the town's Negro Beale streets, in one room and using a kitchen in common with others, after having grown up in a big country house in East Texas. We reviewed the experiences of my aunts and uncles; those who passed for white in northern and southern cities, those who remained in East Texas—some being able to exploit the fact of a white father—to hold a job, to stay out of jail, or to live reasonably unoppressed—while others barely eked out a living as poor cotton farmers.
>
> In these conversations, I became aware of social processes and social forces, and recognized that the nature of the interaction that exists between human beings—the kinds of societies in which they live and the ways in which these societies became organized—provides more fruitful bases for understanding what men do, what they say and what they think than explanations which lay all the weight upon the goodness of men or their perversity.

Samuel Adams is one of Park's many students who have lived and worked in foreign countries and studied their peoples. Since receiving a Ph.D. from the University of Chicago in 1952 and entering the Foreign Service, Adams has lived in twenty-seven countries and was at one point United States Ambassador to Niger. Addressing the students of the American School in Tangier in 1967, he said: "Don't miss seeking in someone else the man you would like to be. The man in whose footsteps I dreamed of walking was a man who made the world literally his doorstep. . . . He read avidly. He had worked in the Congo, in China, in many of the countries of Europe. . . . He also had the art of knowing that the world around him was filled with secrets, waiting to be understood. . . ."

Between 1905 when he went to Tuskegee and 1936 when he came to

Fisk, Park had been in continuous touch with black history in the making. By 1936 the mood and temper of the black community had changed and neither Tuskegee nor Washington were as highly regarded as they had once been. Of the two great black leaders of 1905, only Du Bois was still alive. Washington had died in 1915 and the management of Tuskegee had passed to other hands. In 1935—a year before he came to Fisk—Park had received an estimate of Tuskegee's situation from Charles S. Johnson, then teaching at Fisk, who thought he might be asked to shift to Tuskegee. "I do not believe," Johnson said, "that Tuskegee is as yet interested in adapting its program to the new frontier of American and Negro life. I seriously doubt whether anyone realizes that there has been a new frontier since Washington died."

There was no reason why Johnson should be interested in going to Tuskegee. His primary interest was sociological research, and the new frontier he speaks of, he himself had helped to bring into existence as an editor of *Opportunity*, one of the principal organs of the Negro Renaissance movement.

While in residence in Nashville, Park entertained W. E. B. Du Bois at a luncheon party. Edgar Thompson, who was also present, reports that the relations between the two men were "very amiable." Park had been critical of some of Du Bois's behavior during 1905–12 because of the tension that then existed between Washington and Du Bois. He had, however, always admired Du Bois's writing, especially *The Souls of Black Folk*, to which he often referred. Werner Cahnman, who had studied ethnic relations in Austro-Hungary and had come to Fisk at Park's suggestion so that he could study American race relations there, gives his version of how Park regarded Du Bois and Washington during the Fisk period:

> He retained a lively appreciation of Booker T. Washington's shrewd and folksy personality, his sharp insight into human nature, his realistic appraisal of the situation in which the American Negro found himself, and his diplomatic skill in striking the water of life from the barren rock of prejudice and hostility. But he was likewise appreciative of W. E. Du Bois' courage, intellectuality and power of expression, gifts which he saw more as complementary than as antagonistic to those possessed by Booker T. Washington. Park's judgment of the Washington-Du Bois controversy was that "the American Negroes were lucky to have had both these men as leaders."

A confirmed traveler, Park used trains and ships until late in life. He never learned to drive, but when the Parks returned to Chicago from their world travels he bought a Ford V–8, then new. He loved its power and speed. Family members and younger colleagues drove the Parks on long trips—even on a journey through Ontario and Quebec with a house trailer to sleep in. After one of these long journeys, in 1936, Clara had a heart attack. The car was then used to take her on shopping errands. When they went to Fisk, one of the several chauffeurs (in addition to the students Harry Walker and Horace Cayton) was Helen Pierson, wife of a research fellow who had come to Nashville at Park's urging. Park had met Donald Pierson in Brazil, where Pierson was studying Brazilian blacks, and had proposed that the Piersons come to Nashville and live with him and Clara in the Morena Street house; Helen could drive the Park car while Donald wrote up his Brazilian researches. He added that Donald could also read masters' theses for him and assist in a seminar on racial contacts. The Piersons accepted.

Mrs. Pierson found that she had quite a task. Park knew nothing about cars. Once a service man advised that they buy new tires before making a trip to New Orleans. Park refused to consider it, and, of course, shortly they had a flat. His only desire was to go fast. He frequently urged his driver to pass the car ahead of them. During the Christmas rush in Nashville, Mrs. Pierson once extricated the Park car from near-collision on a crowded icy street. When Park exclaimed, "That certainly was accomplished with luck," Mrs. Pierson spoke up. The relief of tension undoubtedly made her a little bolder than usual for she replied dryly, "And with a little know-how." Dr. Park turned and gave her a sharp look but said nothing. "After that," she said, "I seemed to sense a greater awareness on his part of the manual capabilities of others."

The Park-Pierson arrangement was a success. Donald Pierson, during his two years at Fisk, finished his work and published *Negroes in Brazil: A Study of Race Contact in Bahai.* Mrs. Pierson's driving contributed to her husband's career and the Parks and Piersons enjoyed each other's company.

During his years at Fisk, Park did what he could to help the university. In March 1938 Charles Johnson in the *American Journal of Sociology* announced the acquisition by the Social Science Department of Fisk of 1,000 volumes on race in Hawaii, Japan, China, Africa, South America, and the United States—the gift of Robert E. Park, "visiting professor." Park's son Robert reports: "Once Pop wanted me to suggest a field of research in physics for Fisk and I suggested infra-red spectro-photometry and they did enter that field."

Fisk University had financial difficulty during the depression years, and so Park wanted only a nominal salary and the small house in which he lived. In appreciation for all that Park was doing for Fisk, Charles

Johnson asked the students who had graduated to write him letters for his seventy-seventh birthday in 1941.

These letters are sometimes very moving. Hermann D. Burrell believed that he succeeded in business partly because Park taught him to understand the mind of white Americans:

> I have been successful in turning big deals among all races in spite of the fact that my employer expected me to confine my work to the Negro Market. 99 and $^{44}/_{100}$ths per cent of the reason why I have been a success is that you equipped me with the proper tools to analyse a social situation; I have been able to vizualize my role in society both from the point of view of others and as I wanted it to be. With your method I try to cope with the social forces which threaten my prestige. I believe that my conception of myself in relation to the rest of society enables me to work agreeably side by side with persons from all over the world.
>
> That conception evolved from your lectures on race relations. I decide my "place" in society, and respect all persons as I would have them respect me. My employer congratulated me on my ability to get along exceptionally well with persons of diverse cultures without resorting to self-subordination. People are very interesting to me. Thank you for much "knowledge about" them.

Joseph H. Douglass said:

> Oftimes I recall how . . . you would come in the classroom and show us just how well we didn't have the point. Neither can I forget that under you and Dr. Pierson I wrote the first chapter of my thesis 11 times. I appreciate it all so much now. I believe I am strong. I am deeply serious when I say "Thank you" for preparing me for life.

Although Robert and Clara Park had friends in Nashville and in nearby colleges, they missed their children. On Thanksgiving 1940 they tried to compensate by having a party to be held at a house where a group of Fisk students, earning their way through college, lived cooperatively. Clara Park wrote to her son Edward: "We were feeling a mite lonely, after all, we had no children at all around . . . so we wondered whom to invite for we always have a party of some kind. And Pop said: 'I have an idea.'" Lewis Jones, one of their special friends, helped to arrange the party. There were speeches, toasts, flowers, and superb food. At its close Park reminisced about his first Thanksgiving away from home, when a freshman at the University of Minnesota. As Mrs. Park tells it: "After the dessert came in, Pop told the story of how he ran away from home and earned his own way and got so hungry and then his mother sent the box with the turkey and mince pie etc. and then my friend and I waited for hours till the other boys would get home and finally at four o'clock could stand it no longer and pitched right in. . . . It was a very nice, soul warming day. . . ." Of Park's concern for her, Mrs. Park added: "I used to wonder what I would do when all the children were gone, and Pop and I alone, and I would have been sad, because Pop used to be too busy to play around much with me, but when you were all gone, Pop became responsible for my and his happiness and he took over and I have not had a chance to be lonely very long."

Park attended the meetings of the Southern Sociological Society a number of times. A young black sociologist drove Park to the first meeting in Atlanta to attend the society's dinner in a leading hotel where usually blacks were not admitted. The young man was feeling very uncomfortable until Park caught his eye and gave him a reassuring wink.

Park was accorded considerable esteem at these meetings where, according to Edgar T. Thompson, he became a familiar figure after his retirement from Chicago and his move to Fisk. Thompson, one of Park's former students and a professor at Duke University, has related how Park would be driven to the meetings in Atlanta or Chattanooga or Knoxville by Harry Walker, Lewis Jones, or some other Fisk student. In the following excerpt from a speech made at Fisk, Thompson recalls that at one of the meetings a spontaneous tribute was paid to Park:

> On one occasion I read a paper on the perennial and irrepressible plantation . . . with Dr. Park in the audience. . . . Guy Johnson was slated to discuss my paper, but instead . . . he began to reminisce about his student days at Chicago with Dr. Park. . . . For a few years, you remember, we were getting a stream of Texans all interested in race relations—Guy Johnson, W. O. Brown, Lewis Copeland and maybe others. Prof. Brearley . . . told me that someone else from the audience rose when Guy had finished speaking and began telling about how Dr. Park had gotten him started investigating some problem. . . . I gather from Brearley that what we began having was something like what the Methodists in camp meeting called a "love feast." Dr. Brearley tells me that Dr. Park several times expressed his special interest in our society and its special promise of achievement because discussion of sociology in it went on among a relatively small number of people who knew each other personally and talked a great deal of shop in an atmosphere of personal friendship. He was especially interested in the Race and Culture section of our Society freely participated in by both white and colored.

On 19 April 1942 Mrs. Park told her son Edward what happened at another meeting of the Southern Sociological Society in Atlanta that Park did not attend:

> Some one had sent out a questionnaire . . . it was called Evaluation of Sociological Research and was sent out by Prof. Logan Wilson of Tulane University, New Orleans. He had 65 replies. It was reported that Park had the top position in the cumulative rank order and was mentioned most frequently for his pioneering in the field and for his stimulating influence on other sociologists.

For nearly a quarter of a century, the University of Chicago had been Park's intellectual home. Now, although Ernest Burgess and two of his own students, Louis Wirth and Herbert Blumer, were leading members of the Department of Sociology, Park was in the position of the retired professor who has a title but fades off the scene. He later told Hughes that he went to Fisk so he would not be "an old man in the way."

Park probably went to Fisk largely because Johnson was there. He had had considerable influence on Johnson's career ever since they met in 1917. An article on Johnson by Preston Valien says: "A graduate of Virginia Union University, he received his sociological training at the University of Chicago, primarily through an unusual apprenticeship which he served under Robert E. Park. On Park's recommendation, he became secretary of the Chicago Urban League and one of the two directors of the Illinois Commission on Race Relations."

Johnson learned from Park almost everything that Park could teach anyone. Park also learned a great deal from Johnson, who not only was in touch with all the research going on concerning race relations but was also well acquainted with the black elites of both the North and South. Johnson had a profound regard for Park both as a sociologist and as a man; Park had much respect and affection for Johnson. It was an ideal example of the kind of relation that can exist between an older scholar and a younger one.

Of the three great black sociologists of the 1900–60 period—Du Bois, Johnson, and Franklin Frazier—Johnson was the only one who did not have a Ph.D. degree. But his industry and productivity were remarkable. By 1946 he had written or helped write seventeen books, and at this time, he moved from being head of the Social Science Department to being Fisk's first black president. He received honorary degrees from Columbia, Glasgow, and Harvard.

Park sometimes thought of leaving Fisk for a larger university that would offer him more stimulating contacts. In 1939 he wrote to Clara, suggesting that they might go elsewhere—"perhaps Baton Rouge would be best." But they stayed at Fisk. Earnest E. Neal, a Fisk graduate who once drove the Parks to Roaring Brook and who in 1941 was listed in *Who's Who in American Education*, says in one of the 1941 birthday letters:

> I appreciate so much the personal sacrifice that you are making to be at Fisk University in order that Negro students who are unable to go to the more expensive universities will have the benefit of a great teacher. I am grateful that your interest in the Negro is not one of sympathy. You are trying so hard to develop sociologists at Fisk and not Negro sociologists. Because of that I have been able to stand on my feet and not have the slightest feeling of inferiority in the presence of other sociologists regardless of the schools in which they received their training.
>
> In conclusion may I paraphrase what Plato said on his deathbed: I am glad that I was born an American and not a barbarian; a freeman and not a slave; a man and not a woman; and above all, that I was born in the time of Robert E. Park and was one of his students.

Charles Johnson also repudiates the notion that Park had any special sentimentality about blacks or was burdened with a sense of *noblesse oblige*:

> If anyone ever made the verbal mistake of calling him a "race benefactor," or humanitarian, or friend of the Negro, Dr. Park would be likely to let loose an impatient torrent of an old reporter's private and uncensored vocabulary of digust. Vigorous, sturdy, commanding in appearance, and often, on the surface, brusque in manner, he detested sentimentality and unctuous professions of sympathy for the Negroes. Yet he was at heart as gentle as a mother. . . . He occasionally stunned sophisticated Negro audiences by saying that he was not "interested in the race." Similarly he could stun white audiences by saying that he was not interested in the Negroes but in America, adding that his concern about Negro status and injustice in America was the highest expression of his patriotism.

Chapter 17. Ecology and the Moral Order

A year after Park moved to Nashville, Howard W. Odum of the University of North Carolina asked him what he considered to be his main contributions to sociology. In a letter dated 20 January 1936, Park replied that he had four main sociological interests:

My dear Odum,

My first studies in the field of what I should now call sociology were during the period of my service as a reporter on a newspaper. I was one of the first and humbler of the muckrakers.

As a result of this experience I became convinced that the reporter performed a more important function than the editorial writer in bringing about needed reforms, that facts were more important in the long run than opinions.

My experience as a reporter led me to study the social function of the newspaper, not as an organ of opinion, but as a record of current events. In fact, with a group of others of the same mind I started out to reform the newspaper, by making it more accurate and scientific, something like *Time* and *Fortune*.

I spent six years at home and abroad at that task. Out of that grew my thesis on the crowd and the public (Masse and Publikum) and my interest in collective behavior. I think my principal theoretic interest is still the newspaper as a social institution.

One thing that I discovered in the course of my studies was that there was no adequate and no precise language in which to describe the things I wanted to study, "collective behavior," for example.

As a reporter I had learned a good deal about the city and I had used my position as city and Sunday editor to make systematic studies of the urban community. During my connection with Booker Washington and Tuskegee, I learned a great deal about the Negro. It was from these two sources mainly that graduate students found materials for the researches which I directed after I went to Chicago.

It was these researches that revealed to me that we had in sociology much theory but no working concepts. When a student proposed a topic for a thesis, I invariably found myself asking the question: what is this thing you want to study? What is a gang? What is a public? What is a nationality? What is a race in the sociological sense? What is graft? etc.

I did not see how we could have anything like scientific research unless we had a system of classification and a frame of reference into which we could sort out and describe in general terms the things we were attempting to investigate. Park and Burgess' *Introduction* was a first rough sketch of such a classification and frame of reference.

My contribution to sociology has been, therefore, not what I intended, not what my original interest would have indicated, but what I needed to make a systematic exploration of the social world in which I found myself. The problem I was interested in was always theoretic rather than practical. I have been mainly an explorer in three fields: Collective Behavior, Human Ecology and Race Relations.

If the newspaper was Park's first sociological love, human ecology was his last. He had done his early thinking about the newspaper by 1898, about collective behavior by 1903, and about race relations by 1912. He did not, however, mention human ecology in his writings until 1921.

During World War I, Park was reading the biologists who wrote about plant and animal ecology. It was clear to him that there was something which could be called human ecology, but what was its nature? How did it differ from plant and animal ecology? In a 1936 paper called "Human Ecology" he defined the difference: "Human ecology, in so far as it is concerned with a social order that is based on competition rather than consensus, is identical, in principle at least, with plant and animal ecology. . . . Human ecology has, however, to reckon with the fact that in a human society competition is limited by custom and culture."

In the Park and Burgess *Introduction to the Science of Sociology*, Park used the term "human ecology" for the first time in his writings and discussed it in a number of contexts, especially its relation to biology and economics. Three years later, when he was on the Pacific Coast as director of a race relations study, his interest in human ecology was stimulated by his conversations with a former student, Roderick D. McKenzie. At Chicago, McKenzie's Ph.D. thesis had been "The Neighborhood: A Study of Local Life in Columbus, Ohio." McKenzie told Park he was planning a book on human ecology. Park urged him to consider a joint book. On 19 July 1924 McKenzie replied: "I am in accord with your suggestion that a volume on ecology, to be worthwhile, must be a joint product."

During the fall semester of 1924 McKenzie gave a course in human ecology at the University of Washington. This was the first such course given in the sociology department of an American university. On 21

November Park wrote to McKenzie asking him to give the same course at the University of Chicago.

In 1925 at the annual meeting of the American Sociological Society, Park and McKenzie presented their notions about human ecology to their colleagues. Park wrote his wife:

> I had three of my former students in the section on ecology and every single one of them did well. There were Dawson of Montreal, McKenzie of Seattle, and Wirth, whom you know. Prof. House was in charge of the division on methods. It was one of the best sections we have had. . . . It seems that we have succeeded in making ecology popular. We are almost the founders of a new science, McKenzie and myself. Every one, I learned from New York, is now talking about the "ecological" aspect of everything.

Between 1926 and 1932 Park gave a course in "Human Ecology" three times. During the summer of 1933, immediately after Park's return from South Africa, Park and McKenzie worked at Park's summer home at Roaring Brook and outlined the book on ecology they planned to write. A memento of this session is forty-two pages of typed notes by Park inserted in the 21 August 1933 copy of *Time* magazine.[1] While these notes were rich in ideas, there was at this point no completed table of contents and no clear-cut division of labor between the two men. Park summed up the problem that confronted them: "From the point of view of sociology and human ecology the question is twofold: (1) Does there exist below the level of what is ordinarily called society a system of vital and functional relationships between human beings which can be properly described as symbiotic or ecological? (2) How does one distinguish between those relationships that are symbiotic and ecological and those which are political and moral, i.e. social in the narrower sense of the word?"

Since the University of Chicago Press was publishing a book on ecology by the Hindu sociologist Mukerjee, Park and McKenzie signed a contract with the Ronald Press in 1933. However, no joint book by Park and McKenzie was ever published. The difficulties that arose were due mainly to the situation and temperament of the two men.

In 1933 Park was sixty-nine years old and retired. He had only such teaching obligations at Fisk as he cared to assume. If he had wished to give all or a major amount of his time to the book on ecology, he could have done so. However, he preferred the free, roving life he was living, visiting various colleges and universities, traveling, and writing

1. These notes are now in the Chicago Archives, like most of Park's papers.

steadily—but always papers, not books. Perhaps he did not write books because, between 1887 and 1898, as reporter, editor, and critic, he had written so much. When he became a newspaper editor, he had discovered that it was possible to share the labor of writing with someone else. At Tuskegee, for instance, he was delighted to find that Washington's secretary, Emmett Scott, had some literary ability. He persuaded Scott to work with him in putting together Washington's books. Later, as a professor, he explored many subjects with the aid of graduate students who valued his creative ideas. In putting together the 1,000-page *Introduction to the Science of Sociology,* he had the assistance of his young colleague Ernest Burgess.

McKenzie, like Scott and Burgess, seemed an ideal collaborator, especially for a book on human ecology. He was young and able, and Park considered him the best of the university research staff he had directed on the Pacific Coast study. He had already written a great deal about human ecology. He was all the things Park thought him; but he was, during the 1930s, in financial difficulty and not well. In 1930 he had accepted the chairmanship of the Sociology Department of the University of Michigan and been promised enough financial support to build a first-rate department, but because of the depression this support was not forthcoming. On 11 March 1933 he wrote Park: "Conditions here are almost in a state of chaos. No one knows what will happen to universities in the coming year. Michigan was the first state to collapse financially. . . . We received only part of our February salary and nobody knows whether there will be any more money for us the rest of this year."

It was that summer that Park and McKenzie first worked on the human ecology manuscript. In spring 1936 they had their second working session, at the University of Michigan, where Park was also doing some teaching. McKenzie hoped for further sessions that summer and fall, but they had none. Instead Park taught at Harvard that summer and moved to Nashville in the fall. From the spring of 1936 on, the two men were, in the main, working separately, although still committed to the project of writing a book together.

The ecology book was not the only book Park had on his mind during the 1930s. He also wanted to publish a book embodying his final thinking on sociology. He did not intend to write it alone; he planned to act as editor and to select able sociologists—mostly former students—as contributors. After signing a contract in 1935 with Barnes & Noble to publish a book called *An Outline of the Principles of Sociology,* Park asked McKenzie to write the section on human ecology. On 23 September 1935 McKenzie explained that he could not: "I am returning the contracts unsigned, for in looking over my contract with the Ronald Press—I am editor of a series of books on Sociology—I find that I have agreed not to undertake any publication for royalty with any other company during the period of my contract."

Park turned the chapter on human ecology over to a University of Alabama student, A. B. Hollingshead, with whom he had corresponded. He also asked three of his ablest Chicago students to contribute to the book: Edward Byron Reuter, Everett C. Hughes, and Herbert Blumer. Hughes says:

> He [Park] intended it to be the textbook to end all textbooks, a book of ideas. . . . It was Park's idea to continue the tradition of an "idea" book, leaving it to others to publish facts in monographs. More correctly to keep the research monograph separate from the idea book. . . . Reuter did Race. Blumer did Collective Behavior. I did Institutions. Hollingshead actually did Human Ecology. A man named Fuller did a section on Social Problems.
>
> After Park died, the publishers gave the editorship to Alfred McClung Lee. The book has been edited and more or less rewritten several times. It is in the College Outline Series . . . and is just now [1972] being re-published. Few are the books that continue to sell after 30 years.

When the Ronald Press learned of the coming publication of an *Outline of the Principles of Sociology*, they canceled their contract to publish the projected Park and McKenzie book on human ecology. To Park's great distress, McKenzie broke off relations with him. This had been a shock to both men. But, according to Amos H. Hawley, a student of McKenzie's, "The reason the Park-McKenzie volume was not finished lies mainly with McKenzie's progressive illness, which made it impossible for him to do sustained work."

McKenzie now asked Hawley to write the book on human ecology that he was not able to finish and Hawley did so. Later, in 1968, Hawley also edited a University of Chicago Press book, *Roderick D. McKenzie on Human Ecology*. For both McKenzie and Park, the attempt to create the great book they had in mind came too late in their lives. However, their association in the 1930s stimulated their separate writings. One of McKenzie's achievements was to create a strong interest in ecology at the University of Michigan, which was carried on by a succession of students after his death. Among them were Hawley and Otis Duncan. Hawley says: "In my youth, the 1930s, there was no other source than Park and his students, notably McKenzie, from which one could obtain so clearly defined and promising a program for intellectual development."[2]

2. Letter to the author, date unknown.

The contributions made by sociologists and other social scientists to the subject of human ecology has been noted by Odum and Odum in their *Fundamentals of Biology*, published in 1959. At one point, they define ecology as "the structure and function of nature, it being understood that man is part of nature." Of the social scientists, they say:

> In recent years the ecological approach to the study of human society had developed into the distinct field of human ecology in which sociologists, anthropologists, geographers as well as ecologists have found a meeting ground. The books of Hawley (1950) and Quinn (1956) summarize the development of the field from the sociological side, which began with Galpin's (1915) work in rural sociology, and with the studies in the "ecology of cities" made by Robert E. Park, R. D. McKenzie, E. W. Burgess and their students in the 1920s.

Yet a more complete statement of the contributions made by both biologists and social scientists to this interdisciplinary field needs to be made. In a 1959 paper, "The Ecological Complex," Otis Dudley Duncan says:[3] "There has never been written a decent historical account of the rise of human ecology and the sources which influenced its direction." When that account is written, the work of Park, McKenzie, and their students will be an important part of the record.

The discipline of human ecology evolved, for Park, from the cross-fertilization of the biological and social sciences. Arriving at the University of Chicago in 1914, Park began talking with his biological colleagues about Ernst Haeckel, a German zoologist who first used the word "ecology" in 1866. "Ecology" derives from the Greek word *oikos*, "the place where one lives." As a traveler and field naturalist, Haeckel had observed how dissimilar plants and animals nevertheless manage to coexist on the same piece of territory. Biologists began to study plant and animal communities. Park, in turn, studied human communities and called this branch of inquiry human ecology:

> Ecology conceives society as fundamentally a territorial as well as a cultural organization. So far as this conception is valid, it assumes that most if not all cultural changes in society will be correlated with changes in territorial organization, and every change in the territorial and occupational distribution of the populations will effect changes in the existing cultures.[4]

In 1921, in the *Introduction to the Science of Sociology*, the authors said: "The economic organization of society, so far as it is the result of free

3. Unpublished manuscript.
4. Robert E. Park, in *Human Communities*, vol. 2 of *The Collected Works of Robert E. Park* (Glencoe, Ill.: Free Press, 1950–55), p. 231.

competition is an ecological organization. There is a human as well as a plant and animal ecology." In 1926 Park gave his first course in human ecology which was listed in the University of Chicago catalog as follows:

No. 361 *Human Ecology*: Geographic and economic factors which determine the location and growth of communities. Types of communities, trade and market zones, significance of changing forms of transportation and communication, popular selection, and segregation; community structure; distribution and segregation of utilities and inhabitants. A background for the study of community problems.

During the 1930s Park wrote six papers on human ecology. Some dealt with concrete examples of life on the ecological level. Two abstract papers, "Human Ecology" (1936) and "Symbiosis and Socialization: A Frame of Reference for the Study of Society" (1939), are important. In them Park explored a number of relevant ideas: the web of life, the struggle for existence, competition, symbiosis, freedom, collective action, long-time biotic and social processes, the biotic base of society, and social equilibrium. To these familiar concepts, he added one of his own: "The fact seems to be then, that human society, as distinguished from plant and animal society, is organized on two levels, the biotic and the cultural."

Competition is the outstanding characteristic of the biotic or ecological level. Among plants and animals, it is unrestricted. Among people, competition is free in some areas, restricted in others. Park commented:

Competition on the biotic level, as we observe it in the plant and animal communities, seems to be relatively unrestricted. Society as far as it exists, is anarchic and free.

In human as contrasted with animal societies, competition and the freedom of the individual is limited on every level above the biotic by custom and consensus.

It is when and to the extent that competition declines that the kind of order which we call society can be said to exist. In short, society, from the ecological point of view . . . is just that area in which biotic competition has declined and the struggle for existence has assumed higher and more complicated forms.

Competition on the ecological level sometimes takes the form of dominance or succession, a type of competition which Park explored in two papers, "Dominance" and "Succession: An Ecological Concept." He had begun talking to his classes about succession as early as 1918. To illustrate the concept as it is applied in biology: if, in the North Carolina

Piedmont, a farm field is first destroyed by fire and then abandoned, biologists can predict that in the first five years there will be grasses, crabgrass, horseweed, fall asters, and broom sedge, and in the sixth year pine seedlings. After 100 years, pines will be dominant; after 150 years, pines and hardwoods; after 250 years, hardwoods. In 1933, while in South Africa, Park observed and studied this process going on there—not among plants but among people:

> First came the Bushmen; they were hunters. . . . The Hottentots followed. They were hunters to be sure, but herdsmen also and they had a great deal of trouble with the Bushmen who killed their cattle with poisoned arrows. So the Hottentots drove the Bushmen into the Kalahari desert. The Bantu were next. They were hunters and herdsmen, but they were more. They cultivated the soil and raised Kaffir corn.
>
> Later still came the Boers, who settled the Transvaal and the Orange Free State, conquered and enslaved the natives, settled on the land, raised large families and lived on their wide acres in patriarchal style. . . . Then, finally, came the English. They were a sophisticated city folk and they came in force only after diamonds were discovered . . . in 1867 and gold was discovered . . . in 1884. They built Johannesburg, a cosmopolitan city. . . . In this way they drew South Africa out of its isolation into the current of international trade and the new world civilization.
>
> What makes this instance of succession ecologically interesting is that it illustrates a principle familiar to ethnologists: the principle, namely, that the more primitive the culture of a people the larger the territory needed, in proportion to its numbers, to support its population. A corollary of this is the principle that the land eventually goes to the race or people who can get the most out of it.

The process of succession in South Africa had been going on for centuries. Park felt that it is the special function of the scholar to study such long-time processes and to keep people informed of how they may affect the future. "Studies of succession," he said, " . . . seek less to predict the course of change than to make it intelligible, so that it can eventually be controlled by technical devices or political measures. For this reason studies of succession are concerned not only with the form change takes, but even more with circumstances and events which preceded, accompany and follow change."

In his 1936 paper on "Human Ecology," Park created a graphic image of the two levels of human life: the biotic, symbiotic, or ecological level, and the social level. The image was of a pyramid whose base was the ecological order. The three upper levels were the economic order, the political order, and the moral order.

One of his most provocative ideas about the levels of society was that there is more freedom on the ecological than on the social level. He said:

> It is interesting . . . that these divergent social orders seem to arrange themselves in a kind of hierarchy. In fact they may be said to form a pyramid of which the ecological order constitutes the base and the moral order the apex. Upon each succeeding one of these levels, the ecological, economic, political and moral, the individual finds himself more completely incorporated into and subordinated to the social order of which he is a part than upon the preceding.
>
> Competition, on the biotic level, as we observe it in the plant and animal communities, seems to be relatively unrestricted. Society, so far as it exists, is anarchic and free. On the cultural level, this freedom of the individual to compete is restricted by conventions, understandings and law.

Park was aware that people on the social level had a great craving for freedom. As far as the individual was concerned, Park said, freedom was often related to age. The child has little freedom, the adolescent struggles to get free, while the more mature individual has usually accepted some modifications of his freedom. In a speech, "The Domain of the Social," made to a University of Chicago audience in 1934, he said: "Man is constantly in rebellion against the claims society makes upon him. People have always been struggling for freedom against something or other. What they wanted was freedom—not anything else, just freedom. Freedom from what? Freedom from just these claims which have become conventionalized and fixed in society."

Most of Park's writing on human ecology was done in the late 1930s, when the equilibrium of the Western world was showing signs of great stress. In 1938 he said:

> What the present trend and movement of the modern world suggest is . . . that Europe's economic imperium and the modern world are destined to repeat the same cycle of events, or something comparable to it, which accompanied the rise and decline of the Roman empire and the ancient world. . . . Commerce, in progressively destroying the isolation upon which the ancient order of nature rested, has intensified the struggle for existence over an ever widening area of the habitable world. Out of this struggle a new equilibrium and a new system of animate nature, the biotic base of the new world-society is emerging.

Park did not believe that any state of equilibrium is permanent. Change is constant and the world is constantly "in the process of becoming." Nevertheless, he felt that the maintenance of some measure of equilibrium is important. In the world of nature, which includes plants, animals, and man, equilibrium may be affected by climate changes, weather, overpopulation, starvation, migrations, insect invasions, diseases, revolutions, wars, and some technical inventions. He believed it was the function of human ecology to study such matters and said: "Human ecology is, fundamentally, an attempt to investigate the processes by which the biotic balance and the social equilibrium (1) are maintained once they are achieved and (2) the processes by which when the biotic balance and the social equilibrium are disturbed, the transition is made from one relatively stable order to another."

Park first wrote about human ecology in 1921. Although the term "human ecology" has been in existence since then, the field remains only partially explored. Such explorations as exist have been carried out mainly by biologists and sociologists working in universities. However, by 1967 two American foundations had caught up with this trend in the study of man and on 30 January 1967 the *New York Times* reported: "Without fanfare the Ford and Rockfeller foundations, the biggest and most influential in the United States, have been revising their philosophies and policies to cope with a changing world. The most important changes derive from a realization that many of the needs and challenges of this shrinking planet are interrelated. Dr. J. George Harrar, President of the Rockefeller Foundation, described the new approach as 'human ecology.'"

Chapter 18. So Little Time

In the eighty years of Robert Park's life, the United States fought three major wars. His father served in the Civil War; his oldest son, Edward, in World War I; and his youngest son, Robert Hiram Park, and six grandchildren, in World War II. Robert Hiram Park, an engineer and inventor, received a citation from the navy "for distinguished service to the United States Navy in time of war for the designing of magnetic mines." Commenting on this, Robert says: "Pop first knew what I was doing in Washington when I received a citation from the Navy. . . . The mines . . . had the merit that they were fully as sophisticated as any German mines."

On 21 August 1941 Park's colleague, Louis Wirth, asked him to sign a petition relating to the war. Park did so, but reluctantly, explaining: "I find it difficult to sign petitions urging the government to do things. . . . I am, however, unreservedly in favor of supporting the President and the policy of the government in this crisis. . . . I am in favor of militarism in the United States, not only for the present emergency but for all the other emergencies I see looming up." He was not, however, "in favor of any permanent or temporary alliance with England or Russia which will impose on us the necessity or the moral obligation of enforcing terms of peace that require us to police the world."

In a 1941 paper on "The Social Function of War," Park said, commenting on Sherman's "War is hell": "Problems that can be fairly described only in terms of epithets are notoriously hard to deal with. In so far as this is true in the case of war, it seems to be because we have no adequate conception of what war is."

He was concerned about the postwar world. He felt that commerce would create "the biotic base of the new-world society" but that society itself—cut up in a jigsaw sprawl of hundreds of countries—would be unable to function as a unit. In a 1939 paper on "Symbiosis and Socilization," he wrote:

> It seems that every possible form of association is or should be capable . . . of collective action. But there are types of communities, the individual members of which live in a state of interdependence that is sometimes described as social, which are, nevertheless, quite

incapable of collective action. . . . One may perhaps say that the whole world is living in a kind of symbiosis; but the world community is at present, at least, quite incapable of collective action.

In his 1944 paper, "Missions and the Modern World," he reflected the doubt that people customarily feel in a period of great change about whether the persons who are supposed to guide them have valid answers. "We stand," he said, "as the Greek thinkers stood, in a new world. And because that world is new, we feel that neither the sectional observations of the special student nor the ever accumulating records of the past nor the narrow experience of practical men nor the technological devices of science—not even the techniques of this new social science—can suffice us."

Park's instinct during the war years was not to be content with merely writing some papers but rather to initiate experiments which might ease the adjustments that would be necessary in the postwar world. Some of these experiments concerned art, others religion. His own relation to religion and the church was nominal for some time. In Red Wing he had attended the Episcopal church to which his parents belonged. In Wollaston the Parks belonged to the Unitarian church, although Park was rather inclined to spend the Sabbath reading aloud to the family—mainly poetry. Once he got to Chicago and formed a strong friendship with Dr. Edward Scribner Ames, pastor of the Church of the Disciples of Christ and a professor of philosophy at the university, he began to enjoy his contacts with Ames's church. He even belonged, for a time, to a Sunday School class which was studying Gilbert Murray's *The Rise of the Greek Epic*. So when Samuel Kincheloe, a former student of Park's and later a professor in the Chicago Theological Seminary, wrote to Park and inquired about his religious feelings, Park replied with a long letter:

My dear Dr. Kincheloe:

Standing on a street corner in Petoskey, Michigan, last summer I was accosted by a middle aged woman, wearing a gingham apron, who handed me what was obviously a tract. Now it happens that for a number of years past I have been allergic to tracts, either religious or secular. . . . At any rate I accepted, a little warily, the paper which the good woman handed me, explaining quite unnecessarily and unwisely . . . that I would take it home with me if she wished, but that I could not promise to read it. I discovered my mistake in a moment when my interlocutor—if I may use so innocuous a term to describe so positive a character—fixing upon me an eye in which there was, it seemed to me, a gleam of evangelical exaltation, said: "Why? Don't you believe in the Bible?"

Now it happened that I had at that very moment your letter in my pocket which invited me, as I understood it, to make what amounted to a confession of faith. It happened that I had been pondering the question: How it was I came to join up with the Campbellites; how had I managed to become a member in good standing in the Church of the Disciples of Christ; how, considering all the transfigurations of thought I had gone through in the course of a long life, had I ever managed to become a member of, and feel at home in any church? I was therefore not as unprepared as I might otherwise have been to answer this sudden and soul-searching question. At any rate I was able to say that I did believe in the Bible and that my faith in its teachings was probably at the moment as firm and unshakable as her own.

I was able to say this because, after a good deal of reflection, I had come to the conclusion that, except for the language in which I might express it, my creed was and is essentially and fundamentally orthodox. . . . Whatever my individual predilections for one creed or another may have been at different times in my life, I had come finally to believe in religion itself; believe in it, that is to say, as an essential element in a wholesome individual and social life.

Perhaps I have always held to that belief. I have had moments of perplexity and doubt, to be sure, but I have come finally to agree with Dr. Ames, that the only mortal sin is—not doubt, but cynicism; and the antidote for cynicism is faith in man and God—whatever gods there be. At any rate what I attempted to convey to my street corner evangelist was that we were after all fellow travelers, and that essentially and for all practical purposes, I was saved.

And this was actually the way I came to join the church. I was already "saved" when I met Dr. Ames. At any rate I was no longer what the Quakers called a "seeker." I was no longer greatly concerned either about my own or other souls. I was in fact more concerned about the world because I had come to realize that it was in this world that souls are lost and saved; and that the church and organized religion, however imperfect they at any time may be, are still important and essential though by no means the only agencies for the redemption of the world, whatever that means. . . .

I was interested in the University Church of the Disciples because Dr. Ames seemed, as I did, to regard the church itself as a social problem. . . . He described his as an experimental religion. I was interested in social experiments and I wanted to participate in an experiment in religion. . . . Once identified with the church I became interested in the Disciples of Christ as a religious denomination because it had grown up on the frontier and among the people the likes of whom I had known all my life; whose virtues and faults I understood and shared.

I was,—to conclude my story,—so successful in convincing my street corner evangelist that she was wasting her literature on me that I did not discover what was the particular gospel she preached. . . . It seems to be characteristic of every religious faith, when it is new born, that it propagates itself with a kind of naive arrogance; an arrogance which assumes that it has a monopoly of God's grace and that every soul is lost which has not, or cannot, accept its particular formula. I recognize this as one of the normal manifestations of religious life and so accept it, as Margaret Fuller accepted the universe. . . . I recognize also the significance of those forms of organized dissent in which protestant churches have sought to shake off the fixed forms and beliefs of an older and hampering tradition. However, I do not, at present, cherish, as I once did, my right to dissent. On the contrary I am inclined to accept Santayana's dictum that, finally and fundamentally, orthodoxy is always right and heterodoxy always wrong. . . .

Cordially yours,
Robert E. Park

One of Park's wartime experiments relating to religion was facilitated by his connection with Scaritt College near Fisk. A colleague of Park's at Fisk says:

It may not be known that Dr. Park had a rather ambitious investigation in mind when he came here, and he took some steps to implement it. He thought whatever friendship Asia, Africa, and South America had for the people of the United States was generated by the missionaries who had lived in these parts of the world. He thought our military and commercial representatives had created unfavorable attitudes towards us. He proposed to test part of this view by collecting letters from and to missionaries. He planned to organize this intensive search through the personnel of Scaritt College—a college of the Methodist Church engaged in training missionaries of this and other churches. There are regional and national church functionaries located in Nashville for Presbyterian, Baptist, Methodist, and other denominations. I do not think that Dr. Park got very far with this plan because of the magnitude of it in relation to his declining strength.

In a 1942 letter to Everett Hughes, Park explained:

I have been greatly impressed with what missionaries have done and are doing for Americans in the present crisis. I am thinking of Pearl Buck for one and of Henry Luce of *Time* and *Fortune*. It seems to me that it has been our great good fortune that we have men and women like them and others who have lived in and know other cultures to guide and direct our cultural policies in the present emergency. . . .

As a matter of fact I am giving a seminar on missions at Scaritt College, a neighboring college, and have an interesting project which I am directing which is going to get right at the heart of the missionary issue. My interest in the missionary is based on the fact that everyone whom I have known who has been a missionary seems to be right on the race problem. . . .

Fisk University had had for over a decade a springtime Festival of Music and the Fine Arts. In 1943 Park proposed that the 1944 festival be dedicated to furthering the sense of world community and this was done. In the Foreword to the 1944 program, he said:

A world order that is based on machinery must eventually be superseded by a world that is based on understanding. An international society that has been created by commerce and diplomacy must be supported by one that is informal, personal and moral.

Music, drama, and art, since they are forms of expression more universal than speech, are able to achieve understandings that are more elementary and immediate than rational forms of communication.

During the 1940s Park carried on at Fisk a third experiment which concerned listening. The same Fisk colleague who described Park's experiment with missionaries says:

Dr. Park was so anxious to engage in intellectual encounter that he formed a group, mostly professors from the Nashville area, to meet at his home about once a month for a year or so. . . . One very interesting program that he suggested was carried out at Vanderbilt University. He felt that sociologists talked too much within the professional group and that they should listen more. So a day was devoted to hearing leaders from several rural and small town communities hold forth on their view of a number of matters. This might have been somewhat like the meetings held by Booker Washington in connection with his procedures with rural populations in Alabama.

In 1942 Park made his last trip to Tuskegee and delivered an address about Booker Washington on the annual celebration of Founder's Day. It is his most complete statement about Washington's qualities as a black leader, covering both his deficiencies and his virtues. Simultaneously, Park mentioned Washington in an unpublished paper, "Methods of Teaching," which Louis Wirth had asked him to write. His final tribute in this second paper to what Washington and his seven years at Tuskegee meant in his own life is impressive:

> I have studied, first and last, under some very eminent teachers. . . . However, after reviewing my experiences in more universities than I care to mention, I came to the conclusion that I learned most about methods of teaching and most about life while I was studying at Tuskegee under the general supervision of Booker Washington.[1]

Park refused to slow down. He was so tired after delivering the Founder's Day address that he had to spend a day in bed recuperating. And, although he was often fatigued on his travels, he did not stop traveling. On 18 June 1943, when he was seventy-nine, he made yet one more of his many surveys in the field—concerning South Dakota and the role the potato crop played in its fortunes. "I am now better informed about farming in South Dakota than most people in the state," he boasted, " . . . South Dakota was the poorest state in the Union a few years ago. . . . Dakota is no longer in the 'dust bowl.' The country is green again. The fields are alive with game. The birds are singing madly in the trees."

Later that summer he had a heart attack. His friend John Nef, who often visited him at Roaring Brook, says:

> Then the day came . . . when death laid its first heavy threat upon him—on the lawn of that cottage in the north where—as he remembered only too strongly—his father-in-law had fallen before him.
>
> In a sense he was ill prepared. How could he leave when everything, as always (only more so now) was beginning? He was doing better than he had ever done before. No paper he had written had quite the fire of the one he read in Ida Noyes Hall in the summer of 1942.

The country doctor diagnosed his condition as "the breaking up" of age. However, by the end of October, he seemed to have recovered. Clara Park wrote to her son Edward on 23 October 1943:

> I have had you on my mind a good deal, because I see so many things I would like to talk to you about—just special things, like the way Pop has suddenly seemed to bloom out again . . . The way Pop seemed to get his second or third wind seems a good deal to me like

1. Louis Wirth, Special Collections, the University of Chicago Library.

the way I seemed to gradually send out new shoots and deeper roots, and I have faith that we will have another summer in Roaring Brook, at least one more!

There was a final task Park set himself after the doctor had warned him that he did not have much time left; it was to make a start on his autobiography. He told his friend Everett Hughes: "I want to write the natural history of my mind." The "natural history" was one of his most important concepts. Lewis Coser says: "Park conceived of the process of social change as involving a three-stage sequence or 'natural history,' beginning with dissatisfactions and the resulting disturbances and social unrest, leading to mass movements, and ending in new accommodations within a restructured institutional order." [2] He recognized that in his own mind there was a constant dissatisfaction so that he was forever reshaping his conception of human nature, its potential and its limits. He traveled a long distance from the time he expected the world to be saved by better communication to the point where he saw society organized on two levels, the biotic and the cultural.

In two letters, one to his daughter Margaret Redfield on 10 February 1943, the other to his granddaughter Lisa Redfield Peattie on 13 March 1943, he further defined the kind of autobiography he wanted it to be:

> I want to make it a short human document and put in it all the things that have given me insights into the nature of human beings and human society. . . . It is not intended to be something of personal history for the benefit of the family or in order to preserve the memory of my deeds, but rather a document presenting interesting personal data which might have significance for students of social psychology or sociology.

He had hoped that Lisa might come and work with him, she did not. Instead, he dictated some notes, found among his papers after his death.

Having early decided that his own small self was not of primary importance, Park enjoyed an inner calm not everyone would have suspected and, with it, moments of gaiety, zest, and joy that sustained him throughout his life. On 18 October 1943 he was telling his granddaughter to enjoy life as much as he had:

My dear Lisa:

> Your letter of September came to me at Roaring Brook. I attempted to answer it at the time but I was in no condition I found, at the time

2. Lewis Coser, *Masters of Sociological Thought* (New York: Harcourt, Brace, Jovanovich), p. 362.

your letter arrived, to answer anything. My heart was flurrying like a kitten, my blood pressure was up and it was cold and I was unhappy. Now I am in much better condition and I would like to write you some of the things that have occurred to me in regard to your project of writing a small book that grown people and children might profitably read to understand a war in the Pacific.

Well, I think that is a very good project even if you don't succeed in producing anything that will measurably achieve the purposes you have in mind.

The first thing to do, of course, is to learn Chinese. I was thinking last night, while I was not able to get asleep, of how I should proceed to produce the sort of book you suggest. I think I would go to Peiping, if the Japanese would let me, and get acquainted with the city. Peiping is one of the most marvelous cities in the world. No one has ever given anything like an adequate account of it. There are three or four walled cities in one: there is the Chinese city, the Manchu city, there is the Forbidden city, and there is the more or less Europeanized city. Three of them have their own walls, one inside the other. Chinese walls themselves would make an interesting topic. Peiping underworld, of which I gained some acquaintance while I was there, is a wonderful place. I got my acquaintance with it partly by visiting the Thieves' Market and partly by reading an account that a professional thief gave of his adventures in seeking to escape the police, but I can't begin to tell you the things I think are interesting about that city. You and Pete should go there and find out for yourselves. Well, I won't attempt to tell you any more about Peiping because I really do not know much about it, but I have an immense desire to extend my acquaintance with it. The trouble is there is "so little time." I am reading a book by John Marquand entitled "So Little Time." He keeps reiterating that phrase and I find myself uttering it or thinking it every day, almost every hour "so little time." But you and Pete have some time and I advise you to get on the job as quickly as possible and go as far and as fast as you can and be sure to enjoy every bit of the journey.

Always yours,
Robert E. Park

In mid-December 1943 Park was again seriously ill. His family decided he would be better off at home than in the hospital. At home, during the final two months of his life, he was visited by his friends from Fisk and by all his four children, who came to Nashville to spend time with him. H. C. Brearly of Peabody College reports: "Until a few weeks before his death, Park was actively engaged in pursuing his studies, being then engaged on the sociology of law, the sociology of knowledge, and the role of the missionary in the process of acculturation." In an article for *Psychiatry* magazine, Charles Johnson notes that "his mind never ceased to work with ideas and he had not lost his zest for life and work and the still uncharted frontiers of human behavior even when, in his final illness, he could no longer speak." Park died at his home, 1809 Morena Street, 7 February 1944, seven days before what would have been his eightieth birthday. He was survived by his wife, four children, fourteen grandchildren, and one great-grandchild. Horace R. Cayton, in the Pittsburg *Courier*, wrote the following tribute:

ROBERT PARK—A Great Man Died, But Leaves Keen Observation on our Democracy

Last week a great man died. His name was Robert E. Park. He was a white man, but he probably knew more about the American Negro than anyone in the country. He was a professor emeritus from the University of Chicago and had spent his last few years at Fisk University where he died. Robert Park was a strange and colorful character. . . . I first met Park on the Pacific coast, when I was an undergraduate at the University of Washington. . . . Later I knew Park at Fisk University and as my office was next to his we spent a great deal of time talking together. On one occasion I drove him and Mrs. Park from Fisk to New York on a Christmas holiday. As we were driving through New Jersey, near the end of our journey, Park and I got into an argument about the capitalistic system. From an economic point of view, Park was conservative if not reactionary. The argument got hotter and hotter and finally Park told me to stop the car and get out (it was his car). I answered just as warmly that it was three below zero and that he, Park, couldn't drive a car and that I wasn't going to get out. We continued in silence for an hour or so until the lights of New York began to appear, and suddenly, without warning, he launched into a lengthy discussion of his theory of the growth of a city, and for an hour delivered one of the most brilliant lectures I've ever heard. We'd both forgotten our difference by the time we got through the Holland Tunnel and he was again the great teacher and I his humble student.

A Treatise on our Democracy

One of the last visits I had with Park was a few years ago when he had dinner in my apartment in Chicago. After dinner Richard Wright was to come by, as Park had expressed an interest in meeting him. When Wright finally appeared, Park and I had finished dinner, and

Park was sitting in a very large and comfortable easy chair. He was old by that time, way up in the 70's, and it was difficult for him to get around. When Wright walked into the room Park began a painful struggle to get out of his chair. Wright impulsively asked him not to rise, and I, too, went over to protest. He muttered between pants, "I want to get up; help me, Cayton." After Park had struggled to his feet he extended his hand to Wright and said, "I want to shake hands with a great writer. I don't agree with much that you write but it's honest and great writing." The old man recognized talent, ability, perhaps genius, and he, as a scholar, wanted to stand up to this young 34-year-old Negro boy whom he recognized as a peer.

The last letter I had from Park was typical of his rugged mind and intellectual honesty. He wrote in criticism of a paper I had submitted for his criticism and ended the letter with the following observation on democracy:

"Democracy is not something that some people in a country can have and others not have, something to be shared and divided like a pie—some getting a small and some getting a large piece. Democracy is an integral thing. If any part of the country doesn't have it, the rest of the country doesn't have it. The Negro, therefore, in fighting for democracy for himself is simply fighting the battle for our democracy. . . . I think the liberals realize now that the Negro's cause must in the long run win. The only thing is they don't want it to win too soon and they don't want the change to be so rapid as to result in the disorders that we have had. Personally I don't agree with these liberals. In fact I've never been a liberal. If conflicts arise as a result of the efforts to get their place it will be because the white people started them. These conflicts will probably occur and are more or less inevitable but conditions will be better after they are over. In any case, this is my conviction."

Chapter 19. Epilogue: Park and the Department of Sociology

The University of Chicago had been devoted to research and publication of new knowledge from its founding in 1891. Some early professors came with Ph.D.s from the Johns Hopkins University, where economics and politics were studied in a naturalistic way. One of them, Albion W. Small, appointed professor of sociology at the opening of the University of Chicago, had studied theology in New England, then history and economics in Germany, before taking his Ph.D. in welfare economics under Richard T. Ely at Johns Hopkins. Still in his thirties when he came to Chicago, he made sociology a lively enterprise with the motto, "Remember the research ideal, to keep it holy." Some of his writing had been so abstruse that Park admitted he couldn't read it. Yet Small had translated and published some of the work of Park's only teacher of sociology, Georg Simmel; and it was Small who, after Park had come, called together the social scientists of the university to propose that they take the city of Chicago as their laboratory. They did so and it became Park's enterprise. Some of Small's own writing had been very close to Park's muckraking about American cities. Small was known in Chicago then as a fiery, eloquent speaker on reform. His novel *Between Eras: From Capitalism to Democracy*, which told the story of Chicago tycoons and their wayward sons and grandsons, was assigned to generations of his students.

Starting in 1895, the Chicago Department of Sociology and Anthropology had granted 35 Ph.D.s before Park came. In 1896 William I. Thomas and George E. Vincent got their doctorates. Both remained as members of the department. Vincent, son of the Methodist bishop who founded Chautauqua, was perhaps closer to Small in interests. He became important in the administration of the university, was president of the University of Minnesota, and became the first president of the Rockefeller Foundation. Thomas stayed at Chicago as its great pioneer in social psychology and in the study of immigrant communities. Small, Vincent, and Thomas were enterprising men. Others of the Chicago Ph.D.s in sociology were already well known before Park came to the university.

Small, with the university's support, founded the *American Journal of*

Sociology in 1895; it was and remains the property of the University of Chicago. The university statutes provide that a department has the duty of editing its journal if it has one. Thus for many years all members of the sociology faculty were listed as editors of the *Journal*, with Small "in general charge." Park was not listed as an editor of the *Journal* even in 1923, nine years after he came to Chicago, presumably because of his uncertain official status as a "professorial lecturer," but he produced and selected articles for the *Journal* from the moment of his arrival. Before then his writing had all appeared in periodicals of more general circulation.

The *American Journal of Sociology* soon became the recognized organ of American sociology:

> By agreement with the *American Sociological Society* the officers chosen by that body become, during their term of office, the *Advisory Council* of this *Journal*. This arrangement makes neither the *Advisory Council* nor the society which elects them responsible for the conduct of this journal. Through the co-operation and advice thus secured, however, it is hoped that the *Journal* may gain increased success in serving as a clearing house for the best sociological thought of all schools.[1]

The advisory council apparently included all living ex-presidents of the American Sociological Society. Members of the society received the *Journal* by this arrangement until the founding of society's own organ.

The American Sociological Society itself was founded in 1905, with a good deal of initiative from the Chicago department. Its office was maintained on the Chicago campus; the secretary-treasurer was a member of the Chicago faculty. This arrangement, too, continued until the founding of the *American Sociological Review* in 1936. For a number of years thereafter the society's office was peripatetic.

Although the society had been housed at Chicago, its three earliest presidents were Lester F. Ward of Brown University, William G. Sumner of Yale University, and Franklin H. Giddings of Columbia University. Small himself was the fourth president; he was succeeded by E. A. Ross (Wisconsin), George E. Vincent (then president of the University of Minnesota), and soon after by C. H. Cooley of Michigan. This is almost the complete roster of prominent sociologists of the time, though they were by no means all of the same school of thought. They were, rather, pioneers in the various lines of thought that came to be called

---

1. Taken from the front inside cover of the *American Journal of Sociology*. This statement appeared in all issues of the journal to and including May 1933.

sociology. It is doubtful whether they could have been brought together except under very enterprising leadership, such as that of the University of Chicago.

Park came to this department when it was successful not only within the University of Chicago but also as the organizing force in American sociology. Vincent had gone, but Thomas was still there. He and Park had already become colleagues.

Thomas had studied in Germany and had taught English at Oberlin College before coming to Chicago to study sociology. Although he was, like Small and Vincent, reared in pious surroundings, he was much less attached to religion than those and other colleagues at Chicago. He was, rather, attracted to social causes and philanthropic leaders. From 1908 until 1919, Thomas was director of the Helen Culver Fund for Race Psychology. He had written on the psychology of race and sex. He and Park had in common their interest in race, but Park in the main stuck to the effect of race relations on "the American system" and later on other societies. He took little interest in the arguments over the relative intelligence of the races.

Soon after Park came to Chicago he wrote a brochure on *The Principles of Human Behavior* in a series edited by Thomas and published by the Zalaz Corporation of Chicago in 1915. This was the most psychological of Park's writings. Selections from it appear in the Park and Burgess *Introduction to the Science of Sociology* (1921), which was mostly written when Thomas was still at Chicago and Park and Thomas were in close contact.

Thomas left the University of Chicago in 1918. The newspapers published on their front pages the story of his arrest on a charge of disorderly conduct, having been "found" in a downtown hotel room with a woman. (Park once commented: The preacher can drive the soprano home from choir practice, but he should take care not to run into a telephone pole.) Nothing came of the case in court, but publicity of that sort was enough to end a university career in those days. Thomas resigned. Park was one of his few defenders in the university.

Ellsworth Faris succeeded Thomas as professor of social psychology in the Department of Sociology. He had been a missionary in Africa before taking his Ph.D. in psychology at Chicago. He continued courses bearing Thomas's imprint but put his own stamp on them. Ernest Burgess, turning thirty, was just beginning his thirty years of colleague-ship with Park and his fifty years in the University of Chicago community. Small, Faris, Park, and Burgess, with occasional help from others, were the Chicago sociology team for ten years until Small's retirement in 1925 and his death in 1926. The department from then on had no member who had taken his degree there in its first two decades. If there was a "Chicago School" it was not made up of the early Chicago doctors of sociology. William F. Ogburn, of Barnard College, joined the team in 1927. George H. Mead, a professor of philosophy, was the fountainhead of social psychology in the Department of Sociology and in the university. Sophonisba Breckenridge (Ph.D. political science) and Edith Abbott (Ph.D. economics) were also listed in the department; they were the founders of the School of Social Service Administration in the university, and they considered their approach to the study of the city superior to that of the sociologists. Park's relations with the social workers was not close, yet he admired Jane Addam's *The Spirit of Youth and the City Streets* and Graham Taylor's *Satellite Cities.*

The two anthropologists then in the department were not close to the sociologists. Their successors, Fay Cooper-Cole and Edward Sapir, were closer to the sociologists in interests. Sapir was especially influential through his work on language and culture. But the anthropologists eventually went to their own department in 1928. All students took a course in statistics with a member of the Department of Economics. Many took other courses in economics, especially in labor relations. Departmental lines were not rigid; the number of teachers and of courses in each department was limited. Sociology students were encouraged to read widely and a good number did so, in English, in German, and in French.

Park, in these early Chicago years, obviously found teaching an adventure. Accustomed to writing for newspapers and magazines, he had the habit of meeting deadlines. He turned to publishing in scholarly journals in 1913 at the age of forty-nine; by 1940 he had published forty-eight articles and many book reviews. Several more appeared in the early 1940s, some after his death. In addition he had written introductions to a number of monographs produced by his students.

His favorite topics were collective behavior, news, race relations, cities, and human ecology. They were not all new topics in the department to which he came. In 1914, Manuel Elmer had presented a thesis on "Social Surveys of Urban Communities." Other theses had treated Marx's thought, the social and economic policies of churches, capital and labor, industrial morale, industrial accidents, the poor law, and social services. Studies of sectarian communities had been made in the Divinity School and in sociology. Immigrant communities and contacts of ethnic groups were an early object of study. Thomas's work on the *Polish Peasant in Europe and America,* already under way, was the high point in the study of European immigrants to America.

Park's influence did not show immediately in Ph.D. thesis titles. In 1915, Jesse F. Steiner presented a thesis on Japanese immigrants. When it was published in 1917, Park wrote the foreward. Steiner evidently had finished his Ph.D. before he had had significant contact with Park; but he and Park were brought closer together by common interest in the Oriental problem of the West Coast.

Not until 1919, after World War I, did students who had worked with Park and on his kinds of problem appear among the Ph.D.s. In 1919 Kawabe presented a dissertation on the Japanese newspaper, and E. B. Reuter one on "The Mulatto." In 1921 R. D. McKenzie presented a survey of the city of Columbus, Ohio; he went on to broader ecological studies, leading to his major book, *The Metropolitan Community* (1931), to which Park contributed a chapter. Park was gathering a nucleus of sociological colleagues. It was the time that the Midwestern and Western state universities were expanding. The sociologists trained in Chicago became professors, often chairmen, of sociology departments in the same pattern of spread from Chicago as in grubstaking and cattle trading.

In the early 1920s a new generation known as Park's students came to Chicago. In fact, they came first to Burgess, whose interest in social problems—as defined in sociological courses—was somewhat more in the tradition of the Chicago department. Burgess had some hand in the connection of Nels Anderson with Ben Reitmen, M.D., the famous doctor and friend of homeless men; Wirth credits Burgess with the suggestion that he study the Chicago Jewish community. Thrasher, whose book on boys' gangs is still the classic, and Shaw, who published a book on delinquency areas, were both probation officers and students and proteges of Burgess, who specialized in crime and prisons. They came to study social problems—thus, by way of Burgess, to Park. A number of them lived in settlement houses, like Burgess, who had lived at Hull House. Park and Burgess shared an office; it was easy to start talking to Burgess and end up talking to Park.

Burgess said of the office arrangement that "it was most fortunate for me, because Park had a most creative mind. He lived and slept research. I never knew when I would get home to dinner, because we would spend whole afternoons discussing both theoretical and practical aspects of sociology and social research."[2] Eventually many another young sociologist could make the same complaint or boast about talking with Burgess.

Burgess and Park were a teaching team. Burgess often made the connection with a local problem and an agency. Park never bypassed the reporting of the local facts, but he redefined the problem in more general,

---

2. Robert E. Lee Faris, *Chicago Sociology: 1920–1932* (San Francisco: Chandler Publishing Co., 1967), p. 39.

theoretical terms. Their partnership continued throughout Park's years at Chicago, although after a time many students came directly to Park. And, of course, Burgess had his own continuing students in increasing number.

Nels Anderson, whose monograph *The Hobo* was published in 1923, describes how the Burgess-Park team worked. Anderson says he was not of the same middle-class background as other students in the department. He came with less than $20 in his pocket, got a job in a home for incurables, and was admitted by Albion Small to graduate study. Burgess put him to work on the homeless man, a social type which Anderson knew from experience. He found himself at sea. He writes:

> What I was doing was keeping a kind of journal which was being done without having any plan. Often when writing something down an idea would come about getting some other kind of information: what five cents would buy in the way of food or drink, how many ways one could get something for ten cents, how one could get through the day with twenty-five cents. I showed some of these writings to Burgess for discussion but it did not lead to any precise work plan. Once Park, who had seen some of these materials, asked how I was getting on. When I said I was not sure, he came back with, "Write only what you see or hear." After a pause, he added, "or know." Another time he stopped me in the hall and asked, "Why not write the typical day of a panhandler or other characters?" I did that, also for clerks in flophouses, landladies, bartenders, mission workers, policemen.

When he had a report ready on hoboes, he showed it to Burgess in the office Park and Burgess shared. Park showed interest in the document and spent hours going over it and making suggestions. Finally, he announced that it would be published by the University Press. Anderson went home that night, made the changes Park suggested, and brought the document back next day. It was indeed published soon.

At the end of Anderson's oral examination for the M.A., Small told Anderson that, although he did not know sociology "In here (among the books) he knew it out there." He did not continue at Chicago, but took a Ph.D. in the school of education at New York University, with Harvey Zorbaugh, author of *The Gold Coast and the Slum.* During the depression he worked for the government relief program and was head of labor relations in WPA for seven years. When Hughes was teaching at the University of Frankfort on the Main after World War II, Anderson brought a labor leader to have lunch. Although Anderson had failed his German examination at Chicago, and the German did not speak much

English, that meeting went well, as did the research program Anderson organized in the heavily bombed city of Darmstadt. He directed the UNESCO Institute for Social Science in Cologne for seven years. Eventually he became a professor at the University of New Brunswick. The man who didn't know sociology "in here" wrote books about people "out there"—Mormons on the frontier, workers in and out of work. He hadn't passed his German examination; but he eventually worked successfully with German labor leaders to restore their unions from the Hitler shambles. He quickly became very well read on the history of Canadian labor and industry. He was in his office with his students all days and all hours, as Burgess said of Park. Anderson, who says that "much of Park which I absorbed was after leaving," is one of several people who did not finish degrees at Chicago and who did not agree with Park on many points but who consider themselves Park's students in the fullest sense and whom Park respected as such.

Park often walked the floor on the night before some special lecture. Helen MacGill, who lived with the Parks when she was a graduate student, says that once, when she and Park were walking from home to his 8 a.m. lecture, he asked her to walk on the other side of the street so he could think about the subject of the class. Edgar Thompson reports that he got more out of Park's slow think-as-he-went talk than out of the elegant finished lectures of Edward Sapir. Park's teaching always gave the sense of something in the making; he said in a handwritten note, "Science is not knowledge. It is the pursuit of knowledge."

Park's teaching often took the form of editing a student's writing; he was a professional writer who expected his apprentices to meet professional standards. Sometimes his editing was devastating. Pauline Young, author of "The Pilgrims of Russian Town," about Molokans—a Russian sect which was having trouble in adjusting to city life in Los Angeles—recalls her difficulty with Park:

> Once, as a graduate student, I had rushed into print with an article on occupational attitudes of a sectarian group of laborers. I proudly sent a copy of this article to Dr. Park hoping to please him with my "conceptual thinking." His reply put ashes in my mouth. "You have ruined meticulously gathered data by couching them in concepts that sound like the grips and passes of a secret society. Come to my office, I think I can teach you something." He started by taking the concept *competition* apart, and showed how a number of events are condensed under one general heading. I grasped that a concept is in reality a definition of a social situation in shorthand, an analysis of a class or group of facts isolated from other classes on the basis of definite classification systems.

She learned. She produced a good monograph and later a good book on how to study a community. She continued to seek Park's editorial advice:

> Watch if these sentences march along! They must be so simple and carefully written that the man in the street readily grasps their meaning. *You* are not writing for professors, train yourself to write for the general public. To this day I examine every page of my textbook manuscripts and ask myself: "Do these sentences march along?"

Many students have reported that in their first days, or even weeks, they had little or no idea of what Park was talking about and what was expected of them.

Bingham Dai, a social psychologist, relates:

> I went to the University of Chicago in the fall of 1929 as a graduate student of education on a Chinese Government fellowship. . . . I came, therefore, with a serious purpose and burning zeal to learn all I could about human nature and education. With considerable trepidation I went to the first meeting of the class. To make matters worse for me, Dr. Park gave us a list of his favorite concepts and required each of us to write down what he had learned about them. Since all these concepts were strange to me, I turned in a completely blank answer. I felt so perplexed and downhearted that I would have withdrawn from further academic effort . . . had it not been for the next test Dr. Park sprang on us. This time he gave each of us a mimeographed copy of the life history of a delinquent girl and required us to give an account of her problem behavior. This assignment seemed to appeal to me a great deal. Being still unfamiliar with the sociological concepts that we were supposed to use for this task, I went at it with ample naivete but not without native insight and was able to hand in something of a paper.
>
> Weeks went by, it seemed, before Dr. Park remembered to return those papers to us. When he did, he gave me the biggest surprise of my life, for he said that of all the students in the class—mostly candidates for the Ph.D. degree—I was the only one who had given an adequate analysis of the problems of the delinquent girl.
>
> Ever since then whenever Dr. Park spotted me on the campus, he would first ask if I was Mr. Dai, and when I said yes, he would add, "Your mind is analytical." He said this so many times that I began to believe it and gradually gained back my self-confidence. The result was that I stayed in sociology till I completed my Ph.D. work in 1935.
>
> It was at Dr. Park's suggestion that I wrote my M.A. thesis on "Glossalalia or Speaking with Tongues." And it was under his inspi-

ration that I began to formulate my Ph.D. dissertation on "Opium Addiction in Chicago." Both of these are interdisciplinary studies and require a broad conceptual frame of reference, which Dr. Park helped make familiar to me and which I later characterized as the socio-psychiatric approach in my writings—long before social psychiatry as a discipline came to be in vogue.

As was seen earlier in chapter 11, some students were quickly drawn into close and eager interaction with Park and he, in turn, encouraged them in the pursuit of their own interests. One of them was Charles S. Johnson, later president of Fisk University, whose first course with Park was "Crowd and Public." This course brought into American sociology Scipio Sighele's *Psychologie des Sectes*, the classic on revolutionary sects and crowds (Park had well-marked copies of the French and German editions); George Sorel's *Reflections on Violence* and Gabriel Tarde's *Les Lois Sociales*. The course helped prepare Johnson for his role as codirector of the famous study of the Chicago race riot of 1917 published under the title, *The Negro in Chicago*.

Park encouraged a student to draw upon his own experience and helped the student perceive that experience in new ways. At Yenching University in 1932 (see chapter 14), he told the class he was going to teach them "how to write a book." Because Chinese learning had, he felt, committed the error of excess reliance on rote learning, he instructed his students to go out and collect facts, form hypotheses, and check back and forth constantly between facts and books. This may seem a special adaptation to Park's perception of Chinese students, but the method was not much different from what he did in Chicago and in the South. Although in his Chicago classes he often started with quite abstract and conceptual discussion, sooner or later he asked the student to record what he had gathered from his own experience, or to go out and make observations and have experiences which he could then put into some broader and more systematic frame of reference.

Not all students, of course, accepted Park's interpretation of their own experiences. W. O. Brown, the son of a tenant farmer from Texas, thought Park's view of the relations between the black and the white did not take sufficiently into account the Texas situation of poor white and poor black; Park's view was based too much on the plantation. Brown has written of himself:

> My education was a series of emancipations. First I got emancipated from the church, mostly because the good respectable Christians of Fayette county were such hypocrites, and then from the caste system notions of the south.

He wrote a thesis on "Race Prejudice" which he said was a reaction against Park's theories; yet he says that Park was sometimes irascible but never mean, and that he respected his students. Brown was a militant enemy of racial prejudice and inequality—perhaps the most militant among Park's white students. He suffered for it at the University of Cincinnati. Then he devoted his life to study of race relations in America and Africa, using very much the scheme which Park had developed.

Instances in which Park exerted great influence or provided aid have been abundant. Edgar Thompson, in the same group of students as Brown, was born and reared on a small plantation in South Carolina, and later, encouraged by Park, made it his life work to study the plantation system—wherever entrepreneurs had recruited and used large numbers of people of a race different than their own to produce a single crop or raw produce for a world market. E. Franklin Frazier is another example. Frazier came to Chicago from Atlanta, where he had taught at Morehouse College and had worked with W.E.B. Du Bois. He had published an article on the psychopathology of racial prejudice and a consequence was that he had to leave Atlanta—or, at least, teaching in a white-supported black college. Park invited him to come to Chicago to study the black family, although Park had received hate letters telling him what a "bad nigger" Frazier was. Frazier himself was of a middle-class family. He had spent some time in Denmark studying the folk school, a device to promote social equality by having all young people given practical as well as more academic education. He thus came to study sociology with Park with a good academic background. He became one of Park's favorite students. After *The Negro Family in Chicago*, he published a broader study of the black family in the United States. Much later he wrote a book on *Race and Culture Contacts in the Modern World*. It follows Park's work rather closely by perceiving race relations as a product of the colonial expansion of Europe. Still other examples are Roderick McKenzie, who made a community study of Columbus, Ohio, then moved—with Park's teaching and stimulation—to world ecology, especially in the racial and ethnic division of labor in Malaysian rubber plantations; and Donald Pierson, who was encouraged by Park to study race relations in Bahia and who has spent his whole career in research on race in Brazil in the entire demographic and economic setting.

Park's genius was to arouse a student's interest in a small project and develop it into a large one, stated in universal terms. Sometimes the student turned the project around. Park encouraged Everett Hughes to make a study of land values as an index of the growth of a city. Hughes started on it but became interested in another problem. Chicago had been one of the fastest growing cities in the world; the real estate agents flourished and eventually organized, and some of them tried to turn their business into a profession. Park had noted the tendency for trades of all kinds to become professions in the city; Hughes studied not the land values but the values of the dealers in land, looking at them as businessmen trying to be professionals. This led him to the study of professions, and since race and ethnic relations always include an ethnic division of labor and professional problems and conflicts, Hughes saw this as a key to analyzing the relations between the French and English populations of urban eastern Canada.

There are stories of Park's sharp criticism of a student's work. When Park was angry it was impersonally; he had no pleasure in anyone's failure. And he never excused himself if he failed to arouse response and participation. After a class on news and public opinion, Hughes remembers, Park once took him to his office, sat down heavily, and said dejectedly, "I wonder what is wrong with this course. These people are not getting what I am trying to do." It was the course in which Hughes discovered the press agent. He wrote a paper about the members of this new occupation and how they changed the name of their activity to public relations as they became more respectable. Many students wrote interesting papers in that course.

He was a tireless teacher. He insisted that data gathered for research should not be used for social casework or individual therapy. He tried to understand and guide his students in their efforts to learn and to communicate clearly what they were learning.

Eventually his teaching by editing bore fruit in the University of Chicago Sociological Series. He had this project in mind when he wrote his introduction to Anderson's *The Hobo*: "The present volume is intended to be the first of a series of studies of the urban community and of city life." Shortly afterwards the trustees of the university did establish that series. Faris, Park and Burgess were the editorial committee, but Park wrote the introductions. Several of the books were theses, edited for publication in the series. Wirth credits Burgess with the suggestion that he study the Jewish community of Chicago, but it was Park who wrote the foreward to *The Ghetto*, perhaps the best known of the series. These volumes show Park's gifts and persistence as a teacher. Every book in that series was written by someone who was in spirit, and generally by paying tuition, a student of Park. The last of the series—but not the last work published by a student of Park—seems to have been *News and the Human Interest Story*, on which Helen MacGill worked with Park from 1927 until 1940. Frances Donovan, a schoolteacher who took courses but took no advanced degree, was inspired to write three books, *The Woman Who Waits* (about waitresses), *The Saleslady*, and *The Schoolma'am*. She was one of the many people who attended seminars and the meetings of the Society for Social Research, and who were taught by Park. He spent hours with them, and some of them kept in touch with him for years.

A further step in the development of the teaching-research-publication enterprise was the establishment of the Local Community Research Committee, financed by the Laura Spelman Rockefeller Fund. The committee consisted of representatives of several departments of social science and of the School of Social Service Administration. In 1924 and 1925 a number of fellows were appointed, supported by the committee's funds. They were assigned to studying various areas and institutions of the city. They met in seminars at least once a week. Burgess and Park were in the seminar but the students reported on their projects from the beginning. Vivian Palmer was the coordinator of these studies; she arranged for the fellows and other graduate students to supervise undergraduate students who studied different communities, groups, and institutions. Palmer produced an outline to be followed in such studies. In 1928 she published *Field Studies in Sociology,* based on the collection of materials by members of the seminar and the students they supervised. She names seventeen students who contributed material. Zorbaugh, in *The Gold Coast and the Slum,* names fourteen students (only one of whom is in Palmer's list) who supplied him with data. This was the work of students whose teachers—Park, Burgess, and Faris—believed that students learned by participating in the search.

In 1925 Burgess had arranged for a number of students of sociology to take civil service examinations for positions as directors of the Chicago South Park System's neighborhood parks which had fieldhouses serving as active community centers. These positions—afternoons and evenings five days a week—paid much more than the fellowships, and they supplied another contact with communities and ethnic groups. Not all of the students who held these positions finished their degrees but some did, and they contributed material to the Palmer book. They also went on to study with Park, using the positions as a base from which to undertake larger research projects. Of course, not all students who started at Chicago were content there; some went to finish their degrees at other institutions.

The Local Community Research fellows quickly became a sort of club. They were young and most were unattached; they spent several hours together in seminars each week; they studied German with one of their number as tutor. The projects they undertook were more or less assigned to them. Their morale and that of the other graduate students was high. Park was settled, having finally been made a professor (he had been a professorial lecturer without tenure for nine years); he was about to be president of the American Sociological Society. The Park and Burgess *Introduction to the Science of Sociology* was becoming well known. A lively series of monographs was being published under his editorship. The Park enterprise was at its height.

His students' projects kept Park in touch with the city and with many people and communities in this country and abroad. Louis Wirth became the leader of the students who were studying Chicago. Roderick McKenzie set the model for ecological studies. Many people branched out into studying race and culture relations in the United States and elsewhere. A few worked on collective behavior and social movements; the monograph series included a volume on *The Strike* and one on *The Natural History of Revolution.*

The teaching continued. Reports by students of Chicago and of various movements, institutions, sects, and communities were made in Park's classes. The reports were interspersed with questions and with comments that sometimes grew into lectures. A Protestant missionary to Brazil was reporting in class—Park asked him if he was Christianizing the Catholics. A man who was living in what is now Israel gave an interesting and sophisticated report on Zionist education. Once a student was reporting on a church that was having difficulty getting people to church on good golfing days and on evenings when interesting movies were being shown nearby. Park spoke up: "You mean religion is a leisure activity?" This led to a discussion on the competition between religion and other activities. If they are in competition, said Park, it is because their function is the same. This was a most astounding idea to the young theologian who was reporting. An outrageous idea dropped into a discussion; a new angle; an unexpected comparison—these often contributed to new turns in the thinking and even in the careers of students. Louis Wirth started, as a social worker, to study the Chicago ghetto before ghetto had lost its specific meaning; he went on, as student and colleague of Park, to see it as a worldwide urban phenomenon. Andrew Lind, who had first found Park frightening, went to Hawaii to study the relations of the races there; he became, with much encouragement and collaboration from Park, a lifelong student of the racial contacts around the Pacific. Clarence Glick and Bernard Hormann, also students of Park, joined the team, using Honolulu as headquarters for studies which continue and which include China, Japan, and Australia.

At the 1925 meeting of the American Sociological Society—which Park, as president, organized—a number of Chicago students who had worked with both Burgess and Park read papers showing the two men's influence. Harvey Zorbaugh, then at work on his study of the Near North Side (*The Gold Coast and the Slum*), read a paper on "The Natural Areas of the City," and another on "The Dweller in Furnished Rooms." Walter Reckless had a paper on "The Distribution of Commercialized Vice in the City"; Louis Wirth, on "Some Jewish types of Personality." These and other Chicago students gave each other credit for data·and ideas. They also thanked their teachers and the Local Community Research Committee for support.

Park, after only ten years in the sociological community, had been elected president of the American Sociological Society. The chief prerogative of that office is to determine the topic of the annual meeting. Park's topic was "The City." *The City* was published in November of that year. The American Sociological Society's meeting was held in December. Park invited W. I. Thomas to read a paper on "The Problem of Personality in the Urban Environment." Thomas, who had not been at a meeting of the society since his resignation from Chicago in 1918, was given an ovation. A large contingent of graduate students had come to the meeting, partly because of Park's prestige and partly to support the return of Thomas, whom they considered a victim of academic injustice. Solidarity was demonstrated by the participation of Thomas and his successor, Ellsworth Faris, in the same program. At this meeting human ecology, especially as a method of urban research, came to the fore. Stuart Chapin, of the University of Minnesota, organized a session on statistical sociology, with eight papers concerning cities. Gehlke of Western Reserve led a session of eight papers on social research. The movement toward a more scientific study of cities and urban social problems was not confined to Chicago or to sociology. That meeting was a high point for Chicago and a maturing point for American sociology. It was the acme of Park's sociological career. It brought Burgess into his own as editor of the volume in which this meeting was reported, *The Urban Community*, although his youth and continuing role as secretary of the American Sociological Society probably delayed his election to the presidency.

Almost immediately after this meeting, there was a change in the Chicago department. Small was retired and died. Faris became chairman of the department and William F. Ogburn came to Chicago. Of Burgess's age, and already known for his *Social Change*, Ogburn brought the study of population and stronger use of statistics as an instrument of research. Both the Department of Sociology and the new Department of Anthropology added some of their new generation of Ph.D.s to the staff. Wirth, Blumer, and Redfield were the first, with Stouffer soon to follow. Graduate students were more numerous and had more possible mentors to choose from. Park, already past sixty when he was president of the society, had his share of new students, but that share was a smaller fraction of the total. But Park's students were especially among the Ph.D.

candidates. Forty-nine doctorates were granted after Park's arrival and before the separation of anthropology; another twenty-eight in sociology by 1934 when Park was finally listed as emeritus. A few students had written theses in the Divinity School under Park's direction. Not all these people had direct contact with Park, but many were influenced by him. He continued to teach, by letter and by conversation. The last straggling Park student, Helen MacGill, took her degree in 1936 on a topic dear to Park, *The Human Interest Story in the Newspaper*. By that time many universities had strong departments of sociology. The Chicago solo was over.

The Publications of Robert E. Park

Books

Introduction to the Science of Sociology (with E. W. Burgess). Chicago: University of Chicago Press, 1921.

Old World Traits Transplanted (with William I. Thomas and Herbert A. Miller). New York: Harper & Brothers, 1921.

The Immigrant Press and Its Control. New York: Harper & Brothers, 1922.

The City—Suggestions for the Investigation of Human Nature in the Urban Environment (with E. W. Burgess and R. D. McKenzie). Chicago: University of Chicago Press, 1925.

An Outline of the Principles of Sociology (Editor). New York: Barnes & Noble, 1939.

Ph.D. Dissertation

Masse und Publikum, Eine Methodologische und Sociologische Untersuchung. Bern, Switzerland: Lack and Grunau 1904. Later translated and published in *Robert E. Park: The Crowd and the Public and Other Essays.* Chicago: University of Chicago Press, 1972.

Articles

"Negro Home Life and Standards of Living." *Annals of the American Academy of Political and Social Science* (September 1913).

"Racial Assimilation in Secondary Groups with Particular Reference to Negro." *American Journal of Sociology* 19 (March 1914), 606–23.

"Racial Assimilation in Secondary Groups." *Publications of the American Sociological Society* 8 (July 1914), 66–83.

"The Principles of Human Behavior." *Studies in Social Science* 6, pamphlet edited by William I. Thomas. Chicago: The Zalaz Corp., 1915.

"The City: Suggestions for the Investigation of Human Behavior in the City Environment." *American Journal of Sociology* 20 (March 1915), 577–612. Also appears in *The City,* edited by Robert E. Park, Chicago: University of Chicago Press, 1925.

"Education in Its Relation to the Conflict and Fusion of Cultures." *Publications of the American Sociological Society* 13 (March 1919), 38–63.

"The Conflict and Fusion of Cultures." *Journal of Negro History* 4 (April 1919), 111–33.

"Sociology and the Social Sciences." *American Journal of Sociology* 26 (January 1921), 401–24.

"Sociology and the Social Sciences: The Social Organism and the Collective Mind." *American Journal of Sociology* 27 (July 1921), 1–21.

"Sociology and the Social Sciences: The Group Concept and Social Research." *American Journal of Sociology* 27 (September 1921), 169–81.

"The Natural History of the Newspaper." *American Journal of Sociology* 29 (November 1923), 273–89. Also appears in *The City*, pp. 80–98.

"Negro Race Consciousness as Reflected in Race Literature." *American Review* 1 (September–October 1923), 505–16.

"The Significance of Social Research in Social Service." *Journal of Applied Sociology* 8 (May–June 1924), 263–67.

"The Concept of Social Distance as Applied to the Study of Racial Attitudes and Racial Relations." *Journal of Applied Sociology* 8 (July 1924), 339–44.

"Experience and Race Relations." *Journal of Applied Sociology* 9 (September–October 1924), 18–24.

"Magic, Mentality, and City Life." *Publications of the American Sociological Society* 18 (September 1924), 102–15. Also appears in *The City*, pp. 132–41.

"Culture and Culture Trends." *Publications of the American Sociological Society* 19 (October 1925), 24–36.

"Communication from the President of the American Sociological Society." No. 30 (1924–25), 594.

"Community Organization and Juvenile Delinquency." *The City*, pp. 99–112.

"The Immigrant Community and Immigrant Press." *American Review* 3 (March–April 1925).

"The Mind of the Hobo: Reflections Upon the Relation Between Mentality and Locomotion." *The City*, pp. 156–60.

"Behind Our Masks." *Survey Graphic* 56 (May 1926), 135–39.

"Our Racial Frontiers on the Pacific." *Survey Graphic* 56 (May 1926), 192–96.

"The Urban Community as a Spatial Pattern and a Moral Order." In E. W. Burgess, *The Urban Community*, pp. 3–18. Chicago: University of Chicago Press, 1926.

"Human Nature and Collective Behavior." *American Journal of Sociology* 32 (March 1927), 733–41.

"Topical Summaries of Current Literature: The American Newspaper." *American Journal of Sociology* 32 (March 1927), 806–13.

"Human Migration and the Marginal Man." *American Journal of Sociology* 33 (May 1928), 881–93.

"The Bases of Race Prejudice." *Annals of the American Academy of Political and Social Science* 140 (November 1928), 11–20.

"The City as a Social Laboratory." In T. V. Smith and L. D. White, *Chicago: An Experiment in Social Science Research*, pp. 1–19. Chicago: University of Chicago Press, 1929.

"Sociology." In *Research in the Social Sciences*, edited by Wilson Gee, pp. 3–49. New York: Macmillan Company, 1929.

"Urbanization as Measured by Newspaper Circulation." *American Journal of Sociology* 35 (July 1929), 60–79.

"Murder and Case-Study Method." *American Journal of Sociology* 36 (November 1930), 447–54.

"Human Nature, Attitudes, and the Mores." In *Social Attitudes*, edited by Kimball Young, pp. 17–45. New York: Henry Holt and Company, 1931.

"Mentality of Racial Hybrids." *American Journal of Sociology* 36 (January 1931), 534–51.

"Personality and Cultural Conflict." *Publications of the American Sociological Society* 25 (May 1931), 95–110.

"The Problem of Cultural Differences." Proceedings of the Institute of Pacific Relations, 1931. Problems of the Pacific, data paper #15.

"The Sociological Methods of William Graham Sumner, and of William I. Thomas and Florian Znaniecki." In *Methods in Social Science*, edited by Stuart A. Rice, pp. 154–74. Chicago: University of Chicago Press, 1931.

"The University and the Community of Races." *Pacific Affairs* 5 (August 1932), 695–703.

Abstract in Racial Contacts and Social Research. *Proceedings of the American Sociological Society* 28 (1933), 101–102.

"Newspaper Circulation and Metropolitan Regions." Prepared in collaboration with Charles Newcomb, in *The Metropolitan Community*, edited by R. D. McKenzie, pp. 98–110. New York: McGraw-Hill Book Company, 1933.

"William Graham Sumner's Conception of Society." *Chinese Social and Political Science Review* 17 (1933), 430–41.

"Industrial Fatigue and Group Morale." *American Journal of Sociology* 40 (November 1934), 349–56.

"Race Relations and Certain Frontiers." In *Race and Culture Contacts*, edited by E. B. Reuter, pp. 57–85. New York: McGraw-Hill Book Company, 1934.

"Assimilation, Social." *Encyclopaedia of the Social Sciences* 2 (1935), 281–83.

"Collective Behavior." *Encyclopaedia of the Social Sciences* 3 (1935), 631–33.

"Social Planning and Human Nature." *Publications of the American Sociological Society* (August 1935).

"Succession, an Ecological Concept." *American Sociological Review* 1 (April 1936), 171–79.

"Human Ecology." *American Journal of Sociology* 42 (July 1936), 1–15.

"The City and Civilization." Reproduced in Syllabus and Selected Readings, Second-Year Course in the Study of Contemporary Society (Social Science II), pp. 204–20. Fifth Edition, September, 1936. Distributed by the University of Chicago Bookstore.

"A Memorandum on Rote Learning." *American Journal of Sociology* 43 (July 1937), 23–36.

"Reflections on Communication and Culture." *American Journal of Sociology* 44 (September 1938), 187–205.

"The Nature of Race Relations." In *Race Relations and the Race Problem*, edited by Edgar Thompson, pp. 3–45. Durham, N.C.: Duke University Press, 1939.

"Symbiosis and Socialization: A Frame of Reference for the Study of Society." *American Journal of Sociology* 45 (July 1939), 1–25.

"Social Contributions of Physics." *The American Physics Teacher* 7 (October 1939), 327–29.

"News as a Form of Knowledge: A Chapter in the Sociology of Knowledge." *American Journal of Sociology* 45 (March 1940), 669–86.

"Physics and Society." *The Canadian Journal of Economics and Political Science* 6 (May 1940), 135–52.

Introductions to Books

The Japanese Invasion, J. F. Steiner. Chicago: A. C. McClurg & Company, 1917.

The Natural History of Revolution, Lyford P. Edwards. Chicago: University of Chicago Press, 1927.

The Gang, Frederick M. Thrasher. Chicago: University of Chicago Press, 1927.

The Strike, E. T. Miller. Chicago: University of Chicago Press, 1928.

The Ghetto, Louis Wirth. Chicago: University of Chicago Press, 1929.

The Gold Coast and the Slum, Harvey W. Zorbaugh. Chicago: University of Chicago Press, 1929.

The Pilgrims of Russian-Town, Pauline V. Young. Chicago: University of Chicago Press, 1932.

Shadow of the Plantation, Charles S. Johnson. Chicago: University of Chicago Press, 1934.

Negro Politicians, Harold F. Gosnell. Chicago: University of Chicago Press, 1935.

Interracial Marriage in Hawaii, Romanzo Adams. New York: Macmillan Company, 1936.

The Marginal Man, Everett Stonequist. New York: Charles Scribner's Sons, 1937.

The Etiquette of Race Relations in the South, Bertram W. Doyle. Chicago: University of Chicago Press, 1937.

An Island Community, Ecological Succession in Hawaii, Andrew W. Lind. Chicago: University of Chicago Press, 1938.

News and the Human Interest Story, Helen MacGill Hughes. Chicago: University of Chicago Press, 1940.

Collected Papers

The Collected Papers of Robert Ezra Park, edited by Everett C. Hughes, Charles S. Johnson, Jitsuichi Masuoka, Robert Redfield, and Louis Wirth. Three vols. Glencoe, Ill.: Free Press, 1950–1955.

Vol. I. *Race and Culture*, 1950

Vol. II. *Human Communities* (The City and Human Ecology), 1952

Vol. III. *Society* (Collective Behavior, News and Opinion, Sociology, and Modern Society), 1955

Manuscript Sources

Robert E. Park. Special Collections, The Archives, University of Chicago Library.

Robert E. Park. Manuscripts. Social Science Research Institute, Fisk University, Nashville, Tenn.

Booker T. Washington Papers, Library of Congress, Washington, D.C.

Writings Referring to Park

1927   *Life Histories of William I. Thomas and Robert E. Park*, with an Introduction by Paul J. Baker. *American Journal of Sociology* 79 (September 1973), 243–60. Written by Park for Luther L. Bernard, 1927.

1931   *The Sociological Theories of Robert E. Park*, by students in Yenching University, China. Text in Chinese.

1943   An autobiographical note dictated to Park's secretary shortly before his death in 1944; appears in *Race and Culture*, 1950.

1944   Ernest W. Burgess. "Robert E. Park." *American Journal of Sociology* 49 (March 1944), 478.

1944   Ellsworth Faris. "Robert E. Park." *American Sociological Review* 9 (June 1944), 322–25.

1950–55   Everett Cherrington Hughes. Three Prefaces in *The Collected Papers of Robert E. Park*, 3 vols. Vol. I, *Race and Culture*; Vol. II, *Human Communities*; Vol. III, *Society*. Glencoe, Ill.: Free Press.

1951   Howard W. Odum. *American Sociology*. New York: Longmans, Green & Company.

1955   Andrew W. Lind, ed. *Race Relations in World Perspectives*. Honolulu: University of Hawaii Press. Dedicated to Robert E. Park, Edgar T. Thompson, and Everett C. Hughes.

1961   *Race Relations, Problems and Theory*. Essays in Honor of Robert E. Park, edited by J. Masuoka and Preston Valien. Chapel Hill, N.C.: University of North Carolina Press.

1967   Robert E. L. Faris. *Chicago Sociology: 1920–1932*. San Francisco: Chandler Publishing Company.

1967   Ralph H. Turner. *Robert E. Park on Social Control and Collective Behavior*. Chicago: University of Chicago Press.

1968   Helen MacGill Hughes. "Robert E. Park." *International Encyclopaedia of the Social Sciences*.

1968   References to Park in the biographies of Franklin Frazer, Louis Wirth, and Robert Redfield. *International Encyclopaedia of the Social Sciences*.

1970   Edward Shils. "Tradition, Ecology, and Institution in the History of Sociology." *Daedelus* 99 (Fall 1970), 760–825.

1970   "In the Parkian Tradition," section 2, pp. 69–150 of *The Black Sociologists: The First Half Century*, edited by John H. Bracey, August Meier, and Elliott Rudwick. Belmont, Calif.: Wadsworth Publishing Company.

1971   Lewis A. Coser. *Masters of Sociological Thought*. New York: Harcourt, Brace & Jovanovich. Reprinted 1977. Pp. 357–84.

1972   Stanford M. Lyman. *The Black American in Sociological Thought*, chap. 2. New Perspectives on Black America, New York: G.P. Putnam's Sons.

1974   John Higham. "Integration vs. Pluralism: Another American Dilemma." *The Center Magazine* 7 (August 1974), 67–73.
1977   Fred F. Matthews. *Quest for an American Sociology: Robert E. Park and the Chicago School.* Montreal: McGill-Queens University Press.

Chronology. Robert E. Park

1864	Born February 14 in Luzerne County, Pennsylvania
1881	Graduated from Red Wing Minnesota High School
1882	Attended University of Minnesota, one-year science course
1887	Graduated from University of Michigan, Ph.B., Phi Beta Kappa; majored first in philology, then philosophy
1887–97	Newspaperman: Minneapolis *Journal*, Detroit *Times*, Denver *Times*, New York *Journal*, New York *World*, Detroit *Tribune*, Detroit *News*, Chicago *Journal*
1894	Married Clara Cahill
1897–98	Graduate student in philosophy at Harvard
1899–1903	Graduate student in philosophy, Friederich-Wilhelm University, Berlin; University of Strasbourg (then Strassburg); University of Heidelberg
1903	Ph.D. in philosophy from University of Heidelberg; thesis: *Crowd and Public*
1903–1905	Assistant in Harvard philosophy department; Secretary of the Congo Reform Association
1905–12	Director of Public Relations at Booker T. Washington's Tuskegee Normal and Industrial Institute
1913–22	Professorial Lecturer, Department of Sociology, University of Chicago
1922–24	President National Community Center Association
1923–33	Professor of Sociology, Department of Sociology, University of Chicago
1925–26	President, American Sociological Society
1925	Delegate to Institute of Pacific Relations, Honolulu
1927	Member of Social Science Research Council
1927–31	University of Chicago Delegate to Institute of Pacific Relations
1929	Delegate to 4th Pacific Science Congress, Java
1929–30	Travels in Japan, Indonesia, the Philippines, China
1931–33	Visiting professor, University of Hawaii; travels in China, India, South Africa
1933	Retired from University of Chicago and University of Hawaii
1936	Teacher in Harvard Summer School; moved to Nashville, Tennessee; visiting professor at Fisk University
1937	Visited Brazil
1944	Died in Nashville, February 7, 1944

Member of: Phi Beta Kappa

American Academy of Political and Social Science

International Institute of African Language and Culture

Population Association of America
Ecological Society of America
Southern Sociological Society
American Statistical Association
Sociological Research Society
National Economic and Social Planning Association
Disciples of Christ Church, Chicago

Index